100 THINGS
UCLA FANS
SHOULD KNOW & DO
BEFORE THEY DIE

Ben Bolch

TRIUMPH
BOOKS

Library of Congress Cataloging-in-Publication Data

Names: Bolch, Ben, author.
Title: 100 things UCLA [fans] should know & do before they die / Ben Bolch.
Other titles: One hundred things University of California, Los Angeles [fans]
    should know and do before they die | Hundred things University of
    California, Los Angeles [fans] should know and do before they die
Description: Chicago, Illinois : Triumph Books LLC, [2018]
Identifiers: LCCN 2018023914 | ISBN 9781629374741
Subjects: LCSH: UCLA Bruins (Basketball team)—History. | University of
    California, Los Angeles—Basketball—History. | UCLA Bruins (Basketball team)—
    Miscellanea. | University of California, Los   Angeles—Basketball—Miscellanea.
Classification: LCC GV885.43.U423 B64 2018 | DDC 796.323/630979494—
dc23 LC record available at https://lccn.loc.gov/2018023914

This book is available in quantity at special discounts for your group or organization. For further information, contact:
    Triumph Books LLC
    814 North Franklin Street
    Chicago, Illinois 60610
    (312) 337-0747
    www.triumphbooks.com

Printed in U.S.A.
ISBN: 978-1-62937-474-1
Design by Patricia Frey

To Emma and Max,
who amaze me every day.

Contents

Foreword

My love affair with UCLA began in the spring of 1960, following my junior year in high school. That was when I received a letter from Jerry Norman, UCLA's assistant basketball coach, expressing interest in my basketball potential. In late October of that year, coach John Wooden invited my dad and me to visit the UCLA campus and watch practice. Wooden also offered me a basketball scholarship. Needless to say, I was thrilled. My dream growing up in Southern California, only 16 miles from The Hills of Westwood, was to play college basketball. Coach Wooden had just given me the opportunity to pursue my dream.

UCLA is a very unique institution—a school with a reputation for excellence in academics, research, and diversity as well as tremendous athletic accomplishments. My parents always stressed the need for higher education and knowledge. UCLA was perfect for me. It was the place where I was able to experience college life, grow as an individual, expand my horizons, and begin the journey that would enable me to meet challenges later in life.

During my years at UCLA, the basketball program began to excel. We won consecutive national championships in 1964 and '65. We were a group of players from totally diverse backgrounds who came together and coalesced into a real team to reach a common goal. Life lessons were learned from Coach Wooden in the pursuit of perfection. Who could forget Coach's annual tutorial on how to put on your socks and lace up your sneakers? Furthermore, never to be forgotten are Wooden's daily afternoon practice admonitions: "Be quick, but don't hurry," "Make every day your masterpiece," and "Goodness gracious sakes alive" with every mistake.

Our team formed lasting friendships. A special bond of shared experiences and enduring respect exists to this day. The 1960s were a time of unrest in the country, but there was a sense of pride and excitement among the students when it came to UCLA basketball. It was the beginning of 10 championships in 12 years for the Bruins. UCLA became the most prestigious college basketball school in the country.

UCLA also experienced athletic excellence on the football field, with Rose Bowl appearances, as well as track and field championships and national titles in other sports. Such notable athletes as Arthur Ashe, Jackie Robinson, Rafer Johnson, and Kenny Washington provided outstanding performances while at UCLA and in the years to follow. Since the 1960s, the Bruins have in many ways dominated college sports, becoming the first university to reach 100 NCAA championships.

UCLA provided me with incredible memories I will always cherish. There were enjoyable times spent with teammates, fraternity brothers, and friends with whom I shared both campus life and leisure time in Westwood Village, which was a huge part of college life. Whatever the interest, UCLA offers something for everyone.

The school has grown tremendously through the years with the expansion of its facilities. College athletics has changed in recent years with emphasis on athletics as a business. For me, however, college athletics will always be about preparation, competition, and perseverance toward victory on the playing field.

This book is a series of vignettes of famous UCLA players, coaches, games, and things to do. It documents many of the accomplishments by the Bruins in all sports and is a must read for all of the school's alumni and fans.

—Gail Goodrich

Foreword

As a senior at Oscar Smith High School in Chesapeake, Virginia, I'd told anyone who would listen that I was going to attend and play football for the University of Michigan. However, in the presence of my high school classmates and teachers assembled in the high school auditorium one morning in February 1977, I announced that I would attend UCLA. Gasps could be heard. Confusion reigned. Asked by friends and coaches afterward why I said "UCLA," I told them I did not know. Perhaps it was divine intervention, but as they say, the proverbial cat was now out of the bag and there was no turning back.

I walked onto the campus of UCLA for the second time in July 1977, a few days before my first college football training camp was to begin. My first trip to UCLA had been during my official visit as a recruit in December 1976. My goal was to survey the area and take in the beauty of the campus. I was housed with the other freshman football players in Dykstra Hall, upwind from Drake Stadium (where the track and field team practiced and competed) and Spaulding Field (where football practices would be held). It was an easy walk down the hill going to practice, but a torturous walk up the hill after two-a-day practice sessions.

Fall classes wouldn't commence until after we'd played two games in September, winning one and losing one. The Monday morning after the second game—a 17–7 victory for the Bruins against the University of Kansas—a mass of humanity of all stripes was now moving about the campus of UCLA. I remember my first class, History 101b, where there were more people in the lecture hall than in my entire high school at Oscar Smith. Blew my mind! However, I was now also the starting free safety for the UCLA Bruins and playing with only a minimum amount of confidence,

xi

as I had to speed learn the defensive coverages because I was also charged with making the secondary calls. And that was much harder than starting as a freshman free safety.

Although my freshman season was literally a blur, I managed to lead what was then the Pacific-8 Conference with seven interceptions. I was named first team All-Pac-8 and Freshman Defensive Player of the Year, but we lost a nail-biter to Southern Cal, 29–27, and a chance to play in the Rose Bowl. In fact, my biggest disappointment over my four years as a Bruin football player was that I never played in a Rose Bowl game. After the '77 season, I worked really hard to build up my body, as I had entered UCLA weighing only 177 pounds. I now knew I would not last long at this level if I did not add some weight and muscle to my frame.

Reminiscing now about the 1978 season, when I was a sophomore, we were good enough on defense to make a run at the national championship. I had put on 12 pounds (now weighing 189), shaved probably 1.2 seconds off my 40-yard-dash time, grown two inches, and was a much stronger player. We started the season with a great 10–7 victory over the Washington Huskies in Seattle, as I blocked a punt and Brian Baggott recovered it in the end zone for a touchdown and the win. (Interestingly, this would also be when Jack Patera, the Seattle Seahawks' coach, said he started thinking about drafting me.) After eventually improving our record to 7–1, we lost back-to-back games against Oregon State (15–13) and Southern Cal (17–10) that we should have won. We went to the Fiesta Bowl and finished in a 10–10 tie with Arkansas to conclude our season with an 8–3–1 record, Oh, well! Anyway, I made my first consensus All-American team in 1978.

I did six things really well over the next two years at UCLA—I played good, confident football; I got bigger; I got better; I got stronger; I got faster; and I made All-American teams in '79 and '80. When the pro scouts came to UCLA for my pro day in March 1981, I was 6'2½" and 210 pounds of sheer terror coming at a ball carrier from a 12-yard head start. UCLA had given me an opportunity to compete and play free safety as a freshman and I seized it and put a stranglehold on the position for the next four years. In 1980, we finally defeated Southern Cal, 20–17, and that was the best gift I could have received as a departing senior.

As a four-year starter from the second game of my freshman season, I had also left a legacy with UCLA football that every free safety afterward for at least the next 10 years would try to duplicate. Free safeties Don Rogers (1980–83), James Washington (1984–87), Eric Turner (1987–90), Shaun Williams (1994–97), and Rahim Moore (2008–10) were each All-American players and high draft picks in the NFL. For a time, UCLA was producing so many quality free safeties that pro scouts started calling it "Free Safety University."

Anyway, I may have slipped and said "UCLA" in 1977 when announcing where I would go to college, but I now have no doubts, UCLA is where I was destined to be.

—Kenny Easley

Introduction

The moment I learned I would no longer be covering UCLA basketball for the *Los Angeles Times*, I did what came naturally.

I cried.

It was the summer of 2011 and I was returning from the Las Vegas summer high school club basketball tournaments, where I had been following Bruins prospect Shabazz Muhammad and other top recruits. As I walked down the packed aisle of a Southwest Airlines flight toward the jet bridge at Los Angeles International Airport, my cell phone buzzed. It was *Times* sports editor Mike James.

With a tone that told me he was not calling to exchange pleasantries, he said a heavy hello before delivering the news: Hall of Fame national NBA writer Mark Heisler had been laid off and I was being tabbed to replace him. I wasn't able to fully process the meaning of it all in the moment, overcome by a jumble of emotions. I was relieved to be keeping my job but devastated that one of my favorite writers was being forced out the door in the latest wave of gut-punching layoffs (thankfully, Heisler would soon be inundated with more work than he could handle).

It wasn't until the cab was inching along a few miles up Interstate 405 toward home that it hit me and the tears began to flow. The worst part wasn't that my heart wasn't in the NBA at the time. Nor was it that the prospect of replacing Heisler was a bit like journeyman Pete Myers trying to replace Michael Jordan with the Chicago Bulls. The biggest disappointment was that there would be no more UCLA. No more Pauley Pavilion. No more NCAA tournaments. No more of the fun that can only come from covering the most storied team in all of college athletics.

I also knew that UCLA basketball was just part of a much broader legacy. I had come to learn bits and pieces of the history of

Bruins athletics since first writing about the school's football and basketball teams on an occasional basis for the *Times* in 2004. It wasn't until starting my research for *100 Things UCLA Fans Should Know & Do Before They Die* that I became fully aware of just how impressive that legacy is.

A thought struck me one day while flipping through stacks of yellowed newspaper clippings and rumpled photos inside UCLA's athletic archive room. The Bruins could boast of having produced not just the Jackie Robinson of the NBA (Don Barksdale) and the Jackie Robinson of the NFL (Kenny Washington), but Jackie Robinson himself. What other college athletic program could claim such a pioneering trio?

"My dad used to tell me that UCLA was a university for the people and what he meant was, a person that was an African American, a person that was Hispanic, or someone that was a minority would be welcome at a place like this," UCLA athletic director Dan Guerrero told me in January 2018. "And that resonated with me. So I was always a UCLA fan when I was a young boy."

There has been plenty to cheer. John Wooden is widely considered the greatest coach in the history of college sports, but there was another man on his own campus who won nearly twice as many NCAA championships, in volleyball coach Al Scates. The Rose Bowl is the most picturesque and storied setting in college football and Pauley Pavilion has been home to more men's basketball national championship teams than any other college venue.

When I interviewed Jackie Joyner-Kersee for a chapter on herself and fellow Bruins track star Florence Griffith Joyner, I asked if she had become a celebrity upon returning to campus after winning a silver medal in the 1984 Summer Olympics. I was stunned when she suggested it was no big deal. "One of the great things about UCLA was that there were Olympians across the board in every sport," Joyner-Kersee said. "It was like being part of a family."

There are so many amazing players and coaches to have come through UCLA that, given a few more years, I could have written *1,000 Things UCLA Fans Should Know & Do Before They Die*. The list of luminaries *not* included in this book includes Hall of Famers and Olympic gold medalists. UCLA's athletic tradition is so rich that I couldn't make room for scores of deserving stars and coaches. There were just too many. And perhaps that's my only regret in writing this book.

But I'm thrilled to be back around the Bruins on a daily basis. *Times* sports editor Angel Rodriguez granted my request to return to UCLA in the summer of 2016 as the beat writer for all Bruins sports. I had asked off the NBA not only to travel less but to return to a place where my heart belonged, covering the world's top college athletic program. I hope I'm just getting started.

—Ben Bolch
April 2018

1 John Wooden

In his final years, as he sat in a recliner inside his condominium penning monthly love letters to his late wife and autographing fan mail that he sometimes paid the postage to return, John Wooden answered a telethon's worth of phone calls from his former UCLA players.

Sometimes they would call just to check in on the coach. On other occasions they wanted to hear his reassuring words of wisdom. There was a telepathic tone when Wooden said "Hello."

"Whenever you called Coach Wooden, it was like he was just expecting your call," said Jamaal Wilkes, who went by Keith Wilkes when he starred at small forward for the Bruins. "I mean, to a man, that's what all the guys say about him. It was like he knew you were going to call."

It must have been a skill that Wooden developed late in life, because he never anticipated the call that would have drastically changed the course of UCLA history, not to mention the power structure in college basketball for parts of four decades.

In 1948, Wooden was a fast-rising coach at Indiana State Teachers College mulling tentative job offers from Minnesota and UCLA, when the Golden Gophers, his preferred choice, called to tell him they would meet his condition that he hire his own assistant. Wooden wanted to accept. Problem was, the call came later than expected after a snowstorm had prevented Frank McCormick, Minnesota's athletic director, from reaching Wooden at the scheduled time.

Only minutes earlier, Wooden had fielded a call from UCLA and, figuring that Minnesota was not interested in his services, agreed to coach the Bruins. A man of conviction, Wooden kept his word even after the offer he truly wanted came from Minnesota.

Wooden would go on to guide UCLA to an unprecedented 10 national championships, including seven in a row from 1967 to 1973. He was equally iconic as a life coach whose Pyramid of Success transcended basketball and inspired a nation.

"He saw himself as a teacher first, which he was," Wilkes said. "He was an English teacher and he had a way with words. He could say so much in so few words and it applied to so many different situations."

The man who liked to be called "Coach" had developed a taste for simplicity growing up on a farm in rural Indiana. The family home had no running water or electricity and the first basketball Wooden used consisted of old rags stuffed into black cotton stockings. He would shoot at a tomato basket with the bottom knocked out inside the hayloft of a barn.

Wooden showed an early aptitude for baseball as well as basketball but had to give up the former sport because of injuries. He starred in basketball at Martinsville High before going on to Purdue, where he learned many of his detail-oriented ways from coach Ward Lewis "Piggy" Lambert. A wiry 5'10½" and 178 pounds, Wooden earned a reputation for tenacious play and became the first three-time consensus All-American.

He graduated in 1932 and married his high school sweetheart, Nell Riley, while accepting his first coaching job at Dayton High in Kentucky, where he also taught English. A coaching stop at South Bend Central followed before Wooden provided fitness training to combat fighters as a Navy lieutenant in World War II. Wooden's first college coaching job came after the war at Indiana State Teachers College (now Indiana State University), where he led the Sycamores to a 44–15 record in two seasons.

The call to coach UCLA in 1948, at age 37, was hardly akin to assuming control of a basketball power. The Bruins had posted

March 31, 1975: Coach Wooden wears the net around his neck after UCLA defeated Kentucky 92–85 to win the national championship. (AP Photo/File)

a winning record in only three of the 21 seasons immediately preceding Wooden's arrival, so their capturing the Pacific Coast Conference's Southern Division in his first season was widely viewed as a breakthrough. The Bruins posted a winning record in each of the next 12 seasons but never made it past the first round in any of their three NCAA tournament appearances.

Wooden was laying the groundwork for something much bigger. It came in the way he taught his players to pull their socks tight to avoid blisters and repeated sayings such as "Be quick but don't hurry" and "Failing to prepare is preparing to fail."

"When I went there as a 17-year-old, I knew he would make me a better basketball player, but I didn't realize how much influence he would have on [me] in terms of how I approached life, because he was a teacher," said guard Gail Goodrich, who played for Wooden from 1962 to '65. "He taught us principles and things like that that you could carry on in your life."

Goodrich was the leading scorer on the team that finally broke through during the 1963–64 season, going from unranked in the preseason to stunning Duke in the national championship game while posting a 30–0 record. That started a run of unparalleled success, with the Bruins winning back-to-back titles to transform Westwood into Title Town for more than a decade.

Players respected Wooden but didn't always like him or his strict adherence to a set of principles that often ran counter to the desires of young men yearning to fully explore the freedoms of college life.

"He had all these rules and all this stuff and he was very subtle, but he was very demanding and strict," recalled forward Sidney Wicks, who played on three national championship teams. "He would tell you, 'Hey, this is how we play here, this is what we do, so I'm just letting you know this is how we do things.' And then you had to find your way in that system; the system doesn't change for individuals. It expands for you, but it doesn't change and you have to stay within the parameters of what they were trying to do."

Wooden was a master of psychology, sternly pushing those who needed prodding while taking a softer approach with players whose psyches were more delicate. Everyone knew to be on their best behavior when Coach blew his whistle and yelled, "Goodness gracious sakes alive!"

"He knew how to communicate and motivate players based on their personality," Goodrich said. "I was the type of person who probably didn't take a lot of yelling nicely. I would drop my head, so he wouldn't embarrass me in front of the other players."

Wilkes once went to see Wooden, fully intending to quit the team over the intense pressure he felt, before being calmed by an impromptu poetry recital.

"I came away so refreshed and I just couldn't believe he did that," Wilkes said. "Then, of course, the next day it was back to practice, but that's what I remember most. The only thing that made it sane was Coach Wooden, his approach, his philosophy—'Do your best.'"

The Bruins usually did, beating Kentucky to win a 10th national title in Wooden's final game in 1975 after he had surprised many two days earlier by announcing his retirement. Some argued that he became even more influential after leaving the sideline, inspiring a legion of admirers with his philosophies, which were applicable to many other endeavors besides basketball.

Wooden became the first person inducted to the Naismith Memorial Basketball Hall of Fame as both a player and a coach. In 2003, he was awarded the Presidential Medal of Freedom, the highest honor given to a civilian. That same year, the court inside Pauley Pavilion was rededicated as Nell and John Wooden Court.

Wooden remained a fixture at UCLA home games long after his retirement, sitting behind the Bruins bench. He died at the Ronald Reagan UCLA Medical Center on June 4, 2010, prompting the school to permanently retire his seat. A statue of Wooden clutching a rolled-up program stands outside Pauley Pavilion, the coach still inspiring to this day.

"He really saw himself training young people first and foremost," Wilkes said. "Now, he wanted to win, don't get me wrong—he was a very competitive, feisty guy—but he truly saw himself as a teacher first and that was how he ran his program. With all the expectations, the stresses, the winning streak, the undercurrent of everything that's going on when you basically have a group of teenagers in a major media market with all the distractions, it was him that held it all together."

2 Jackie Robinson

The man who would go on to break Major League Baseball's color barrier did not represent a racial first for UCLA athletics.

When Jackie Robinson transferred from Pasadena Junior College (as Pasadena City College was known then) to join the Bruins' football team in the fall of 1939, UCLA already had black stars Kenny Washington and Woody Strode gracing its roster. Robinson's arrival did represent confirmation of the school's forward-thinking ways, which were not shared nationally… or even locally.

Robinson and Ray Bartlett, who accompanied Robinson in making the move from PJC to UCLA, picked their new school in part because they did not feel welcome at crosstown rival USC. "We knew USC was prejudiced over there because they didn't have Negros playing sports," Bartlett told the *Daily Bruin*, UCLA's student newspaper. "UCLA was more friendly and gave us the area and type of opportunities that we wanted."

Prejudice proved an inescapable part of their experiences, however. UCLA had to play all of the Texas schools on its schedule at the Los Angeles Memorial Coliseum because black players were not accepted in the South. Robinson and Bartlett also encountered racism in Northern California during a trip to play Stanford in 1939 when they were the only two players who were refused service. The entire group departed together, leaving one penny as payment.

Robinson once groused that he never felt fully embraced at UCLA except when he was starring on the field. Of course, given his prowess as the first four-sport letterman in school history, that was a good chunk of his time on campus.

Robinson, the grandson of a slave and son of sharecroppers, was born in Cairo, Georgia, in 1919. He moved to Pasadena with his mother and siblings in search of a better life when he was just an infant. Though he would famously ignore physical and verbal abuse while playing for the Brooklyn Dodgers years later, young Jackie had no tolerance for racist insults.

When a white girl called him the n-word, he responded by calling her "cracker." When the girl's father emerged and began throwing rocks at Robinson, he picked them up and threw them right back. Willa Mae Robinson, Jackie's sister, would say that his talent for throwing a football and baseball came from those less-than-sporting exchanges.

Robinson gave fans a teaser of sorts when he played four sports at Muir Technical High School before going on to Pasadena Junior College, where he attained national fame by leaping 25'6⅓" in the long jump. Duke Snider, who would later become Robinson's Brooklyn teammate, recalled Robinson once leaving one of his junior college baseball games in the middle of an inning to go compete in the long jump while still in uniform, only to return to the baseball game as if nothing unusual had happened.

Robinson's exploits were so well known that a Stanford alumnus, realizing Robinson could shatter his alma mater's hopes

That First Game

He went 0-for-3 on that cloudy and frigid day in April 1947, grounding out, flying out, and laying down a sacrifice bunt. One of his at-bats ended in a double play.

It had been a most remarkable debut for Jackie Robinson.

The first black player to compete in Major League Baseball—when he played first base and batted second for the Brooklyn Dodgers that day—had irrevocably changed the course of a nation's history.

Robinson quelled the doubts of his own teammates, not to mention the will of every other team, by merely stepping onto the field. Dodgers president and general manager Branch Rickey had supported the subject of his "noble experiment" through years of strife, leading to his breakthrough moment.

When Rickey signed Robinson in 1945 and sent him to the Dodgers' top minor league team in Montreal, the manager, Clay Hopper, asked, "Do you really think that a nigger is a human being?"

Before the 1947 season, Rickey ignored baseball's owners, who had voted 15–1 against Robinson being allowed to play for the Dodgers. When Rickey brought Robinson to spring training, Dodgers star Dixie Walker started a petition asking that Robinson be left off the roster. A furious Rickey ended the internal dissent by lambasting his players but could not protect Robinson from the racist taunts and threats he would face over his 10-year career.

"Baseball tortured him, tormented him," legendary broadcaster Howard Cosell told *The Sporting News*. "What he had to live with was the greatest debasement of a proud human being in my lifetime."

Pee Wee Reese was the first Dodgers teammate to openly support Robinson, walking across the infield and placing a hand on Robinson's shoulder when he faced insults during games in Cincinnati and Boston.

Robinson would eventually be embraced by a nation, his legacy enduring long after his retirement, when April 15 became Jackie Robinson Day in the majors.

"He, like the mythical great Greek Gods, had his Achilles heel through no fault of his own; he had to bear the burden of all black men," Marian B. Logan wrote in the memorial program commemorating Robinson upon his death in 1972. "When he ran, he had to run for all blacks, thus for all humanity; when he hit the ball, it was for all the poor; he caught for all the dispossessed. He played the game for all the downtrodden; he went to bat for all the neglected and his home runs were for all mankind, his victories were for all humanity."

in four sports, offered to pay for his education in "any Eastern college you choose, so long as it's not on Stanford's schedule."

Robinson starred primarily in football and basketball at UCLA and did what he could for the baseball and track teams in the spring, given the overlap in schedules, not to mention growing fatigue. The shortstop's finest moment on the diamond was undoubtedly his debut, when he went 4-for-4 and stole four bases, including home, against Los Angeles City College. But he would hit only .097 in his first and only baseball season, prompting many to regard it as his weakest sport.

Robinson enjoyed far more success in football. He averaged 12.24 yards per carry as a wingback in 1939 for the first unbeaten team in school history. The Bruins went 6–0–4, tying for first place in the Pacific Coast Conference while being ranked as high as No. 7 nationally.

Gifted with a natural burst of speed, the 6-foot, 195-pound Robinson almost single-handedly engineered UCLA's 34–26 triumph over Washington State in 1940. He passed for one touchdown, returned a punt 60 yards for another touchdown, and had scoring runs of one and 75 yards.

"I still marvel at the way Jackie Robinson evaded three Cougar tacklers who apparently had him cornered on his first touchdown run," Bob Ray wrote in the *Los Angeles Times*. "They all wound up falling flat on their faces, grabbing nothing but night air. Jackie has more than a change of pace—it's a change of space."

Robinson used his shiftiness to lead the nation in punt returns in each of his two seasons, averaging 20.1 yards in 1939 and 21.0 in 1940.

He also found plenty of success on the basketball team, twice leading the PCC's Southern Division in scoring with averages of 12.4 points and 11.1 points per game. In his first season with the Bruins, Robinson scored the winning basket to help his team complete a 35–33 upset of California.

In track, Robinson won the PCC long jump competition with a leap of 25 feet before going 24'10¼" to capture the event at the NCAA championships.

Robinson dropped out of school after the 1941 basketball season, taking a job with the National Youth Administration. He later became a second lieutenant in the Army, being stationed close enough to Pearl Harbor to hear the exploding bombs, before receiving a medical discharge and joining the Kansas City Monarchs of the Negro League.

That preceded his historic signing with Branch Rickey's Dodgers, largely made possible by his time at UCLA. It was those two years that gave Robinson the credentials as "a college man" who had played with and against integrated teams that Rickey had sought in a player who could break baseball's color barrier.

Robinson compiled a lifetime average of .311 with the Dodgers from 1947 to 1956, was Rookie of the Year in 1947, National League Most Valuable Player in 1949, and elected to the Hall of Fame in 1962. After his baseball career ended, Robinson was a director on the national board of the NAACP and served as first vice president of People United to Serve Humanity.

He died in 1972 at age 53 after having been in failing health for some time, but his legacy endured. In 1997, Major League Baseball retired the No. 42 that Robinson had made famous with the Dodgers. (UCLA announced it was also retiring the number in 2014, even though it remained unclear whether he had worn it as a Bruin. Robinson wore No. 18 in basketball and No. 28 in football, with no definitive records of his baseball jersey number.) UCLA had earlier named its baseball facility Jackie Robinson Stadium, where a statue of the player sits inside the venue on the concourse. Another statue of Robinson was unveiled outside the Rose Bowl in 2017. He was also awarded the Congressional Gold Medal of Honor and the Presidential Medal of Freedom.

UCLA athletic director Dan Guerrero said retiring Robinson's No. 42 across all sports was his most memorable achievement at his alma mater because of what Robinson meant to him and his father. "My dad used to tell me that UCLA was a university for the people," said Guerrero, who, like Robinson, played baseball for the Bruins. "And what he meant was, a person that was an African American, a person that was Hispanic, or someone that was a minority would be welcome at a place like this."

3 Lew Alcindor

Lew Alcindor had been an outsized presence long before he entered UCLA at 7'1⅜" and 230 pounds. Born to a mother who was 5'11" and a father who was 6'3", Alcindor weighed 13 pounds and measured 22½ inches from his first breath. He edged over 6 feet in the sixth grade, was 6'8" when he finished grammar school, and sprouted to 7 feet by the 10th grade.

Tall jokes became routine. "You've heard them all," Alcindor said as he prepared to start college. "'Watch your head.' 'How's the weather up there?' 'You must have trouble sleeping.'"

He certainly didn't have trouble dominating on a basketball court. Coming out of Power Memorial Academy in Manhattan, Alcindor was perhaps the nation's most widely coveted recruit. He picked UCLA because he was enticed by the idea of attending a large urban school away from home that would provide excellence in basketball and academics.

Alcindor had received recruiting letters from prominent Bruins basketball alumni, including Jackie Robinson, and forged a quick connection with contemporary star Mike Warren during his recruiting visit. But there were challenges that made the introspective Alcindor feel like anything but a big man on campus upon his arrival in Westwood in the fall of 1965.

"It wasn't long before I realized that certain cats who hated my guts were giving me the big Pepsodent beachboy smile and saying, 'Hello, how are you?'" Alcindor wrote in a *Sports Illustrated* account titled "UCLA Was a Mistake," which was published in 1969, after he'd finished his collegiate career. "Back in New York City, you knew who liked you and who didn't. You knew where you were. But in California, I felt like I was in the middle of an ocean on a raft."

Alcindor spent one night with teammate Lucius Allen musing about all the other schools they could have attended before an epiphany struck: Alcindor would transfer to Michigan and Allen would go to Kansas.

They never left, of course, the tormented sticking around to become the tormentors on the basketball court during one of the most celebrated runs in college basketball history.

Alcindor's freshman season was eventful even though he couldn't play for the varsity team. In the first game ever played in Pauley Pavilion, he scored 31 points and grabbed 20 rebounds during the freshman team's 75–60 victory over a varsity squad that also happened to be the two-time defending national champions. The freshman games were even less of a challenge, the Brubabes going 21–0 with a roster that included Kenny Heitz, Lynn Shackelford, and Allen, in addition to Alcindor.

Alcindor spent much of that first season working on his conditioning with former Oregon State star Jay Carty, who made his protégé repeatedly jump to touch a line he had chalked on the backboard 18 inches above the basket.

Although he developed a low-post offense that would accentuate Alcindor's strengths, coach John Wooden strived for a balanced attack. But the Bruins always seemed to tilt toward Alcindor. He scored a record 56 points in his first varsity game, while making 23 of 32 shots in a 105–90 victory over USC, one of the last times a team tried to stop him with single coverage. Alcindor broke his own record later that season by scoring 61 points in a triumph over Washington State.

UCLA would have been among the favorites to win the national championship that season even without Alcindor. There was Warren, in addition to all those other super sophomores, and the Bruins romped their way to a 30–0 record that concluded with a 79–64 victory over Dayton in the 1967 championship game at Freedom Hall in Louisville.

Kareem Abdul-Jabbar (then known as Lew Alcindor) easily keeps the ball away from Duke defenders before reeling back to pass to a teammate in a December 1966 game. (AP Photo)

"So awesome were Lew Alcindor and his teammates and so obvious is it that they are destined for two more titles," Frank Deford wrote in *SI*, "that the old moon there over Louisville will doubtless suffer the indignity of conquest by mortal man before the Bruins do."

Dunking was outlawed before Alcindor's junior season, though that only served to force Alcindor to enhance his other moves around the basket. He finally experienced defeat in January of that season during what would be dubbed "The Game of the Century." It pitted the top-ranked Bruins against second-ranked Houston in the Astrodome before 52,693, the largest crowd to see a basketball game in the United States.

Alcindor, having scratched his left eyeball the previous week against California and been forced to sit out subsequent games against Stanford and Portland, had the worst showing of his career, making only four of 18 shots. Houston star Elvin Hayes scored 39 points, including the two deciding free throws, to help the Cougars emerge with a 71–69 victory. Unmoved by the display, Wooden said he would not trade Alcindor for two Hayeses.

Alcindor used the defeat as motivation, posting a magazine cover showing Hayes shooting a jump shot over his outstretched arm in his locker and looking at it every day before and after practice. The Bruins got their revenge in the semifinals of the NCAA tournament during a 101–69 beatdown of the Cougars at the Los Angeles Sports Arena. UCLA stymied Hayes with a diamond-and-one defense that held him to 10 points while Alcindor tallied 19 points and 18 rebounds. Alcindor would go on to score 34 points during another easy victory over North Carolina in the championship game, donning a colorful African robe that stretched to below his knees in celebration.

Always contemplative about the world around him, Alcindor became a Sunnite Muslim during the summer before his senior season, changing his name to Kareem Abdul-Jabbar (though he would not use that name publicly until 1971). His winning ways continued as the Bruins romped their way to another title, beating Purdue 92–72 in the championship game to become the first college basketball team to win three consecutive titles.

UCLA went 88–2 with Alcindor, who was selected Most Valuable Player of all three Final Fours in which he participated. "No one else dominated three consecutive years like he did to win the NCAA [every year]," Wooden said.

Alcindor was selected No. 1 overall by the Milwaukee Bucks in the 1969 NBA Draft and had a professional career befitting his collegiate greatness, becoming the NBA's all-time leading scorer with 38,387 points during a 20-year career. He was a noted author, social activist, and coach after his retirement in 1989.

Alcindor finished his UCLA career as the school's all-time leading scorer with 2,325 points, averaging 26.4 points per game. Wooden was convinced that Alcindor could have been the top scorer in college history, surpassing the 44.2 points per game that Pete Maravich averaged in his three seasons at Louisiana State, but Alcindor was chasing something more significant than scoring records.

"I talked to him once and said, 'I'm sure that we could devise an offense to make you the all-time leading scorer in college history, but if we do that, we're not going to win national championships,'" Wooden said. "And—I'll never forget it—he said, 'Coach, you know I wouldn't want that.'"

4 Bill Walton

Bill Walton's thoughts can seem as random and free-flowing as the patterns on his favorite tie-dye shirts.

"The powers that be—Los Angeles, Santa Monica Bay, Palos Verdes, and three-point jumpers!" Walton gushed during the ESPN2 broadcast of UCLA's basketball game against Washington State in December 2017.

"The Bruin offense is flowing like the 405 freeway with the new Wilshire off-ramp."

"You know that UCLA, this is where the Internet started? With a computer science teacher, Leonard Kleinrock, he laid the foundation for the present-day Internet."

It wouldn't be Walton unless he was dropping references to Bruins legends on the court and in academia, not to mention his favorite books and movies, all the while referring to the Pac-12 Conference as the Conference of Champions.

There was a time when all you had to do to muffle the chatty giant was to ask him to speak in public. Late in a career in which he was a three-time college basketball player of the year who had led his team to 73 consecutive wins, which completed a record 88-game winning streak, Walton rose to speak in front of a speech class.

"Nothing came out," Walton, who had a stuttering problem, told the *Los Angeles Times* many years later. "All I could do was go back to my seat. My classmates just laughed at me, right to my face. It was the lowest moment of my life."

There weren't many other lows during Walton's time on campus. The exuberance he displays as a broadcaster once manifested itself on the Pauley Pavilion court, where the floppy-haired redhead flung outlet passes, tipped in missed shots, materialized for blocks, and sacrificed every limb on his 6'11", 210-pound frame going after loose balls.

"He does so many things that don't show up in the box score," UCLA coach John Wooden once marveled. "Like intimidation? How do you measure that? I know that when we had Lewis Kareem,

Bill Walton goes up for two points in a 1973 game against Loyola (Chicago) in which he finished with 32 points, 27 rebounds, and four blocks in UCLA's 60th consecutive victory during its record 88-game winning streak.
(AP Photo/Fred Jewell)

the other teams had a lower shooting percentage. It went back up during the next couple of years but now, with Bill, it will go down again."

Walton's many talents had been on display in various sports growing up. He played end on the football team in middle school, and it's not unreasonable to imagine a very different trajectory for his athletic career, considering his brother Bruce became an offensive lineman for the Dallas Cowboys team that lost in the 1976 Super Bowl.

Bill had played both center and point guard on his eighth-grade basketball team under coach Frank Graziano because he was also the top ballhandler. It was Graziano who persuaded Walton to stick to basketball, a decision that seemed fortuitous when Walton sprouted from 6'1" to 6'7" between his sophomore and junior years at Felix High in La Mesa, California. He had grown to 6'10½" by his senior year before finally announcing he would enroll at UCLA in the fall of 1970 because of its blend of academics and athletics.

Walton initially majored in engineering before switching to political science, geography, and then history. A fan of the Grateful Dead and left-wing causes, he was arrested while sprawling his body across Wilshire Boulevard in protest of the Vietnam War. He was also known to march his size-15 feet over to Sepi's, a sandwich shop on the edge of campus where Walton devoured subs while chatting up the employees.

Walton gave Bruins fans plenty to talk about. UCLA went unbeaten during his sophomore season in 1971–72, beating its opponents by an NCAA-record 30.3 points per game. Florida State was so worried about Walton in the championship game that it neglected to properly defend Bruins teammate Keith Wilkes (now Jamaal Wilkes), who poured in 23 points to nearly match Walton's 24 during UCLA's 81–76 triumph.

The only thing that seemed capable of stopping Walton was Wooden after his star big man showed up to practice one day sporting a beard. "Bill, have you forgotten something?" Wooden famously asked, prompting Walton to explain that he should be allowed to wear his facial hair however he liked. "Bill, I have great respect for individuals who stand up for those things in which they believe. And the team is going to miss you." Walton shaved and returned to practice, disaster averted.

Walton was unquestionably the star of the Bruins' championship game in 1973 during one of the greatest individual performances in college basketball history. He made 21 of 22 shots—not to mention four dunks that were waved off because they were not allowed at the time—on the way to 44 points during an unprecedented display of catch-and-shoot basketball. Walton also snagged 13 rebounds while powering UCLA to an 87–66 victory over Memphis State, his only blemish being that he made two of five free throws. Wilkes said the Tigers were complicit in Walton's display of might.

"When we saw they were fronting Bill and playing him straight up, we couldn't believe it," Wilkes recalled of a game in which teammates Greg Lee and Larry Hollyfield combined for 23 assists. "They were just lobbing the ball and Bill was just, it wasn't even like he was jumping; he was just gliding from all different angles and twisting. I mean, they were close-in shots but they were not easy shots at all because all the angles, but I always tease Bill that he had a pretty good night, but why did he miss three free throws?"

UCLA's run of seven consecutive national championships ended in 1974, when the Bruins lost to North Carolina State in a national semifinal in Greensboro, North Carolina, but that couldn't diminish Walton's achievements. He finished his career averaging 20.3 points per game and a school-record 1,370 rebounds (15.7 per game) while becoming a three-time consensus All-America selection. The Bruins went 86–4 and won two championships in his three seasons, with Walton winning Most Valuable Player in two Final Fours.

Selected No. 1 overall in the 1974 NBA Draft by the Portland Trail Blazers, Walton's professional career was hindered by a series of foot injuries that limited him to 468 games in 13 seasons, three of which he missed completely. He led the Trail Blazers to the 1977 championship and was the sixth man for the Boston Celtics when they won the 1986 title.

Walton also overcame that stuttering problem when he was 28 with the help of Marty Glickman, a sportscaster based in New York. "The most important thing I told Bill was that he had to express his thoughts in a patient, deliberate manner and not let his head get ahead of his tongue," Glickman told *Inside Sports*. "He had to learn to discipline himself to say things in their order of importance and keep the rest in his head. You can't say it all at once." Often it seems as if Walton still tries, a kaleidoscope of thoughts conveyed to the masses in his own unique style.

5 Arthur Ashe

Arthur Ashe never flinched at those who were uncomfortable playing him because of the color of his skin. He dealt with discrimination like the 140-mph serves he calmly returned for winners, using the same introspective approach that would make him a powerful advocate for human rights and the eradication of the virus that ultimately took his life.

"This doesn't bother me so much," the former UCLA star told *Sport* magazine of the racism he faced in 1966 during the midst of a spectacular rise through the tennis ranks. "You've got to remember I've faced this problem all my life. When these things crop up, I just consider the source and feel much better about myself for having greater tolerance and understanding than others."

The only black man to win Wimbledon, the U.S. Open, and the Australian Open, Ashe championed causes great and small. He boycotted Wimbledon in 1973 in a show of solidarity for a fellow Association of Tennis Professionals player who had been banned from the tournament because he had competed in a doubles event as part of his contract rather than play for his native Yugoslavia in the Davis Cup. He also visited South Africa in support of those who faced the ugly wrath of apartheid four years after himself being denied a visa to visit the country.

Ashe spent the final months of his life in a frantic fight against AIDS. He said he contracted HIV, the virus that causes AIDS, from an unscreened blood transfusion in 1983 during open heart surgery. He did not disclose his condition until 1992, more than three years after he became aware that he had become infected, because he wanted his fight to be a private one. He went public only after a reporter confronted him with rumors about having contracted the disease.

"Just as I'm sure everyone in this room has some personal matter he or she would like to keep private," Ashe said while appearing with his wife on the day he made his announcement, "so did we."

Much of Ashe's life played out in public because of his tennis prowess. He began playing the sport at seven in his hometown of Richmond, Virginia, using a borrowed racquet at a club that welcomed black players. It was there that he attracted the attention of Dr. Walter Johnson, a philanthropist who became his benefactor, giving him a proper racquet and spending thousands of dollars to train the young boy. But Ashe was sometimes forced to travel far from his segregated hometown to compete against whites, prompting a move to St. Louis for his senior year of high school when a tennis official offered a room in his home.

Ashe's scorching serve helped him win the 1960 and '61 indoor junior championships, the latter coming the same year he arrived in

Westwood. Ashe chose UCLA for some of the same reasons as other black athletes from the South—its ideal climate and hospitable atmosphere that felt nothing like the racial discrimination they faced back home. Ashe was also drawn by the presence of Pancho Gonzalez, another tennis trailblazer of Mexican descent who lived within walking distance of UCLA's campus. The two spent hours playing together, Gonzalez helping Ashe perfect all aspects of his game.

Ashe packed a wallop into his lithe 6'1", 158-pound frame. "To look at him," Gonzalez told *Sport*, "you wouldn't think he has the amount of power he does. But I tell you, Ashe is as strong as he ever needs to be for him to be the best." Ashe steadily improved and led the Bruins to an undefeated season as a senior in 1965, becoming the NCAA singles champion and the doubles champion with Ian Crookenden. He rose to a No. 2 national ranking among collegiate players, trailing only Dennis Ralston. "All that's left after that," Ashe said at the time, "is the world." He would go on to attain the No. 1 world ranking in both 1968 and 1975. He won the inaugural U.S. Open in 1968 as an amateur at a time when he was a 25-year-old Army lieutenant.

His greatest triumph might have been his march to the 1975 Wimbledon championship, which included an upset of third-seeded Bjorn Borg in the quarterfinals. He persevered through a five-set semifinal against Tony Roche before heading into the final against Jimmy Connors, a fellow Bruin alumnus who was nine years younger than his counterpart. Few expected Ashe to last four sets, much less prevail.

"Ashe's tactics were inspired," Mike Downey wrote in the *Los Angeles Times*. "He controlled the pace. He found holes in Connors' forehand that no one else had noticed. By the time the royals were rising to pay tribute from their box, he was the Wimbledon winner in four sets, and it was indeed as though he had pulled his tennis racquet from a stone, for on this day Arthur truly was king."

Ashe's health problems started in 1977, with a persistent heel injury and eye inflammation that forced him to sit out most of that year before commencing a comeback. He was ranked No. 8 when he suffered a heart attack in 1979 after conducting a clinic for children in New York City, necessitating a quadruple bypass and prompting his retirement the following year. But his tennis career had one more act remaining, Ashe being named captain of the U.S. Davis Cup team at age 38 and leading it to triumphs in 1981 and '82 before his final retirement in 1985.

He became a central figure in the formation of the National Junior Tennis League, a program designed to encourage the participation of inner-city youths in tennis. He also worked as a tennis commentator for ABC and HBO and won an Emmy for his book *A Hard Road to Glory*, which chronicles the history of black athletes in America.

In the months after he disclosed his health crisis, Ashe founded the Arthur Ashe Foundation for the Defeat of AIDS and served as a board member of the UCLA AIDS Institute. He had been scheduled to speak to UCLA students about AIDS less than a month after he died in February 1993 of pneumonia, a complication of the virus. He was 49 years old.

His legacy lives on, Ashe having donated generously toward the construction of UCLA's Los Angeles Tennis Center, the John Wooden Center, and the James West Alumni Center. Ashe was also a charter member of the school's Athletic Hall of Fame and a name that comes up in discussions of all-time tennis greats, fulfilling a pledge he made in 1966. "When I say I want to be the best," Ashe had said, "I don't mean the best Negro player, I mean the best player—period! I don't consider myself a Negro player, although most everyone also does. I'm a tennis player who happens to be a Negro. I want to be No. 1 without an asterisk next to my name."

His name is uttered countless times every fall, when the U.S. Open is held inside Arthur Ashe Stadium.

6 Gary Beban

The Heisman Trophy was not on Gary Beban's mind heading into the 1967 season. It probably helped that there wasn't much Heisman hype back then.

ESPN did not exist. Neither did 24-hour sports talk radio. Websites such as Heismanpundit.com, which handicap the race for college football's most prestigious award, were decades away.

Beban would have had every right to consider himself the Heisman favorite going into his senior season as UCLA's quarterback. He was the leading vote-getter among returning players, having finished fourth behind Heisman winner Steve Spurrier of Florida in 1966. There had also been recent winners from the West Coast in Oregon State's Terry Baker (1962) and USC's Mike Garrett (1965). Baker had already served as a template for Beban stylistically.

"Even though he was a left-hander," Beban said of Baker, "I still learned on film how to turn your shoulders when you're on the run and even though he was going right and I would be going left, the technique is still the same."

Beban had become a speedy runner thanks to workouts with UCLA track coach Jim Bush and benefited from the play-calling genius of assistant Pepper Rodgers, an offensive mastermind, and head coach Tommy Prothro. Beban had been wowed by Prothro during a recruiting visit to Oregon State while playing for Sequioa High in Redwood City, California, telling his father that he thought Prothro was the finest coach he had encountered, but he was still going to UCLA.

Beban would enjoy the best of both worlds when Prothro left Oregon State to become the Bruins' coach prior to Beban's sophomore season, when the coach and his star quarterback combined to upset top-ranked Michigan State in the Rose Bowl.

Beban's steadying demeanor was just as celebrated as his physical gifts. "The thing he did best for us, I think," Prothro once said, "was give the rest of our kids a tremendous amount of confidence, not only in themselves but in him."

Prothro was quoted in the 1967 media guide as calling Beban "The Great One," though Beban now suggests that nickname probably came from UCLA's PR department given that Prothro was reluctant to openly compliment players.

Beban certainly inspired greatness in the season opener against Tennessee, which featured its own Heisman hopeful in quarterback Dewey Warren. The Volunteers had beaten the Bruins two years earlier in Memphis, angering Prothro because the coach felt the home team had benefited from three questionable stoppages of play on its winning drive. "I'm a born and bred Southerner, and I've always been proud of it," Prothro, a Memphis native, said afterward, "but I'm sorry to say it today."

Tennessee was in position for another victory at the Los Angeles Memorial Coliseum the next time the teams met, holding a 16–13 lead with four minutes left, when Beban and the Bruins faced a fourth-and-2 on the Volunteers' 27-yard line. After asking—and receiving confirmation—that his quarterback was fresh enough to run the ball, Prothro gave Beban his instructions. "I want you to run one more great play for me," Prothro told him. Beban complied, running to his right before cutting across the line of scrimmage and eventually veering back to the left for a 27-yard touchdown that gave UCLA a 20–16 victory.

The top-ranked Bruins eventually took a 7–0–1 record—their only blemish being a 16–16 tie against Oregon State's "Giant Killers"—into their rivalry game against USC, which had only one loss and was ranked No. 2 in the Coaches Poll.

The Trojans had one major advantage: Beban was hurt. He'd been injured the previous week against Washington when he was speared in the ribs—intentionally, he says.

"It would have been a little more comforting if I had not had that injury; it was a strain," Beban recalled. "I had torn the muscle surrounding the rib cage and so when you turned in an unusual way or you got hit, it would take your breath away, which was why I had to come off the field and be able to go back on."

Fortunately for the Bruins, the injury did not hurt Beban when he threw the ball, something he did plenty of that day. The quarterback threw for a season-high 301 yards and two touchdowns with one interception and UCLA led in the fourth quarter. But in one of the great runs in college football history, O.J. Simpson raced 64 yards for a touchdown to give USC the lead with about 10 minutes left in the Trojans' eventual 21–20 victory.

The Bruins were hurt by kicker Zenon Andrusyshyn missing a conversion kick after a touchdown and a field goal, as well as having two other low-trajectory field goals blocked. But Beban mostly blamed himself for a defeat that was followed by a limp loss to Syracuse the following week.

He was still brooding when it was announced he had won the Heisman—edging Simpson—a few days later.

"I don't think anything would have been grand enough to still get the taste out of our mouths of what had happened a couple of weeks before," Beban said, "so I was still in that state of feeling sorry for ourselves and having not won."

Beban's passing statistics were modest by today's standards. He threw for 1,359 yards and eight touchdowns, but he also rushed for 11 touchdowns. Beban viewed the Heisman as a career achievement award after he finished his UCLA career with a 24–5–2 record and guided the Bruins to a victory over top-ranked Michigan State in the 1966 Rose Bowl.

It also meant that everything those teams accomplished would enjoy an eternal spotlight. "I appreciated it and I realized quickly that that the three years we had played there at UCLA would not be forgotten once you are selected for that award," said Beban, who spent two years in the NFL before going on to a lengthy career in global real estate services, "but that took a long time to evolve."

7 Rafer Johnson

Back and forth they went for two days and 10 events, refusing to concede a quarter of an inch or a split second in one of the greatest man-to-man battles in Olympic track and field history.

It was impossible to tell that Rafer Johnson and C.K. Yang were once UCLA teammates given the way they barely acknowledged one another inside the flag-rimmed Stadio Olimpico during the 1960 Rome Olympics. They had trained together for weeks under Bruins track coach Ducky Drake, whose toughest task might have been maintaining impartiality with his two stars vying for a gold medal in the decathlon.

Drake had deadened many razor blades sloughing away the scar tissue that had formed on Johnson's left foot as the result of a terrible accident more than a decade earlier. Johnson was playing on the conveyor belt of a produce packing house near where his family lived in the central California farming community of Kingsburg when he slipped, slicing the ball of his foot. The injury required a lengthy recovery and briefly threatened his athletic career.

Johnson and Yang had competed as teammates under Drake before they became rivals, cementing their bond for two years at

UCLA while helping the Bruins win their first conference and NCAA track and field championships. Johnson, whose friends called him Ray, was named both track and field captains at UCLA. He also played basketball for coach John Wooden for two seasons and served as student body president.

Johnson entered his first decathlon in 1954, during his sophomore year, and in 1955 he won the gold medal at the Pan-American Games. A painful kneecap pad and torn stomach muscle derailed his bid for gold in the 1956 Melbourne Olympics, where Johnson finished second in the decathlon.

Johnson was the U.S. team captain and flag bearer in Rome, not to mention one of the favorites in the decathlon, which featured 30 competitors from 20 countries. But Yang, representing the Republic of China, was the early leader after winning the first two events. Fortified by a lunch of a steak sandwich and two cups of tea, Johnson overtook Yang for the points lead after a dominant showing in the shot put.

It was after 11:00 PM when Yang edged Johnson in the 400-meter dash, 48.1 seconds to 48.3 seconds, to conclude a 14½-hour day that included a rain delay of 90 minutes. Johnson's lead stood at only 55 points and it was down to a two-man race for the gold medal.

Johnson suffered a setback in the first event of the second day when he slammed into the second barrier in the 110-meter high hurdles, staggering and almost pulling up completely. He finished in 15.3 seconds, well behind Yang's 14.6, which gave Yang a 128-point lead. Discus was next and Johnson prevailed with a throw of 159'1" to Yang's 130'8", giving Johnson a 144-point lead.

That left three events to go, with Yang favored considerably in two of them. But Johnson defied the odds when he cleared 13'5⅛" in the pole vault, his all-time best. Yang cleared 14'1¼", leaving him 24 points behind Johnson. Johnson edged Yang as expected in the javelin, his throw of 228'10½" well ahead of Yang's 223'9½".

Johnson was clinging to a 67-point lead going into the final event, the 1,500. Heightening the drama, Johnson and Yang were grouped in the same heat with four other runners. To win the gold, Yang needed to beat Johnson by 10 seconds or more.

As the runners established the pace, Yang led Johnson by two steps. On the final lap, Russia's Yuriy Kutyenko started to pull away and Yang tried to keep pace. But Johnson did not fall back, crossing the finish line only six meters and 1.2 seconds behind Yang. Johnson sliced five seconds off his personal best and won the gold, defeating Yang 8,392–8,334 in one of the narrowest margins in Olympic history.

When it was over, Johnson and Yang leaned on each other in an exhausted show of respect. A breathless Johnson declared that it would be his final decathlon. "The victory compensates for every ounce of energy and every hour of time I spent all along the way," he said.

Johnson would go on to help found the California chapter of the Special Olympics in 1969. He also worked with People to People International, a goodwill agency, dabbled in acting, recruited volunteers for the Peace Corps, and volunteered for Robert Kennedy's 1968 presidential campaign. On the night Kennedy was shot in Los Angeles, Johnson disarmed assailant Sirhan Sirhan.

Johnson would have one more moment in the Olympic spotlight as the final torchbearer in the 1984 Los Angeles Olympics. Hidden in a trailer outside the L.A. Memorial Coliseum to keep his identity secret, Johnson was supposed to watch the ceremonies on television and await his cue. But he was so nervous he moved into the Coliseum tunnel to prepare for his moment.

Johnson ran out onto the track and took the torch from Gina Hemphill, granddaughter of the late Jesse Owens. He stood at the bottom of a hidden stairway that began to rise. The crowd gasped.

"When I lit the torch, the hair on my arms was standing straight out," Johnson told the *Los Angeles Times*. "It was almost scary. It was a moment that I think would be hard to top."

8 Jackie and Flo-Jo

Jackie Joyner never imagined she was making an introduction of sorts for her future sister-in-law when she showed her older brother some photos of her UCLA track and field teammates during her sophomore year.

Maybe she should have realized the possibilities, given Al Joyner's reaction to a picture of sprinter Florence Griffith.

"He told me, 'Oh, I'm going to marry her,'" Jackie recalled with a laugh, "and I go, 'Oh, you're not even her type.'"

Jackie was kidding, not thinking much of the comment. But it was almost as if Griffith was destined to be part of the family. Jackie and the teammate who came to be known around the world as "Flo-Jo" were a superb pairing long before they posed for the cover of *Sports Illustrated* in 1988 under the caption "America's Golden Girls," with a host of Olympic medals draped around their necks.

Jackie would let Griffith do her nails even though she normally wasn't into such things. The two-sport athlete, who also played forward for the Bruins women's basketball team, was not one to risk having a wayward ball split a long nail in painful fashion. It was all part of putting her team before herself while living up to its credo.

"One of the things we always said to each other was, 'We're going to look good, we're going to run good,'" Jackie said.

UCLA did both while winning national outdoor track championships in 1982 and '83 with Joyner and Griffith leading the way.

Joyner won individual titles in the seven-event heptathlon each year while Griffith prevailed in the 200 meters in 1982 and in the 400 meters in 1983, even though the latter event was not among her favorites.

"It was something about just having a winning attitude that we were willing to do whatever we needed to do to help the team win," Joyner said. "Florence wasn't a quarter-miler. She didn't like running that 400, but she ran that 400 and ended up winning a national title in it."

Joyner also made sacrifices, forgoing her beloved heptathlon during her senior year to help out in other events. She was the rare star who didn't mind doing utility duty, once clinching a meet title after already competing in the grueling heptathlon.

"We were out of events," Joyner said, "and I was the only one that was left and I needed to compete in the long jump and all I needed to get was sixth place or something and I ended up getting third.... Everyone just thought maybe I was too fatigued from doing the heptathlon, running the hurdles. I'm telling you, as long as I was able to walk, there was always a will to get it done."

Joyner's greatest challenge was a double gut punch that came late in her freshman season. She was diagnosed as an asthmatic within a matter of weeks of her mother dying.

Joyner stoically powered through the ordeal until hearing her teammates discuss their plans for Mother's Day. She broke down, but soon realized it was a needed turning point for someone who had shepherded her siblings through the pain while neglecting her own feelings. "I was the oldest girl and just trying to make them feel comfortable without realizing the depth of despair I was going through myself," Joyner said.

Joyner was more stubborn when it came to dealing with her asthma. She initially refused to believe that the wheezing that sometimes accompanied her running was anything serious.

"I just could never put in the same sentence at that time 'Jackie Joyner' and 'an asthmatic,'" Joyner said. "It's like, no. Those two don't go together. All my life I've been running, I've been doing this, I haven't had any problems. I had some problems my senior year in high school, but we always equated it to that I wasn't in track shape, like when I went to state and it was cold and it was wet and those were some of the elements that would give me problems."

She began to realize the severity of the problem when she had trouble breathing and started seeing stars after what was supposed to be an easy workout at Drake Stadium. Joyner was rushed to the hospital and told to take better care of her condition, something she now acknowledges she didn't fully do until leaving college.

Her refusal to solve her asthma makes her success at UCLA all the more remarkable. A four-year starter on the basketball team who redshirted during the 1983–84 season to prepare for the 1984 Olympics, where she won a silver medal in the heptathlon, Joyner averaged 12.7 points and a team-high 9.1 rebounds per game as a senior in 1984–85 for the team that twice defeated USC and star Cheryl Miller.

"She was 6'3", I'm 5'10"," Joyner said, "and my claim to fame in a sense was that I was one of our top defensive players and I had to deny her, deny her, deny her."

Joyner graduated in 1985 with a degree in history, fulfilling a pledge to her late mother to complete her collegiate studies. Her Olympics career was just beginning to blossom, with Joyner accumulating a still-standing world record 7,291 points in the heptathlon during the Seoul Olympics in 1988, while also becoming the first American woman to win a gold medal in the long jump.

Griffith amassed three gold medals in the same Olympics, winning in the 100 meters, 200 meters, and 4x100 meter relay.

A family triumph came the previous year when Griffith married Al Joyner, becoming Florence Griffith Joyner. Jackie had already married her track coach, Bob Kersee, in 1986, becoming Jackie Joyner-Kersee.

Griffith Joyner would finish her Olympics career with three gold medals and two silvers while widely being considered the fastest woman of all time because of her world records that still stand in the 100 and 200 meters. Joyner-Kersee won a total of six Olympic medals—three gold, one silver, and two bronze—on the way to being named the greatest female athlete of all time by *Sports Illustrated for Women*.

Griffith Joyner died in her sleep from an epileptic seizure in 1998 at the age of 38, a tragic ending to a fairy tale life. Her exploits live on in the memories of Joyner-Kersee and those who watched in amazement every time she burst out of the starting blocks. Joyner-Kersee's legacy is memorialized with a display at Drake Stadium and in the Rafer Johnson/Jackie Joyner-Kersee Invitational held at the stadium each year.

"Seeing that," Joyner-Kersee said of the display, "it just gives me chills."

9 Troy Aikman

In the moment that changed everything, Troy Aikman did what came naturally. He passed.

He could have returned to Oklahoma and tried to reclaim the starting quarterback job from Jamelle Holieway, though his chances seemed iffy. Holieway had just led the Sooners to the 1985 national championship after taking over for an injured Aikman, allowing coach Barry Switzer to restore the wishbone offense he preferred.

Aikman had agreed to come to Oklahoma two years earlier only after Switzer vowed to scrap the run-heavy formation for a multiple offense that would allow Aikman to fully utilize his passing skills. It quickly became apparent to Aikman that Switzer's pledge had constituted an empty promise.

"Everybody's always saying he changed the offense for me, but that's simply not true," Aikman would later tell *Sports Illustrated*. "He changed the wishbone a little bit, but the only real difference when I played was that we threw the ball 12 times a game instead of seven."

After playing sparingly and unspectacularly as a freshman, Aikman led Oklahoma to a 3–0 start in 1985 and appeared to be on the way to his best day with the Sooners in the fourth game against Miami. He had completed six of seven passes for 131 yards when he broke his left ankle in the second quarter. Holieway took over and Oklahoma went back to the wishbone, a combination that resulted in a national title after the Sooners' 25–10 victory over Penn State in the Orange Bowl.

But even before Aikman was injured, it was apparent that change was afoot. Coaches had told him before the Miami game that they were considering bringing in Holieway on third downs to utilize his speed. "I thought it was just a matter of time before they'd start working him into the lineup," Aikman said.

When it appeared that Holieway would stay the starter in the spring of 1986, Aikman went to Switzer and told him he wanted out. To Aikman's surprise, Switzer readily agreed. The coach called UCLA counterpart Terry Donahue, touting Aikman as a potential No. 1 NFL draft pick.

That was all the selling Donahue needed. "Well, you've had enough of them," Donahue told Switzer, "so I guess you ought to know one."

Aikman's transfer to UCLA was a homecoming of sorts. He had been born in nearby West Covina and bounced from Whittier to

Troy Aikman warms up before a 1988 game. (AP Photo/Al Messerschmidt)

El Monte to Cerritos before moving when he was 12 to Henryetta, Oklahoma, a small town about 50 miles south of Tulsa. His father was a pipelaying engineer whose industry often prevented him from setting down firm roots.

Aikman's first passes at UCLA came on a practice field apart from the rest of his new team. He was assigned to work with Rick Neuheisel, a former Bruins quarterback who had led them to a Rose Bowl victory, while sitting out the 1986 season because of transfer rules. A humble hero who preferred anonymity, Aikman hung out with the offensive linemen because their personalities aligned. "Maybe it's they don't have much of an ego," Aikman said at the time.

It quickly became apparent to those who watched Aikman's workouts what the Bruins were getting in the unflappable quarterback who was blessed with a strong arm and a sturdy build, standing 6'3" and weighing 217 pounds unless he had an unusually large wad of tobacco in his mouth.

When Aikman won the starter's job going into the 1987 season he became UCLA's first junior quarterback in six years, ending a stretch in which the Bruins had gone exclusively with fifth-year seniors. His impact was immediate, leading UCLA to a season-opening 47–14 rout of San Diego State and later its first victory in a Pac-10 Conference opener in six years while completing 19 of 25 passes for 256 yards and three touchdowns against Arizona.

As a senior, Aikman won the Davey O'Brien National Quarterback Award and finished third in the Heisman Trophy balloting after passing for 2,771 yards and 24 touchdowns. In two seasons, he completed 64.8 percent of his passes for 5,298 yards, 41 touchdowns, and 17 interceptions while leading the Bruins to a 20–4 record, including an 11–2 mark in his home stadium. But he never got to play in the Rose Bowl game after twice losing to USC. Instead, his teams won the Aloha and Cotton bowls.

After Aikman led the Bruins to a 17–3 victory over Arkansas in the 1989 Cotton Bowl, Donahue ceded his quarterback to Gil Brandt, the director of player personnel for the Dallas Cowboys, who fully telegraphed their intentions to make Aikman the top pick in the NFL draft. "He's all yours now," Donahue told Brandt with a smile. "But if you don't want him, please send him back."

No chance, even after Brandt was fired by new Cowboys owner Jerry Jones shortly after the draft. Aikman went on to lead the Cowboys to three Super Bowl victories during a 12-year NFL career before being elected to the Pro and College Football halls of fame. He returned to UCLA in 2009 to receive his bachelor's degree in sociology after completing the necessary coursework.

He was far from anonymous in cap and gown after having gone largely unrecognized on the streets of Westwood during his playing days, a welcome departure from his time as a Sooner.

"Everybody in the state of Oklahoma knows if you play OU football," Aikman once told the *Los Angeles Times*. "They know if you're a starter or a backup. They know your stats…. I think I like this better."

10 4.8 Seconds

Long before he faced the outstretched arms of Missouri's Derek Grimm in the 1995 NCAA tournament, Tyus Edney had to get past his brother on a concrete driveway outside their Long Beach home. That's where the move that resulted in perhaps the most iconic play in UCLA sports history originated.

The boys would battle each other on a makeshift basket that stood around 6 feet tall, maybe 6'2"—Tyus never knew the exact height—its wood backboard and metal rim attached to the garage gutter of the Edney home. Tyus, a jitterbug of a point guard, would hoist shots for hours at a time with his older brother, Russell, and their friends, the roughhousing occasionally leading to twisted ankles and other injuries that irritated the boys' father, Hank. "He'd be like, 'I'm not going to let you guys play out there anymore,'" Tyus recalled his father saying. "'It's getting too crazy.'"

One of the house rules was that there was no dunking on the rim unless it was an uncontested play, for fear of breaking the basket. Any time a defender challenged a shot, it required the attacking player to lay the ball up around the flailing arms of whoever stood in front of him. That could be particularly difficult for Tyus, who at 5'10" stood several inches shorter than his brother. Their father would later see his sons execute the same moves they had unveiled in the driveway in games that counted, leading him to soften his stance on the horse-play. "After he saw it was kind of helping us, he just let us play," Tyus said. "He's like, 'Nah, nah, nah, you guys are fine.'"

Tyus might as well have been back in his driveway late in UCLA's second-round NCAA tournament game against Missouri on March 19, 1995, in Boise, Idaho. The Tigers had just scored to take a one-point lead over the top-seeded Bruins with 4.8 seconds left. Missouri players rushed onto the court in celebration as UCLA called timeout. Bruins senior Ed O'Bannon, the team's best player, immediately clamored to take the final shot, but coach Jim Harrick had another idea. "Tyus," Harrick told his team, "get the ball, I want you to go down and make the play."

In case there was any doubt, Harrick repeated his demand as players departed the timeout huddle. "On the way out," Tyus recalled, "he gave me that look that he always did, and he's like, 'You've got to make the play.' So I had my marching orders, I guess you could say."

Tyus knew he was capable of scoring a length-of-the-court basket in 4.8 seconds because the Bruins regularly ran a practice drill in which they did it in only three seconds. The key was not getting stopped. "I knew that I couldn't get slowed down," said Tyus, who was playing on a sore ankle that he had tweaked two days earlier against Florida International. "Even if they were trapping, I probably would dribble through a trap." The play set up perfectly. Tyus took the inbounds pass from teammate Cameron Dollar in stride and took three dribbles to reach midcourt before making a behind-the-back move to change directions and elude the initial defense.

Then came three more dribbles before Tyus neared the basket and found himself confronted by the long arms of Grimm, Missouri's 6'9" forward. All those hours on the driveway had prepared him for this moment. "When he put his arms up," Tyus said, "it was instinctually the shot that I made to make that."

Tyus pushed off with his left leg, twisted his body around the defender, and banked the ball off the side of the backboard and into the basket. Tyus leaped in triumph and was quickly hoisted into the air by teammate Bob Myers, who would go on to be general manager of the Golden State Warriors. The Bruins had survived what would be their toughest challenge on the way to winning their first national championship in 20 years.

Harrick would call the play the defining moment of his coaching career, though it took Tyus a while to grasp the significance of what he had done. "I think at the time I didn't realize how important it was, but then after we won the championship that obviously made it huge," Tyus said. "But still, you don't realize how much that affected people's lives and impacted people's lives until later on, and how many people just remember it and have great memories of it and stories, and Missouri people, bad memories of it. There is the other side. Now, I guess I appreciate how important it was as time went on."

Tyus went on to spend four seasons with the Sacramento Kings, Boston Celtics, and Indiana Pacers before playing professionally in

Europe, where his teams won nine championships. He returned to UCLA in 2010 as director of operations before being promoted to assistant coach in 2017. His nickname back on campus has become "4.8." It was just enough time for Tyus to make the basket that took him back to his childhood driveway. "Four-point-eight seconds is a quick time," UCLA forward Charles O'Bannon said on the day of the storybook shot. "But for Tyus, that's an eternity."

11 Reggie Miller

Some kids hold part-time jobs to make pocket money. Reggie Miller worked the playgrounds of Riverside.

The spindly youngster would survey a couple of guys playing pickup games, walk up, and ask if they wanted to take him and a partner on for $5 or $10. Sure, they would tell him, but where's your other player? "I'd whistle and then here comes some pigtails out of the bushes and they start to laugh, talking about easy money," Miller said.

Those pigtails belonged to Cheryl Miller, his equally slender sister who would go on score 105 points in a high school game before leading USC to two NCAA championships and the U.S. team to an Olympic gold medal in 1984. "The next thing you know," Reggie said, "we're celebrating on the way to McDonald's for a Big Mac."

Word soon got out about the Millers' side business, but there was no stopping Reggie from cleaning up in his own backyard. His mastery in games of H-O-R-S-E and Around the World prompted his father to add more sections of cement to the court as his son's range kept increasing. "I wanted to master the outside shot as much

Reggie Miller holds his trophy in Madison Square Garden after being named the 1985 National Invitational Tournament's Most Valuable Player. (AP Photo/ Ray Stubblebine)

as possible," Reggie said, "so I just kept extending my range all the way back into my mom's rose garden."

While Cheryl, who was a year older than her brother, went from Riverside Poly High to USC, Reggie hoped to become part of rival UCLA's rich tradition after having been wowed by Bruins games on KTLA Channel 5. But he wasn't exactly UCLA's top prospect at small forward; it took Bruins prospects Reggie Williams signing with Georgetown, Antoine Joubert going to Michigan, and Tom Sheehey ending up at Virginia for a spot on the roster to open for the 6'7", 190-pound Miller.

UCLA fans soon got a taste of "Reggie Range" as well as Reggie's temper, which prompted Arizona coach Lute Olson to suggest that perhaps Miller needed a personality transplant. Miller would acknowledge tripping Washington guard Al Moscatel after alleging that Moscatel whined, threw elbows, and grabbed Miller's jersey. "Now that's a dirty player," Miller said at the time. "I can take it, but not from a little guy that comes in the paint."

Miller averaged 15.2 points per game as a sophomore during the 1984–85 season, becoming the first player in that class to lead UCLA in scoring since Bill Walton in 1971–72, after volunteer assistant coach and former Bruins star Sidney Wicks challenged him. "I used to kid him a lot and play him one on one every day and try to get him stronger," Wicks said. "So we'd go to the weight room and he was pumping iron. I was being physical with him and letting him know, 'Hey, when you go to the next level, this is what's going to happen.' He said, 'Don't worry, Coach. I can handle it.' He went on at that time to show me he could." Miller and the Bruins won the 1985 National Invitation Tournament championship with a 65–62 victory over Steve Alford and Indiana, who would go on to win the NCAA tournament title two years later. Miller was selected MVP of that postseason run.

Miller's senior season coincided with the introduction of the three-point line in college basketball, which complemented other aspects of his game. "I loved to shoot long distance," said Miller, who would make 69 of 157 attempts (43.9%) from beyond the arc in 1986–87, "because it set up everything else—my runner, my floater." Miller would launch shots from 30 feet or more, never drawing a rebuke from coach Walt Hazzard.

Miller led the Bruins to an upset of top-ranked North Carolina at Pauley Pavilion and refused to cut his hair during a nine-game winning streak because of superstition. UCLA won its first Pac-10 Conference title since 1983 before avenging two losses to Washington by beating the Huskies in the championship of the conference tournament. A 19-point victory over Central Michigan in the opening game of the NCAA tournament came next, followed by what was expected to be another easy game against Wyoming.

Not so much. Miller scored 24 points but was not a factor in the last five minutes, when Wyoming surged ahead on the way to a 78–68 victory. UCLA scored only four points in the game's last 7 minutes 58 seconds, missing 12 of its last 13 shots. "It's a simple case of us really looking ahead," Miller said more than three decades later. "Because if we win that game, we get to go up against UNLV and that's the matchup everyone wanted to see."

Miller finished his career with 2,095 points, trailing only Lew Alcindor (2,325) in school history at the time. He was drafted No. 11 overall by the Indiana Pacers against the wishes of a large chunk of the franchise's fan base, who wanted the team to pick local-hero Alford—an eventual UCLA coach. The pick turned out to be a wise one, with Miller spending all 18 seasons of his Hall of Fame career with the Pacers before retiring in 2005. He can still be seen wearing a UCLA hat at airports as he crisscrosses the country for his job as a TNT analyst, his pride in his alma mater still evident even if he did not get to hang a banner inside Pauley Pavilion.

"We play a team sport and my four years, we did not get it done other than the NIT championship, which is nice but it's not an NCAA championship," Miller said. "You forged great relationships along the way—we're all friends to this day, but yeah, not winning the big one, that's what it's all about being a Bruin."

12 Gail Goodrich

The kid didn't care that he was smaller than everybody else. Knock him down on a basketball court and you were doing him a favor. He would get right back up, step to the free-throw line, and sink two shots, thank you very much.

"That's the way I was taught to play from my dad," Gail Goodrich said, "so I always played that way."

Goodrich's father, Gail Sr., had been a slightly built standout himself, a 6-foot forward who weighed about 178 pounds when he was USC's captain in 1939. The younger Goodrich grew up in the San Fernando Valley enamored with the Trojans, sleeping with his father's USC letterman blanket.

It was an unrequited love, at least at first. Concerns about Goodrich's size and strength kept most recruiters away. Goodrich was only 5'1" and not even 100 pounds when he played on the junior varsity team as a sophomore at Sun Valley Poly High. As a junior, he was still only 5'8" when UCLA coach John Wooden spotted him at the Los Angeles City tournament.

"I'm watching his team play," Wooden told the *Los Angeles Times* in 2004, "and I notice this little left-hander, sort of small. I see he's a junior and I say, 'I'm going to be watching him.' Somebody tapped my shoulder, so I turned around, and it was Gail's mother, Jean."

Goodrich sprouted to 5'11" and 135 pounds by his senior season, drawing the interest of USC and California, though questions about his size persisted. Goodrich decided he didn't want to be anyone's second prize. "Wooden was really the one who was interested in me," Goodrich said, "and I just felt I should go where I was wanted."

Goodrich was also attracted to UCLA's fast-breaking style, which would play to his strengths as a triple threat who could pass, shoot, and drive. Goodrich's junior team was the first at UCLA to go undefeated after fully harnessing the fearlessness of the little guard with the big-time game. "I had the belief—which many would say was bordering on cockiness—that I didn't think anyone could stop me," Goodrich said.

That's not to say that there weren't adjustments to be made. As a sophomore, Goodrich tried a behind-the-back pass during a three-on-one fast-break before halftime against Washington. The pass went for a turnover and led to a lengthy rant in the locker room from Wooden, a fundamentals fundamentalist. "He was livid," Goodrich said.

But Goodrich's teammates were immediately struck by his courage. "He wanted the ball at all times," UCLA forward Keith Erickson said. "You know how you come down to the end of the game and there's a lot of pressure to take shots? Gail never felt it at all. He wanted the ball and he was a great competitor, he was a great shooter and a great scorer and a perfect complement to Walt Hazzard in the backcourt." Hazzard would acknowledge as much, saying his ballhandling paired perfectly with Goodrich's shooting. "If you passed the ball to him on the break," Hazzard told the *Times*, "you knew he wouldn't pass it back. But he made a lot of shots."

The Goodrich-Hazzard tandem was the driving force behind UCLA's first national championship in 1964, Goodrich's junior season. Goodrich's scoring binges were usually the result of Hazzard continually finding his teammate in the perfect spot. "Any time you're a shooter, a scorer, you want to play with someone who can get you the ball at the right time," Goodrich said, "and certainly he did."

Goodrich became the team's primary ballhandler as a 6'1" senior after Hazzard's departure, but remained a prolific scorer, averaging 24.8 points per game, a school record for guards. Goodrich scored 42 points during UCLA's 91–80 victory over Michigan in the 1965 national championship, a record for a title game that would stand until Bill Walton poured in 44 points against Memphis State in 1973.

The player who was supposedly too small to succeed at the college level had led UCLA in scoring as junior and a senior for back-to-back national championship teams. Goodrich left UCLA as the school's all-time leading scorer, with 1,691 points (a figure that has since been surpassed), and went on to a prolific NBA career, becoming a five-time All-Star who won a championship with the Los Angeles Lakers in 1972.

Goodrich also continued to get to the free-throw line, leading the NBA in free throws attempted (588) and made (508) during the 1973–74 season. After retiring from professional basketball in 1979, he worked in real estate and became president of a company that acquires and manages golf courses before retiring in Sun Valley, Idaho. UCLA retired his No. 25 jersey in 2004.

"Gail was a special booger," Kenny Washington, Goodrich's former UCLA teammate, told the *Times*. "He was a little ol' guy not supposed to do diddly squat. He was not highly recruited, that's the beautiful part of the story. Nobody wanted him, that's real. Nobody wanted him."

13 Lisa Fernandez

The most transformative moment of Lisa Fernandez's career came not in the pitcher's circle or in the batter's box, but on the track. She was working out with UCLA track coach Henry Hines, who had taken a liking to the freshman softball star after spotting her at Drake Stadium one day and discovering she wanted to improve her speed, perhaps the only weakness in her game.

Hines paired Fernandez with Los Angeles Lakers star Byron Scott during workouts, having Fernandez start a few hundred meters in front of Scott and try to outlast him as they raced around the track. After several of these sprints, Fernandez walked off to the side and threw up out of view of everyone. When she returned, she figured they were done running, only to be asked if she was ready to go again. "I was like, 'Uh, what are you talking about?'" Fernandez recalled. "And they're like, 'We're not done yet.' And I'm like, 'Okay.' And they're like, 'Are you all right?'"

Not wanting to let the coach and NBA player know what had happened, Fernandez said only, "Well …" It was enough of a tipoff. "They're like, 'You lost your lunch, didn't you?' And I go, 'Well, yeah.' And they're like, 'Awesome, welcome to the club! You're ready to go.' And I'm like, 'What are you talking about? I'm like, sick.' They're like, 'Oh, no, you're just getting started. Trust me. Your mind will tell your body when to stop. You've got more in you.'"

They resumed running, but the exercise did more than enhance Fernandez's speed. "I credit that moment in realizing just how powerful your mind can be," Fernandez said. "Just when your body thinks it's had enough, your mind can take over. And that probably changed my life, just even as a person in being able to realize you can accomplish whatever you set forth in your mind and how powerful it truly is."

It was why, as a senior, Fernandez told one of her coaches that she wanted to lead the nation in not only pitching but hitting. The coach was skeptical. "There's no way you could do that," he told her. Fernandez was undeterred. "I'm like, 'Why not?'" Fernandez said. "'What do I have to do? Let's set up a game plan and let's see if we can try and tackle this.'" Fernandez tackled it, all right, leading the nation in 1993 with a .507 batting average and a 0.26 earned-run average.

But her team fell short in the championship game of the Women's College World Series, a first-inning run holding up for Arizona during a 1–0 victory over Fernandez and the Bruins. "That's when I probably learned the most valuable lesson, ultimately what it means to be a true champion," Fernandez said. "There are no guarantees in our game. There are no guarantees in our sport; even the best teams, the best players, the most prepared, it doesn't always guarantee that you're going to win. But at the end of the day, once you get done competing, you want to know you gave it everything you had."

Fernandez made a habit of fully exerting herself and constantly improving. Even after a freshman season in which she helped UCLA win the national championship and a sophomore season in which she was the Pac-10 Conference's Player of the Year, Fernandez wanted more. Realizing that hitters were starting to read her best pitch, a drop ball, Fernandez developed a nasty rise ball to expand her arsenal and make her even more dominant. "One of my mottos is to never be satisfied," Fernandez said. "and I'm always looking to change my game and get different looks and make sure at the end of the day, you stay one step ahead of the hitters."

She seemed multiple steps ahead during a junior season in which she went 29–0, holding Arizona to four hits with six strikeouts in seven scoreless innings during the national championship

U.S.A. pitcher Lisa Fernandez celebrates after the final out to beat China 3–1 for the gold medal in the 1996 Olympics. (AP Photo/Eric Draper)

game, her 22nd shutout of the season. She had broken her own previous national record for consecutive victories and finished the season having pitched 65 consecutive scoreless innings, lowering her ERA to 0.14. "What was probably coolest about that time was Orel Hershiser was going through his consecutive scoreless innings streak at the same time that I was," Fernandez said, referring to the Los Angeles Dodgers ace, "and so it was neat to be able to have your name mentioned with some of the greats of America's pastime, and I think that just helped to bring notoriety to our sport."

It could be said that Fernandez was born to be a softball great. Her father played semipro baseball player in Cuba and her mother played slow-pitch softball and spent hours playing catch with her young daughter, tossing her balls that she would dive into a beanbag chair to catch. Fernandez went on to become the most decorated player in softball history. She finished her UCLA career with a 93–7 record and .382 batting average while helping the Bruins to two national championships and two runner-up finishes. She was a four-time All-American, a three-time winner of the Honda Award as the nation's top softball player, and in 1993 became the first softball player to win the Honda-Broderick Cup, given to the nation's top college female athlete.

Her dominance hardly ended there, with Fernandez going on to win Olympic gold medals in 1996, 2000, and 2004. She established an Olympic record in 2000 when she struck out 25 batters against Australia. She was also a four-time ISF Women's World Championships gold medalist (1990, 1994, 1998, and 2002). She returned to UCLA for a second stint as a full-time assistant coach in 2007, serving as a constant reminder of what's possible when one refuses to place any limits on her ambitions.

14 Kenny Washington

Kenny Washington's passes often seemed like the stuff of Hollywood. He unleashed a 72-yard touchdown pass to Hal Hirshon as part of UCLA's frenzied fourth-quarter comeback against USC in 1937, the ball traveling 62 yards in the air. To be verified as the longest pass in the history of college football at the time, the game film was inspected at the Fox Movietone headquarters, frame by frame by frame.

"Washington's pass is the first of those stupendous heaves capable of actual measurement in the movies," Bill Henry wrote in the *Los Angeles Times*. "The Movietone film is remarkably clear, despite the dusk in the stadium, and this will doubtless be accepted once and for all as the longest authentic touchdown pass ever completed by a collegiate team."

Two years before he would become the first All-American football player in UCLA history, the Bruins' good-luck No. 13 already had etched himself into school lore. Washington nearly helped his team wipe out a 19–0 deficit in the final five minutes of that game against USC at the Los Angeles Memorial Coliseum, completing two touchdown passes to Hirshon in less than 30 seconds.

A third touchdown pass was called back after officials ruled the receiver's knee had touched the ground at the 31-yard line, sealing the Bruins' fate during the 19–13 loss. Afterward, UCLA coach Bill Spaulding stopped by the USC locker room to congratulate Trojans counterpart Howard Jones. "It's all right to come out now," Spaulding yelled through the door. "Kenny's stopped passing!"

A triple threat as a runner and a passer who also played defensive back, the tailback moved somewhat ploddingly but did so with great force and developed a strong straight arm, allowing him to dodge or bulldoze his way through defenders. He was also exceedingly tough. "He could smile when his lip was bleeding," UCLA's Ray Bartlett said of Washington while they were teammates.

As a junior, Washington rushed for 688 yards, passed for an additional 214, and scored 10 touchdowns as the Bruins improved upon their 2–6–1 record the previous season by finishing 7–4–1. It was only a prelude to a magnificent senior season alongside teammates Woody Strode and Jackie Robinson, the latter of whom had joined UCLA from Pasadena Junior College.

The Bruins ended Texas Christian's 14-game winning streak with a season-opening 6–2 victory, the only touchdown coming on a third-quarter drive in which Washington completed runs of 12, 17, and seven yards. The next week, Washington set a UCLA record with 142 rushing yards during a 14–7 victory over the University of Washington, only to break it again a few weeks later with 164 yards in 11 carries during a 20–6 triumph over Montana. Washington factored into all three touchdowns during UCLA's 20–7 victory over California, running for one score and passing for two others.

All of this was just a run-up to the drama surrounding UCLA's rivalry game against USC. The Bruins had yet to beat the Trojans, but put themselves in position to do so during a game with a Rose Bowl berth on the line. In the final minutes of a scoreless tie before a crowd of 103,000—at the time the largest to watch a football game west of the Mississippi River—Washington directed a 79-yard drive that reached the Trojans' two-foot line. On fourth down, the Bruins could have kicked a field goal to go ahead but both of their kickers had injured legs, so they instead tried a pass from Washington to Don MacPherson that failed, depriving UCLA of the finish it wanted.

When Washington departed that game, which ended in a 0–0 deadlock—his last as a collegian—Strode recalled deafening cheers that made it sound as if "the pope of Rome had come out."

Washington concluded that season with school records in rushing (812 yards) and passing (582). In his three seasons, Washington averaged 4.2 yards per carry while setting a UCLA career record with 1,915 rushing yards, which would stand for 34 years, until it was surpassed by Kermit Johnson. His total offensive output of 3,206 yards was also a school record.

Washington was named Back of the Year in 1939 by *Liberty* magazine. Of the 664 players polled by the magazine, Washington was the only one to receive a vote from each player who had opposed him. He was widely considered the best player in the nation despite not winning the Heisman Trophy, leading the country in total offense while playing 580 of a possible 600 minutes.

Washington also starred for UCLA's baseball team, for which he hit for a higher average than Robinson and was believed by some to possess a better arm, more power, and more agility than the teammate who would go on to break Major League Baseball's color barrier while playing for the Brooklyn Dodgers. Washington, an infielder, batted .454 as a sophomore in 1937 and .350 as a junior in 1938.

With his college career complete, Washington served as the Bruins' freshman backfield coach in 1940, before graduating from UCLA a year later with a bachelor's degree in letters and science. He eventually became Strode's teammate with the semipro Hollywood Bears after recovering from a knee injury. Together they reintegrated the NFL in 1946 as teammates with the Los Angeles Rams, though Washington's career was beset by being a rookie who had already undergone five knee operations by the time he made his NFL debut at age 28. He played for three seasons, his finest moment a 92-yard touchdown run against the Chicago Cardinals in 1947.

"If he had come into the National Football league directly from the UCLA," Bob Waterfield, one of his Rams teammates, told *Sports Illustrated*, "he would have been, in my opinion, the best the NFL had ever seen."

Washington entered private business after his playing career before dying at age 52 in 1971. Upon learning that Washington was suffering from congestive heart and lung problems, Strode returned from a movie set in Italy with hopes of bringing his old teammate back to Rome to experience the diversity reminiscent of their childhood days in Lincoln Heights. But Washington slipped away at UCLA Medical Center, his room overlooking the Bruins' football practice field.

15 Karch Kiraly

The greatest player in the history of American volleyball chose his college over a hamburger at Denny's. The plan was for Karch Kiraly and the UCLA coach who was pursing him, Al Scates, to talk things over after splitting the distance between Kiraly's home in Santa Barbara and Scates' home in Tarzana. They ended up meeting in Calabasas, only a few minutes from where Scates lived. "I think we traveled about 60 miles," Kiraly said, "and he traveled about three."

Kiraly already knew a good deal about UCLA because it had won six NCAA championships in the previous nine years and Scates had competed against Kiraly's father, also an accomplished volleyball player, in an open championship in Detroit. Scates had never seen the younger Kiraly play but had been apprised of his potential through the coach's network of former players who served as de facto high school scouts. Scates was teaching full-time as well as coaching, so he didn't have time to go watch high school players—or drive far to convince them to play for him.

Scates' recruiting pitch at the casual eatery was successful. "We decided over a hamburger that Karch was coming to UCLA," Scates recalled of the player who made an immediate impression with his court vision in practice. "I remember one of the first plays, he watches the hitter, decides where he's going to hit it and runs about 25 feet to the left side of the court and digs the ball perfectly. I just watched him do this for a while and I said, 'Okay, Karch, play defense wherever you want.'"

Scates laughed at the recollection and then paused. "Maybe I didn't say that, I don't remember," he said. "But he was free to roam. Wherever he lined up was where the ball was." They were instincts Kiraly had learned by playing the game since he was six years old, eventually partnering with his father before starring at Santa Barbara High. One skill Kiraly had not mastered upon his arrival in Westwood was hitting. "I was a pretty horrendous hitter and horrendous attacker my freshman year," Kiraly said. "I didn't follow my stats much at all, Al didn't tell me them much at all. It was probably to keep my confidence up because I don't think I was hitting much above zero efficiency, but part of that was an adjustment to playing the college game and being a more effective hitter and eventually I figured that step out."

Kiraly helped the Bruins in many other ways his freshman season in 1979, combining with Sinjin Smith, Steve Salmons, Peter Ehrman, and Joe Mica to form the core of the first undefeated team in college volleyball history. Smith (then a senior) and Kiraly constantly pushed each other, a prelude to a successful if brief run together on the pro beach volleyball tour. "Sinjin and I would pepper a lot and hit it as hard as we could at each other," Kiraly said, "and if we had some race or some lines to run, neither one of us wanted to lose to the other, so in lots of ways we made each other better."

A come-from-behind victory over USC in the NCAA championship match capped UCLA's 30–0 season and the first of Kiraly's three titles as a Bruin. UCLA would also topple the Trojans in five games in the 1981 championship match, avenging a loss to the Bruins' rival in the finals the previous year, before rolling to a three-game victory over Penn State in 1982 that gave UCLA another undefeated (29–0) season, with Kiraly becoming the first player in college volleyball history to earn Most Valuable Player honors in two consecutive years.

While Kiraly was part of teams that went 126–5 at UCLA, one of his most memorable triumphs came during an exhibition tour of Japan in 1980. UCLA lost the first of five matches, Kiraly recalled, "and everybody in Japan wrote us off a little bit." Scates made a tactical adjustment in which Kiraly became one of two service receivers and the Bruins ran off three consecutive victories, putting them into the final match against a team of college all-stars in the same Tokyo venue where the 1964 Olympic competition had been held.

Kiraly said the building was so cold that the reserve players were wearing both their sweatsuits and the starters' sweatsuits, while steam rose from the heads of the players on the court. The Bruins got off to an equally frigid start, dropping the first two games before Scates changed the way his team attacked its counterparts' outside hitters. UCLA won a close third game, with Kiraly making a diving save on the concrete floor with the Bruins down 12–10. UCLA prevailed a bit easier in the fourth game and then stomped its way to a 15–2 victory in the fifth game. "It was a big block fest and were really excited to finish the tour so strong in challenging conditions, in a cold gym and with Al leading us with his infectious optimism and confidence the whole way," Kiraly said.

Kiraly went on to lead the U.S. volleyball team to Olympic gold medals in 1984 and '88, while keeping the team atop the world rankings for several years with victories in the World Cup, World Championships, and USA Cup. In beach volleyball, Kiraly was a three-time world champion who won Olympic gold in the inaugural beach volleyball competition in 1996 in Atlanta. His 148 career open beach victories and winnings of more than $3 million top the all-time lists.

Going to UCLA had helped teach the outside hitter who would be voted Male Volleyball Player of the Century by the International Volleyball Federation in 2000 how to win big. "We won three times and lost in the final the fourth during my four years there," Kiraly said, "so we were used to championships."

16 Meb Keflezighi

The physical education teacher laid it out in plain terms for the middle schoolers. Run hard and you're going to get an "A" or a "B" in the class. Goof around and you're going to get a "D" or an "F."

Meb Keflezighi didn't want to avoid disappointing just his teacher. His parents had stressed the importance of good grades after moving their family from war-torn Eritrea to Italy and then San Diego when Keflezighi (pronounced Ka-FLEZ-ghee) was 12. The boy retained painful memories of the war, the boom-boom-boom of gunfire and having to collect body parts for burial after they had been shredded by a land mine fresh in his mind.

There were other inducements to finish the mile with a good time. Anyone who ran it in 6:15 or less would receive an "A" as well as a T-shirt and his or her picture in the window of a building at Roosevelt Middle School. Keflezighi ran his hardest around the baseball and soccer fields on campus, finishing in 5:20 while surprising himself and everybody else. His teacher, Dick Lord, told the boy, who was just beginning to learn English, that he was going to go to the Olympics. Keflezighi's reaction: Uh, what? "Growing up without television or electricity," Keflezighi said, "I didn't know what the Olympics were, so I had no idea what he meant."

And so began the career of one of the most prolific distance runners in American history. Keflezighi would star at UCLA before winning a silver medal in the marathon in the 2004 Olympics and finishing fourth in the 2012 Olympics as part of a storied career that also included victories in the 2009 New York City Marathon and the 2014 Boston Marathon, the latter triumph coming one year after bombers killed four people.

Keflezighi didn't realize he had the potential to become a world-class runner until 1997, when he won four NCAA distance titles while at UCLA. He had been recruited by Bob Larsen after the Bruins men's track and field and cross-country coach watched the prospect compete in a high school meet. "To this day, I thought I won the race, but he didn't think I won," Keflezighi said in 2017 with a laugh. "But I don't know. There wasn't Google then, so I don't know who's right."

Larsen came away impressed nevertheless and pursued the young runner who felt that UCLA offered the perfect blend of academics and athletics. Keflezighi often ventured off campus on training runs to Venice, Marina del Rey, and Santa Monica, navigating the roots of overgrown trees on the shoulder of roads as well as Los Angeles traffic. "You've got to put a hand over your mouth or nose," he said, "so you don't inhale the exhaust."

Larsen would push Keflezighi by having him start 10 or 15 seconds behind his teammates in practice while running the mile. It never seemed to matter how far back the coach placed his top runner. "I would get mad and catch them early," Keflezighi said of his teammates. By his final college seasons, no one could catch Keflezighi. In 1997, he won the 5,000 meters (13:52.72) at the NCAA Indoor meet before topping his time by finishing in 13:44.17 at the summer NCAA Outdoor meet while also winning the 10,000 meters in 28:51.18. At the fall NCAA cross-country championships, he ran the 10,000 meters in a record time of 28:54 to become the first Bruin to win the title.

Keflezighi finished his UCLA career as a four-time All-American in cross-country, a five-time All-American at the NCAA Outdoor and a three-time All-American at the NCAA Indoor. He holds outdoor school records in both the 5,000 meters (13:26.85 in 1998) and 10,000 meters (28:16.79 in 1998) as well as the indoor school record in the 5,000 meters (13:52.72). "It was a great honor to be able to have left as the greatest distance runner from UCLA history," said Keflezighi, who considered his having graduated with a degree in communication studies an even bigger achievement.

Keflezighi soon became a U.S. citizen and retained Larsen as his personal coach, calling him a father figure and role model. After running the 10,000 meters in his first Olympics in 2000, Keflezighi shifted his focus to the marathon. He ran his first one in New York in 2002 and vowed it would be his last after he finished ninth and his entire body ached. But he persevered, becoming the first American man in 28 years to medal in the marathon when he took silver in the 2004 Olympics. He is the only runner to win the New York and Boston marathons while also earning an Olympic medal.

Keflezighi did not compete in the 2013 Boston Marathon because of an injury, vacating the grandstands on Boylston Street near the finish line five minutes before the first pressure-cooker bomb went off. A year later, with the names of four victims scrawled in black marker on his yellow race bib, Keflezighi became the first American man to win the race since Greg Meyers in 1983. He hugged his wife, Yordanos Asgedom, and wept after crossing the finish line.

"My 5:20 mile, the Boston Marathon was the conclusion of the peak of that," Keflezighi said, "affirming that I was on this Earth to be a runner and inspire or have an effect on people's life." Keflezighi ran his 26th and final marathon in New York in 2017 at age 42, allowing him to dedicate more time to raising his three daughters and running the MEB Foundation, which promotes health, education, and fitness among youth.

17 Kenny Easley

Nobody won the games that helped mold Kenny Easley into one of the most vicious free safeties in college football history. The closest thing to a victory in dynamite pigskin was walking off the field intact, not having been dragged away because of a bloodied face or a bruised shin.

Dynamite pigskin started with a scrum of young men and a football thrown into the air. Whoever caught the ball took off running; everyone else tried to pulverize him. "If we had 15 players," Easley recalled of the game he compared to rugby that was played on athletic fields in his hometown of Chesapeake, Virginia, "14 of the players were defensive players and one player was the offensive player. So you would have basically 14 players tackling one player. You could catch the ball and try to run and get whacked right in the face, so it was a tough game to play."

Upon getting tackled or being hopelessly corralled by others, the ballcarrier would fling the pigskin, known as dynamite once it became airborne. The game would go on for hours, until only a handful of players remained upright.

Easley brought a similar survivalist mind-set to UCLA after starring at quarterback and free safety for his high school team. He picked the Bruins over Michigan and scores of other suitors in part because UCLA had promised to let him play free safety—his preferred position—from the moment it started pursuing him.

But playing time was anything but guaranteed. Easley was fourth on the depth chart when he arrived in the fall of 1977. On the flight to Houston for the season opener against the University of Houston, UCLA defensive coordinator Jed Hughes approached Easley and informed him of the plan: He would split time with Michael Coulter, a senior free safety. "That's what happened," Easley said. "Michael Coulter started the game and played the first two quarters, I played the second two, and Michael never played again."

To say that Easley was an impact player as a freshman would be an understatement along the lines of saying that Los Angeles enjoys good weather. He finished the season with six interceptions and 93 tackles, both school records for a true freshman. He was part of a

Kenny Easley blocks a Washington punt in the Huskies end zone during a 1978 game. (AP Photo)

Bruins team that went 8–3–1 his sophomore season in 1978, tying Arkansas in the Fiesta Bowl, before UCLA slipped to 5–6 in 1979. Easley rolled up 17 interceptions through the end of his junior season, but one thing he had not done was beat rival USC.

That finally happened in 1980, after Trojans safety Jeff Fisher tipped a pass with less than two minutes to play, allowing UCLA tailback Freeman McNeil to grab the ball and run for a 58-yard touchdown that provided the decisive score in the Bruins' 20–17 victory. Easley called it "the greatest football game I ever played in. Beating Southern Cal, I can't even tell you what it meant to me personally because that's what you play for."

Easley added only two interceptions as a senior and it was no mystery as to why. "They didn't throw the ball down the middle," he said. "If I was playing against Kenny Easley, I wouldn't throw the ball down the middle either. It was just that simple." Easley said he and defensive backs coach Tom Hayes went back and counted only two passes thrown down the middle of the field all season. "That's very unusual," said Easley, whose Bruins did not go to a bowl that season, even though they went 9–2, because the school was on probation.

Easley credited Hayes and his two other defensive back coaches, Foster Andersen and Gary Blackney, with making him a dynamo who would finish his college career as the first defensive four-time first-team All-Pac-10 Conference player and one of only two three-time consensus All-Americans in Pac-10 history. Easley finished ninth in the Heisman Trophy balloting in 1980, and his 19 interceptions still rank first on UCLA's all-time list.

The Seattle Seahawks selected Easley with the fourth overall pick of the 1981 draft and he didn't disappoint, becoming a five-time Pro Bowler whose career ended in 1987 because of kidney problems. What might have been was a question that lingered regarding his NFL career, but not his glorious days as a Bruin. His jersey (No. 5) was retired by the school and in 1991 he was elected

Almost a Michigan Man

Kenny Easley always thought he was going to be a Michigan man. That's what he told his high school coach and most anybody who asked one of the nation's top prospects where he was going to attend college.

Easley enjoyed a recruiting visit to UCLA, his other finalist, but upon his return reaffirmed to his coach that he was still going to Michigan. The night before national signing day in 1977, coaches from Michigan and UCLA attended Easley's high school basketball game in Norfolk, Virginia, with home visits scheduled afterward. On one side of the gymnasium sat Michigan coach Bo Schembechler and on the other was UCLA counterpart Terry Donahue and Jed Hughes, the Bruins' defensive coordinator.

Schembechler received the first home visit, and it didn't go well. The veteran coach talked about Easley being the quarterback of his team until Easley, who had played both quarterback and safety in high school, told Schembechler he would prefer to be on the defensive side of the ball. "He couldn't believe that a guy who was getting the opportunity to be the Big Ten quarterback at the University of Michigan would pass that up just to be a regular old free safety," Easley recalled, "and so he was not a happy camper when he left the house."

Next up were Donahue and Hughes. "Right away—I don't know if they had a heads-up or if they simply were going after me as a safety—but they came in talking about me being a safety at UCLA," Easley said. Nevertheless, Easley still intended to go to Michigan, thinking that he could convince Schembechler to make him a free safety. When he arrived at school the next day for a signing-day event, Easley said, he was certain of his decision.

With his senior classmates at Oscar F. Smith High and a couple of local TV cameramen in the audience of the school auditorium, Easley was asked by his high school coach what he was going to do. "For whatever reason, I just blurted out, 'I'm going to UCLA,'" Easley recalled with a laugh. "So just like that, the proverbial genie is out of the bottle and it's on videotape that I'm going to UCLA." Looking back 40 years later, Easley said he suspected he changed his mind because UCLA was the only school that had said from the start it was recruiting him to play free safety. "So maybe that was deep down and instinctive," Easley said of picking the Bruins. "I don't know. I just know I had told everybody and I felt like I was going to Michigan."

Easley never had any regrets about UCLA, especially four years and a school-record 19 interceptions later. "I don't know why I said, 'UCLA,'" Easley said, "but I said it, it ended up being the right thing to say, and I proved that by the career that I had there that it was the proper place for me to be."

to the UCLA Athletic Hall of Fame and the College Football Hall of Fame. His election to the Pro Football Hall of Fame followed in 2017, a testament to the player that no offense wanted to face, particularly when it was a game that pitted 14 versus one.

18 Al Scates

Inside a display case in the UCLA Athletic Hall of Fame, which is crammed with memorabilia from championship teams and Olympians, is a lion turned backward with "UCLA" etched under its tail. It might be the most remarkable talisman of Al Scates' record-breaking 50-year run as the Bruins' men's volleyball coach.

The trophy is from the 1980 International Friendship Cup, a tournament held in Taipei that involved several national teams. USA Volleyball couldn't sponsor a team because of a lack of resources, so it sent Scates' Bruins, who had gone 30–0 in 1979 while winning the NCAA championship. UCLA was supposed to be no match for the Republic of China, at least according to the perspective of the host team. The Chinese did not invite some of their powerhouse rivals and were so confident in their chances of winning the tournament that they engraved their name on the lion that represented the championship trophy.

The Bruins easily made the championship match, defeating Venezuela, the Republic of China's junior national team, Colombia, and France to set up a finals showdown with the Republic of China's national team. Scates believed in his team, knowing it had beaten Japan earlier in the year in Tokyo and featured Karch Kiraly and Steve Salmons, making it stronger than the team sponsored by USA Volleyball. His belief was handsomely rewarded. The Bruins dispatched China 15–12, 15–10, 15–9, in front of a capacity crowd of 20,000 that was the largest ever to watch a U.S. collegiate volleyball team. UCLA had showed it was among the best teams in the world, winning 18 of 19 games on the way to the title. "That was huge," said Scates, whose upset forced the Chinese to add the UCLA engraving on the lion.

Remarkably, that wasn't even one of Scates' top teams during an epic career in which the Bruins compiled three undefeated seasons and won a school-record 19 NCAA championships, nearly twice as many as John Wooden's 10 titles. Those honors went to the 1984 Bruins, who finished 38–0 and were voted the best collegiate team of all time by coaches in a poll for *Volleyball* magazine. That team included Ricci Luyties, who started and won four NCAA championship matches; Doug Partie, who started for four NCAA championship seasons; and Ozzie Volstad, the middle blocker whom Scates had recruited off a videotape from Norway. Scates considered his 1982 team that went 29–0 behind the strong play of Kiraly, Partie, Luyties, and Dave Saunders—each of whom went on to win gold medals in the Olympics—on equal footing with the 1984 team, but there was no shortage of contenders when you had as much success as Scates did over so many years.

Scates' players said winning big was every bit as attributable to their coach as their vast talent. "We were favored in lots of contests," Kiraly said, "so Al was a master at helping us be good in that sometimes difficult favorite role where the target is always on your back, and that's a skill in itself." He did it with infectious enthusiasm and savvy tactical adjustments, not to mention old-fashioned hard work.

Scates' teams won 24 conference championships and finished with a 1,239–290 record, winning 81.2 percent of their games. He coached 80 players who were All-Americans, 44 who played on the U.S. national team, 27 who participated in the Olympics, and seven who were collegiate player of the year at least once. He

The Event

Al Scates' contributions to volleyball go well beyond the scores of championships and star players he produced. He also helped make it an NCAA sport.

In 1965, his third year coaching the UCLA's men's team, there was no volleyball below the college level except in pickup games. Scates would stage free high school clinics, but he hatched his greatest idea to grow the sport while serving as captain of the U.S. men's national team that traveled to Mexico City to play its Mexican counterparts. It was there that he learned the Japanese men's and women's national teams would be making a stopover in Los Angeles on the way back to Japan after playing in Brazil.

Scates approached UCLA athletic director J.D. Morgan and pitched the idea of holding a tripleheader inside the newly opening Pauley Pavilion in which the school would keep all the gate receipts.

Some might have seen it as a dubious proposition. Just a few months earlier, the U.S. national team had played France at Carson High. The match received no publicity and the only spectators were family members of the participants. "The net broke halfway through the match," Scates recalled. "This was how USA Volleyball put on events—all volunteers, no money, and bad venues."

But Scates had more ambitious plans for the tripleheader. He wrote articles that his wife Sue would type up, and his friend Bud Furillo, the sports editor of the *Los Angeles Herald-Examiner*, agreed to publish. He also went on Furillo's radio show to promote the event and UCLA agreed to distribute posters promoting the tripleheader to its season-ticket holders in football and basketball. Scates also nailed posters to telephone poles in beach towns to generate interest among the volleyball crowd.

All the work paid off in an unprecedented way, the throng of 5,000 who showed up forming a record volleyball crowd. Fans got to see UCLA sweep rival USC in the first match before the Japanese women easily beat their American counterparts. In the featured match, the U.S., benefiting from what Scates described as some friendly calls from an official, defeated the Japanese men, who had won a silver medal in the 1964 Olympics.

Morgan approached Scates afterward, incredulous at the evening's success. "He looked at the crowd and he couldn't believe this many people would come out to watch volleyball," Scates said. "He told me, 'I'm going to make this an NCAA sport!'" Morgan was powerful enough to make it happen, serving as chairman of the NCAA basketball committee. Sure enough, in 1970, UCLA, which had previously competed in the U.S. Volleyball Association, hosted and won the first NCAA championship, sweeping Long Beach State in the finals.

"That's probably the best thing I did, to get that tripleheader together to get J.D. behind this," Scates said. "Volleyball took off from the colleges on down. Once people saw this, all of a sudden teams started multiplying all over the place."

was the only coach in any collegiate sport to guide a team to three consecutive national championships three different times, including four straight from 1981 to '84. He was also national Coach of the Year six times and the first active coach to be inducted into the UCLA Athletic Hall of Fame, in 2003.

The Bruins' success was hardly a function of their resources. Before Scates' first season in 1963, when he served as a player-coach, he told UCLA athletic director Wilbur Johns that he couldn't accept a coaching salary because he wanted to play for the Olympic team. "He just basically jumped out of his chair and said, 'Congratulations, son. You're hired!'" Scates said of Johns. "And he added, 'By the way, here's your budget and it's $100.'" Scates used the money on volleyballs, forcing him to borrow basketball uniforms from Wooden's team, complete with metal belt buckles.

"Fortunately," Scates said, "we didn't do a lot of diving in those days." The Bruins bought their own socks and jock straps as well as meals and gas. Scates spent $25 on a dilapidated Mercury station wagon (complete with trademark wood paneling) that leaked oil, piling in as many players as could fit into the thing. "I mean, we came from nothing," said Scates, who wasn't made a full-time coach until 1979, working as an elementary school P.E. teacher to support his family.

The coach also made the most of his meager practice time, which consisted of only two hours on Wednesday nights when he started. While other coaches carried 12 or 14 players on their rosters, Scates refused to cut anyone and spread his 36 players among three practice courts. He ran drills that simulated game-like conditions, gave his assistants complete authority, and freely demoted players to courts with lesser teammates, once sending Sinjin Smith down for three weeks during his freshman year. "I never just taught one skill like the other coaches did," Scates said. "If I wanted to work on blocking, I would start with a serve and then there would be a pass and a set and then I would focus on the blocking from the referees' stand or actually stand on the court right behind the blockers during a live drill. As I got older and slower I moved off the court and coached the blockers from behind the end line."

Scates would give instant feedback, a tactic he learned from watching Wooden's practices. He also ran grueling 45-minute circle drills that entailed hundreds of sit-ups and push-ups in addition to a series of sprints, dives, and jumps. "Then we would bring the ball out when we exhausted them," Scates said, "and run a practice."

His efforts made UCLA an unrivaled powerhouse. At the time of Scates' retirement in 2012, UCLA held 27 NCAA men's volleyball team and individual records, including consecutive victories (48), consecutive home court victories (83), consecutive NCAA tournament victories (15), and most undefeated seasons (three). Scates led the Bruins to a 52–7 record in NCAA tournament matches, including a 25–1 mark at Pauley Pavilion.

His last national championship, in 2006, prompted some ribbing from Wooden after the Bruins won their final 14 games after starting the season with a 12–12 record. When he returned from State College, Pennsylvania, he had a voicemail from Wooden, who tried to disguise his voice. "He said, 'Well, Al, this is a disgruntled alumnus and it was so embarrassing the way your team started out this year and you finally started coaching and I'm glad to see you won a championship,'" Scates said with a chuckle. "He would give me a couple of zingers from time to time."

19 Russell Westbrook

UCLA didn't initially have a scholarship available for the player who would go on to become an NBA Most Valuable Player.

The Bruins were interested in Russell Westbrook, a raw but undeniably budding talent at Leuzinger High in nearby Lawndale, but their roster was fully stocked for the following season when the early signing period came in November 2005. Westbrook could have signed with a host of smaller schools that were recruiting him, including Wyoming and Creighton, but opted to wait for something better.

UCLA's offer came only after the Bruins knew they were going to lose Jordan Farmar to the NBA draft, allowing Westbrook to sign his letter of intent in the spring of 2006 at a time when most high school standouts had been taken. "They didn't say much about who was going to go," Westbrook later told the *Los Angeles Times*. "I just had a feeling" there would be an opening.

Westbrook arrived in Westwood with an unreliable jump shot and a tendency to overly rely on his freakish physical ability. But he was already exhibiting signs of precociousness for a 17-year-old, winning the job as the backup to point guard Darren Collison in part because of his fearlessness.

"Normally you have times when you have to tell freshmen to shoot the ball," Collison told the *Times*. "We don't have to tell

Russell to shoot the ball. That's a good thing. We need somebody to be aggressive."

Westbrook played sparingly off the bench before making his first career start against West Virginia in February, with Collison sidelined by a shoulder injury. It was not a joyous debut. Westbrook missed 10 of 11 shots while committing three turnovers and fouling out of a 70–65 loss to the Mountaineers, lamenting afterward that he had not played aggressively enough.

He finished his first college season with a modest average of 3.4 points in about nine minutes per game while logging more turnovers (25) than assists (24), but his confidence was already fully formed. As UCLA battled Indiana in the second round of the NCAA tournament, Westbrook collected a loose ball and sprinted toward the basket before elevating for a ferocious one-handed dunk over the Hoosiers' Rod Wilmont. It led to an ugly scene.

"The Indiana players were so pissed they came over and kind of accosted him like, 'Who is this punk freshman?'" UCLA coach Ben Howland recalled. "And little did they know, that's Russell Westbrook."

Westbrook elevated his game over the summer between his freshman and sophomore seasons in stunning fashion. He packed seven pounds onto a frame that would become 6'3" and 189 pounds, while hoisting as many as 800 shots a day, developing a more consistent release point and increasing the arc on his jumper. Westbrook worked out wherever he could find an open court, whether it was at UCLA's men's gymnasium or Ross Snyder Park at 41st and Compton or Rowley Park off 132nd Street in Gardena.

"He absolutely blew up and became dominant," said Howland, noting that Westbrook improved more in one season than any player he had ever coached. "He would go up to the men's gym and they would tell stories coming out of there every day about him dominating everybody, dominating the pros."

Kevin Love and Russell Westbrook celebrate after defeating Stanford to win the Pac-10 Conference tournament title at the Staples Center in Los Angeles on Saturday, March 15, 2008. (AP Photo/Kevork Djansezian)

Westbrook carved a basketball and flames into his hair, dubbing it "the flaming mohawk," and featured an equally flamboyant game. He immediately moved into a more prominent role, often starting alongside Collison in the backcourt.

The results were a massive uptick in productivity. Westbrook delivered a 40-minute, 13-point, three-assist, one-turnover performance during a victory over Michigan State and became a defensive menace capable of stopping even the most prolific scorers. He held Michigan's Manny Harris to 11 points on 3-for-12 shooting and Davidson's Stephen Curry to 15 points, nearly 10 below his average. Curry said Westbrook had played him tougher than anybody at a time when Curry had already faced North Carolina and Duke.

"Westbrook has such long arms," Curry said after the game. "He was just always there."

Westbrook remained a gracious teammate, accepting a temporary move to the bench in January when Michael Roll's foot injury left the Bruins without a reliable reserve guard. Westbrook finished the season as the Pac-10 Conference's Defensive Player of the Year while helping his team advance to a third consecutive Final Four, where it lost to Memphis, 78–63, in a national semifinal.

Westbrook was upstaged by the Tigers' Chris Douglas-Roberts—who scored 28 points—in that defeat, prompting some to believe Westbrook should return for his junior season after averaging 12.7 points and 4.3 assists in 33.8 minutes per game as a sophomore. Westbrook faced doubts about his mid-range jump shot and his ability to run the point on a full-time basis, but they were answered during workouts for NBA teams after Westbrook declared for the draft.

The Oklahoma City Thunder selected Westbrook with the fourth overall pick in the 2008 Draft, leading to a glorious period for the franchise in which it advanced to the NBA Finals in 2012 with Westbrook starring alongside Kevin Durant and James

Harden. Westbrook became a seven-time All-Star during his first 10 NBA seasons, leading the league in scoring by averaging 28.1 points per game in 2014–15 and 31.6 points per game in 2016–17, when he was selected the league's MVP and became the only player in NBA history besides Oscar Robertson to average a triple-double. None of which Howland could have envisioned when the Bruins made Westbrook a late addition to their roster.

"I never could imagine," Howland said, "he could be the best player in the NBA when we were recruiting him at that time."

20 Don MacLean

Don MacLean had a plan for putting up points as a freshman at UCLA. If he could make four baskets in the halfcourt, two baskets in transition, one or two putbacks, and six free throws, he would tally at least 20 points per game. The 6'10" forward didn't want to reach that threshold just to say he got 20 points; he figured scoring was his role on the team, just as distributing the ball was point guard Pooh Richardson's role and rebounding was forward Trevor Wilson's role.

It was apparent by MacLean's ninth game as a Bruin just how good he was at his role. MacLean poured in 41 points against North Texas—a school record for a freshman in a varsity game—prompting Jimmy Gales, the losing coach, to jokingly try to orchestrate a trade for the super scorer. UCLA coach Jim Harrick noted how MacLean could score in four ways: within the framework of the offense, in transition, on putbacks, and with free throws. "He's got an innate ability with a great touch," Harrick told the *Los Angeles Times*.

MacLean had developed a quick release on his shot many years earlier while starring for American Roundball Corporation, his travel ball team based in the San Fernando Valley. When he was in the fourth grade, MacLean competed against sixth-graders and learned he needed to get the ball off against larger counterparts. "I couldn't jump—I was a skinny white kid—but I could shoot and so I had to figure out a way to get that shot off against all these bigger, faster, better athletes and the only way I could do it was to get rid of it quicker," MacLean said. That process started with planting his feet before a defender could be in position to contest a shot, moving the ball to the release point, and letting it fly. MacLean did it better than almost anyone.

A fierce recruiting battle ensued for MacLean once he reached Simi Valley High. He narrowed his choices to UCLA and Georgia Tech and might have very well been a Yellow Jacket had the Bruins not fired coach Walt Hazzard in the wake of a 16–14 season. MacLean had known Harrick, Hazzard's replacement, since playing on a youth team coached by Harrick when he was in the sixth grade; MacLean also attended Harrick's basketball camp at Pepperdine before he came to UCLA. It wasn't long after Harrick was hired that MacLean signed his letter of intent with the Bruins.

Just as newsworthy as MacLean's scoring prowess—he averaged 18.6 points per game as a freshman—was a fiery demeanor that triggered entanglements with referees and opposing players. MacLean traded verbal barbs with Oregon State's Gary Payton, among many others, and fired a ball into the crotch of Arizona's Brian Williams, admitting afterward that it was "a stupid play." But there was a point to MacLean's petulance; it made him the player he was.

"It's almost like you get into a thing where you don't even know what you're doing; it's not really conscious, which may sound like B.S., but it's really the truth," MacLean said. "I was so locked in mentally to play that anything that disrupted what I was trying to do got me going—an official's call, another player talking, saying something, and so I just let it rip and let it fly and there was a lot of debate on that on whether or not it was good, it was good for me, good for our team. But at the end of the day, it's kind of who I was."

Partially as a result of intense pushback, MacLean decided to soften his approach heading into his senior season. He needed only 379 points to surpass Lew Alcindor (now Kareem Abdul-Jabbar) as UCLA's all-time leading scorer, but slumped so badly in the first handful of games that he decided to return to his old approach. "Once I kind of went back to saying, 'You know what, screw this, I'm just going to go play,' is the minute I started playing better," MacLean said.

MacLean pushed past Alcindor with a free throw against Oregon State on February 13, 1992, telling Harrick afterward that he was relieved the pursuit was over. That allowed the team to fully focus on a deep NCAA tournament run, the one thing that had eluded MacLean during his first three seasons, when the Bruins were eliminated in the NCAA tournament by North Carolina in the second round, by Duke in a regional semifinal, and by Penn State in the first round.

That upset loss to the Nittany Lions was one of the primary factors that motivated MacLean to return for his senior season. UCLA returned all five starters and added freshmen Ed O'Bannon and Tyus Edney, leading to hopes of a Final Four run. The Bruins rolled through their first three games in the NCAA tournament before facing Indiana, the same team they had beaten by 15 points in their season opener. There would be no repeat, with the Hoosiers stomping UCLA 106–79 in the worst postseason defeat in Bruins history. MacLean has a pretty good idea what happened.

"That team got selfish along the way for whatever reason and by the end, we weren't playing for each other, we just weren't," MacLean said. "And I hate to say that, I hate to admit that on the record, but it's the truth because talent-wise, there's no reason why we shouldn't have been at least in the Final Four. I mean, that team was really, really good on paper and we were good for most of the year, but as that year went on, individual agendas started coming to the forefront."

MacLean would finish his career with 2,608 points—not just topping the school list but also setting a Pac-10 Conference record—while averaging 20.5 points per game. He fully acknowledged he did it in four years as opposed to the three that Bruins legends Alcindor and Bill Walton completed in the days before freshmen were allowed to play for the varsity team.

"Listen, I would never in a million years compare myself to Lew Alcindor or Bill Walton or some of the greats at UCLA," said MacLean, who went on to spend nine seasons in the NBA, becoming the league's Most Improved Player in 1993–94, "but I have that record for a reason and that's because I came to play every night. And you can talk about my attitude, you can talk about that I barked at the officials too much—you can talk about any of that stuff—but at the end of the day, I have that record because I showed up to play every single night and I think my teammates know that. I know Coach Harrick knows that and so all in all, I think a pretty good career. Do I wish we had gotten to the Final Four that year? Yeah. But we did a lot of great things along the way."

21 See a Game at Pauley Pavilion

The eyes are naturally drawn to the rafters inside Pauley Pavilion. Eleven blue banners with gold lettering signify UCLA's men's basketball national championships and serve as an everlasting testament to the Bruins greats who have called the building home, from Lew Alcindor and Sidney Wicks to Bill Walton and Marques Johnson to Ed O'Bannon and Tyus Edney.

The ears also get to partake in the sensory smorgasbord. As players warm up prior to tip-off, they are serenaded by the student section as part of the roll call. "Lon-zo Ba-aaall!" the fans chanted during the star point guard's one season on campus, prompting him to raise his hand in acknowledgment. Then it's on to the Frisbee Cheer, a student engaging his peers in another pregame ritual. "Is that the loooooosing team?" the student leader asks while pointing at UCLA's opponent. "Yes, that's the loooooosing team!" his fellow students confirm, repeating the gesture.

Then comes the best part—the game itself, which usually involves a Bruins victory. Sports are supposed to be life's great unscripted drama, but UCLA games at Pauley Pavilion have been pretty close to a sure thing for more than a half century. The Bruins went undefeated on their home court eight times in their first 10 seasons and held a 98-game home winning streak that stretched from the 1970–71 season to 1975–76. UCLA had won 86.4 percent of its games there through the 2017–18 season.

UCLA scored a school-record 149 points at Pauley Pavilion in 1990 during a victory over Loyola Marymount and has knocked off a No. 1 team in the Associated Press ranking four times on its home court, beating Kentucky in 2015, Kansas in 2002, North Carolina in 1986, and Notre Dame in 1974. Of course, chances are if there's a top-ranked team inside Pauley Pavilion it's the Bruins.

"That building was magic and magical," Bruin great Reggie Miller said. "The fans and the student section, it was great. And after the game, walking back to your dorm or suite, there's something special about that. There's something special about the camaraderie you have with the student section in that building. I absolutely loved it."

There's been more to love in recent seasons after the building underwent a $136-million renovation that took 33 months, reopening for the 2012–13 season with nearly 1,000 additional seats. UCLA twice set all-time highs for single-game attendance that season, with a record 13,727 fans packing the arena for a victory over Arizona. Cavernous spaces between the basket and the baseline bleachers that had been requested by coach John Wooden, who believed it was unsportsmanlike to have noisy fans too close to the court, were eliminated thanks to the installation of retractable seats.

The refurbished arena features a wide, modern indoor concourse with additional concession stands. There's also new seats, locker rooms, and player lounges as well as a weight room, sports medicine room, film room, equipment room, high-definition video board, and LED ribbon board encircling the interior. Fans were pleased that restroom capacity increased by 154 percent from the old building, greatly reducing wait times. The Pavilion Club on the mezzanine level hosts pregame events as well as other events throughout the year.

The original Pauley Pavilion opened in 1965, with a cost of more than $5 million, giving the Bruins a permanent home after years of being vagabonds playing at a variety of high school and college venues in addition to their own long-outdated Men's Gym. Regent Edwin W. Pauley contributed $1 million toward construction costs, becoming the principal donor and leading to the building being named in his honor. Pauley Pavilion was first used for commencement services in 1965. In the first basketball game played on the court, UCLA's freshman team, led by Alcindor (now Kareem Abdul-Jabbar), defeated the varsity team that had won the national championship the previous season. The Bruins also won their first official game inside the building, a 92–66 victory over Ohio State on December 3, 1965.

The arena would serve as host to the UCLA men's and women's basketball teams, men's and women's gymnastics teams, and men's and women's volleyball teams. The 1984 Olympic gymnastics competition was held at Pauley Pavilion, with Mary Lou Retton's perfect 10s on the floor exercise and vault catapulting her to the all-around gold medal. In 1991, the building played host to the U.S. Olympics Festival basketball and gymnastics competitions.

Notable entertainers to perform inside Pauley Pavilion have included Bob Hope, Frank Sinatra, Bob Dylan, Nirvana, Eric Clapton, Guns N' Roses, the Grateful Dead, and Luciano Pavarotti.

Wooden was a regular in the building long after he retired in 1975, sitting behind the Bruins bench in Section 103B, Row 2, Seat 1. UCLA dedicated the floor inside Pauley Pavilion as "Nell and John Wooden Court" before a game against Michigan State in 2003, with scores of the coach's former players joining him for the celebration. Then the Bruins did what they usually did inside Pauley Pavilion, beating the Spartans.

Another tribute to Wooden came in 2011 when his great-grandson, Tyler Trapani, scored the last basket in the arena before renovations started, when he grabbed an airball and made a layup against Arizona. "I'm still kind of baffled at what just happened," Trapani, a walk-on guard, said of the basket that seemed heaven sent.

22 Walt Hazzard

To play with Walt Hazzard was to always be prepared to catch a pass or risk bodily harm. The UCLA guard was known for faking a jump shot and flicking the ball to a teammate not ready for the blur of leather whirring toward him. "You had to be on your toes all the time," Bruins forward Keith Erickson recalled, "or you'd get hit in the head with the ball because Walt was so awesome with it."

The player who plied his magic with slick passes and fancy dribbling came to be known as the Wizard of Westwood before John Wooden earned that nickname. Hazzard would effortlessly move the ball behind his back or between his legs, earning himself comparisons to Boston Celtics star Bob Cousy.

There was an adjustment period, to be sure, between Hazzard and his teammates—not to mention Wooden, who favored a more fundamental approach. Player and coach eventually agreed to allow the 6'2" ballhandler to display his freewheeling style while embracing Wooden's concepts, to results that were universally appealing. "I always thought of Walt," Erickson said, "as Magic Johnson before his time."

Hazzard was already something of a Philadelphia basketball legend before he made his college debut. He attended Overbrook High—the same school that produced Wilt Chamberlain—and led his teams to an 89–3 record in three seasons. Hazzard faced far stiffer competition on the playground, where he tangled with pros including Chamberlain, Guy Rodgers, and Woody Sauldsberry.

It was a connection made during those encounters that helped steer Hazzard to UCLA. He was the babysitter for the infant son of Sauldsberry, who encouraged UCLA star Willie Naulls to recruit Hazzard. After spending a year at Santa Monica College to satisfy admission requirements, Hazzard was officially a Bruin in the fall of 1961. He led the team to its first Final Four appearance as a sophomore, with UCLA losing to Cincinnati 72–70 in a national semifinal after Hazzard was called for charging in the final minute with the score tied, and the Bearcats' Tom Thacker drained a 25-foot jumper from the right wing with three seconds left.

It was much easier to cut off Hazzard than his passes. He often stunned opponents with a quick flip between defenders to a teammate underneath the basket. Teams eventually sagged toward the basket in anticipation of his passes, prompting Wooden to ask Hazzard to start shooting more. Hazzard increased his scoring output in each of his three seasons at UCLA, even if it wasn't always fun to watch.

"Man and boy, full-court or free-throw line, no one threw in any uglier baskets than Walt Hazzard," wrote Jim Murray, the Pulitzer Prize–winning columnist for the *Los Angeles Times*. "They came from everywhere, under his arms, under his legs, behind his back, underhanded, overhanded, line drives, soap bubbles, rim shots, prayers, fallaways. They would have had to improve merely to be called 'garbage.'"

Of course, Murray also acknowledged the root of Hazzard's unorthodox style—those playground games against more skilled and experienced players. "Man, you had to invent ways to get the ball in the basket," Hazzard explained to Murray, who also pinpointed the skill that would make Hazzard the most exhilarating presence in college basketball. "No one whistled the all-court passes with the velocity and accuracy of a Hazzard," Murray wrote.

UCLA accentuated Hazzard's strengths with a fast-breaking offense and full-court press. As a senior, Hazzard was surrounded by a talented supporting cast that included guard Gail Goodrich, forwards Jack Hirsch and Erickson, center Fred Slaughter, and key reserves Kenny Washington and Doug McIntosh. The Bruins proved unbeatable, going 30–0 for their first national title and undefeated season after a 98–83 victory over Duke in the championship game.

Hazzard finished his career as the leading scorer in UCLA history with 1,401 points after having averaged 18.6 points during his senior season. Wooden called him "undoubtedly the finest ballhandler I've ever coached." Hazzard was a consensus first-team All-American, the Most Outstanding Player of the Final Four, and Player of the Year as selected by the Helms Athletic Foundation and the U.S. Basketball Writers Association. In 1964, he played for the U.S. Olympic team that won the gold medal in Tokyo.

After becoming a territorial draft pick of the Los Angeles Lakers in 1964 and spending 10 years in the NBA, Hazzard returned to UCLA in March 1984 as the fifth coach to try to recapture the Wooden magic. He vowed to infuse his teams with some of the elements of his legendary predecessor but never came close to matching his success. Hazzard's first team won the 1985 National Invitation Tournament and appeared poised for greater things after winning 12 of its last 13 games.

But the Bruins went only 15–14 the next season, getting eliminated in the first round of the NIT. Hazzard's third season was his best, the Bruins winning the Pac-10 title and going 25–7 before losing to Wyoming, 78–66, in the second round of the NCAA tournament. UCLA needed to win the Pac-10 tournament the next year to make the NCAA tournament, but lost in the first round to Washington State. Less than three weeks later, Hazzard was fired after having completed his four seasons with a 77–47 record, his .621 winning percentage ranking as the lowest of any UCLA coach to have followed Wooden.

Hazzard suffered a stroke in 1996, requiring years of rehabilitation, and died in November 2011 at age 69 following complications from heart surgery. He was a special consultant to the Lakers at the time of his death, his passion for the game remaining strong to the end.

The 1963–64 National Championship

John Wooden's UCLA teams achieved consistent but unremarkable success in his first 15 seasons on campus. The Bruins had won or tied for eight conference titles while making the NCAA tournament five times, advancing to one Final Four.

Few outside the program figured the 1963–64 season would be any different. UCLA featured a quality roster led by the backcourt of Walt Hazzard and Gail Goodrich, but the Bruins lacked size in a big way. Center Fred Slaughter and forward Keith Erickson, both 6'5", were the tallest starters. *Sports Illustrated* didn't even rank UCLA in its preseason top 20.

Fortunately for the Bruins, self-confidence was one trait they did not lack. Goodrich had visualized his team playing for the national championship after watching the 1963 title game between Cincinnati and Loyola of Chicago. "I knew we had everybody coming back and I think everybody's going to get better," Goodrich said of his mind-set. "So I said, 'Next year, we're going to play in that championship game.'"

UCLA managed to offset its stature shortage by the presence of something no other team could match: the two-minute explosion, also known as the Bruin Blitz. That was a scoring flurry in which the Bruins would flummox an opponent who only moments earlier had thought it was every bit UCLA's equal. "It happened in every game that season," Erickson said. "We'd run off six, eight, 10, 15 points in a row."

The zero side of those runs was what was most impressive, a result of the newly installed full-court zone press conceived by assistant coach Jerry Norman. It positioned the speedy tandem of Slaughter and Goodrich under the opponents' basket, with

Hazzard and Jack Hirsch behind them and Erickson serving as the final line of defense. Capitalizing on UCLA's quickness, the alignment flustered teams into turnover after turnover, leading to scores of easy baskets. "Nobody could figure out how to break that," Erickson said. "Our press gave us that advantage."

UCLA unveiled its new look in the season opener, a 113–71 rout of Brigham Young before only 4,700 fans in which the Bruins broke the school scoring record. UCLA gained national acclaim two days after Christmas when it throttled No. 3 Michigan by a score of 98–80 at the Los Angeles Memorial Sports Arena. Nevertheless, plenty of room remained on the bandwagon. "We were ranked No. 1 in the country and that was very unusual for us and I certainly wasn't thinking, 'Okay, we can win it all,'" Erickson recalled. "I mean, that never entered my mind."

UCLA ran off victory after victory, its closest call on the way to the NCAA tournament a 58–56 triumph over California in which Hazzard sank two free throws with 12 seconds left. Wooden told his players before they started postseason play that whatever happened could neither increase nor decrease his pride and pleasure in a team that had won its first 26 games. Of course, that seemed hard to believe given what unfolded next.

The Bruins persevered for a 95–90 victory over Seattle in their NCAA tournament opener before trailing the University of San Francisco by 13 points in the first half of their second-round game. But here came the Bruin Blitz, helping UCLA run away in the second half for a 76–72 victory that sent it to a second Final Four in three years.

The last two games at Municipal Auditorium in Kansas City would follow the same formula. UCLA repeatedly missed layups trying to penetrate Kansas State's zone defense in the national semifinal and trailed the Wildcats 75–70 with only 7:20 left in the game. A little more than two minutes and 11 consecutive points later, UCLA was ahead to stay on its way to a 90–84 triumph

March 21, 1964, Kansas City, Missouri: Coach Wooden (right) and members of the team celebrate after defeating Duke to win the NCAA basketball championship. Players in the front row are, from left: Gail Goodrich, Walt Hazzard, and Jack Hirsch (holding the trophy). (AP Photo/File)

in which Erickson scored a career-high 28 points to go with 10 rebounds.

Duke presented an entirely different challenge in the championship game. The Blue Devils relied heavily on two 6'10" players in Jay Buckley and Hack Tison, not to mention star swingman Jeff Mullins. When asked before the game how he looked at Duke, Wooden replied, "Up."

Duke looked like it might be the first team all season to withstand the two-minute explosion. The Blue Devils repeatedly broke the press for baskets in the game's early going. Wooden countered by inserting a pair of sophomores in Doug McIntosh and Kenny Washington, whose hyperkinetic energy increased UCLA's defensive intensity and swung the game in the Bruins' favor by helping to generate a good chunk of the Blue Devils' 24 turnovers. A 30–27 Duke lead was gone after a 16–0 UCLA run that encompassed—you guessed it—two and a half minutes before halftime, the difference in the Bruins' eventual 98–83 victory.

Goodrich finished with 27 points and Washington, who had traveled 2,440 miles to UCLA from Beaufort, South Carolina, while riding in the back of a Greyhound bus, notched 26 points and 12 rebounds off the bench. Unknown to Washington, his father, Fred, had made the trip from South Carolina to Kansas City to watch his son, who had enrolled at UCLA only because black players were not welcome closer to home in the Atlantic Coast or Southeastern Conferences. Father and son embraced afterward, the first undefeated basketball season in UCLA's 45-year history complete and a dynasty unlike any other just beginning to be unspooled. The team that finished 30–0 would go down as Wooden's favorite, even as he went on to win 10 national championships in a 12-year span.

"It is my firm conviction that the 1963–64 basketball Bruins came as close to fulfilling all of the criteria for success as any team has ever come in the history of athletics," Wooden wrote in a commemorative program. "The courage and poise with which they met every challenge through the entire season, their unselfish team play, aggressive defense, fine passing, hustle, and determination should serve as a source of inspiration to UCLA teams of the future in all sports."

24 Keith Erickson

Keith Erickson came to UCLA on a partial basketball scholarship and a partial baseball scholarship. He was so good that one of his coaches risked his job to let Erickson play... volleyball.

It was 1964 and John Wooden, the Bruins' yet-to-become-legendary basketball coach, had barred the forward from playing volleyball because of concerns about his grades. But Erickson still wanted to play and his volleyball coach, Al Scates, agreed to let him participate in a tournament after doing his best to make sure no one learned of his presence.

"I collared the *Daily Bruin* reporter and said, 'You cannot put Keith's name in the article, you've got that?'" Scates recalled with a laugh, referring to the student newspaper. "And they would listen in those days, they would do what you told them. And so Monday, I get a lunch break from teaching and I come over to UCLA and Keith's name is not in the article."

Scates had gotten away with using the 6'5"-inch hitter to help win the tournament, but he was feeling guilty for betraying the wishes of Wooden, a good friend. Scates sought out Wooden to confess but learned he was not in his office. UCLA athletic director J.D. Morgan spotted Scates and asked him what he was doing there.

"I said, 'I'm looking for Coach; I played Keith,'" Scates said. Morgan was apoplectic. "Oh my god," the athletic director said before anticipating Wooden's reaction. "He's going to cut him off the team! He told him not to play." Scates offered to resign, figuring he could coach high school football, and Morgan agreed that was a good idea. So it was official. Scates was finished.

A few days later, Scates received a call from Morgan saying he wanted him back at UCLA with a $200 raise. The coach readily complied. Sometime in the years that followed, Scates, who would go on to win a school-record 19 NCAA titles, had lunch with Wooden and asked if he ever knew about Erickson having played volleyball at a time when the sport was supposed to be off-limits.

"He says, 'Oh yeah. I knew about that,'" Scates recalled. "'I tore up your letter of resignation.' I thought J.D. tore it up. I didn't even know Coach knew about it. So I guess Coach Wooden saved my volleyball career."

Erickson wasn't seen as any sort of savior when he arrived at UCLA after spending one year at El Camino College. That's why Wooden and Arthur Reichle, the Bruins' baseball coach, each agreed to take on only part of Erickson's scholarship. If he didn't pan out in both sports, then neither coach would have utilized a full scholarship.

There was no need to worry about that. Erickson was a more-than-capable shortstop and center fielder, who also starred as a forward on the basketball team. As a first-team All-American in volleyball who could outjump almost anyone, Erickson helped UCLA win the 1965 United States Volley Ball Association championship, its first major title in the sport. "He could do anything," Scates said. "I remember him down at the beach beating me up playing some kind of paddle tennis. He was a total natural."

Erickson would play baseball only one season with the Bruins; he was too busy winning basketball games. As a junior who played the equivalent of a free safety in UCLA's devastating zone press, Erickson helped the team go a perfect 30–0 while beating Duke to win the 1964 NCAA championship. "Coach Wooden realized that

I was going to be able to play on the team," Erickson said wryly, "so he turned me into a full basketball scholarship student."

One of only two returning starters as a senior, Erickson helped the Bruins win a second consecutive national title. He holds the distinction of having played on the first championship teams of both Wooden and Scates, the two most decorated coaches in UCLA history (with a combined 29 NCAA championships). He was a third-team All-American as a senior for the basketball team.

There was little debate as to which sport Erickson would play professionally because there was no money to be made at the time in volleyball. He was selected by the San Francisco Warriors with the 18th pick in the 1965 draft and went on to win an NBA title with the Los Angeles Lakers in 1972 as part of his 12-year career. He also played for the 1964 United States Olympic volleyball team.

Erickson's versatility was among the reasons Wooden would call Erickson the finest athlete he ever coached. "It's pretty remarkable to have heard that," Erickson said. "My comment was always, Coach Wooden was never a drinker, he never drank alcohol, but he must have had a little sangria that day."

The 1964–65 National Championship

John Wooden surprised some by going along with the gag. One day during the 1964–65 season, a photographer suggested that the UCLA coach pose between two of his top players, Gail Goodrich and Keith Erickson, while holding shoes scrawled with the names of the three starters the Bruins had lost from the team that won the national championship the previous year.

While kneeling, the trio held bent fingers alongside their heads, as if scratching them to contemplate who was going to fill the shoes of Walt Hazzard, Fred Slaughter, and Jack Hirsch. The photo appeared in *The Oregonian* (complete with Hirsch's name misspelled on the Chuck Taylor shoe that Goodrich clutched in his left hand) under the heading "THREE HEADS BETTER THAN ONE" as UCLA prepared to defend its title in the Final Four at Memorial Coliseum in Portland, Oregon.

UCLA found its replacements, all right. Their names were Fred Goss, Edgar Lacey, and Doug McIntosh. Goss took the spot vacated by Hazzard, moving into the backcourt alongside Goodrich. McIntosh went from Slaughter's backup to taking his place. At 6'7", Lacey featured better size than the 6'5" Hirsch. Meanwhile, Kenny Washington, who had been instrumental coming off the bench, remained the sixth man. Collectively, the Bruins felt they were almost as good as the team that had finished 30–0 while winning the school's first basketball championship the year before.

"In '65 we were a little bigger, we were maybe a little better rebounding team," Goodrich said. "In '64 we were a better pressing team and I think we converted better in '64 when we were able to generate a turnover. But in '65 we had some better size."

One thing that was nearly identical was the team's trademark full-court zone press. The alignment shifted a bit, the Bruins going from a 2-2-1 formation to a 1-2-1-1, but once an opponent inbounded the ball it became essentially the same press. It featured McIntosh underneath the opponent's basket, with Goodrich and Lacey stationed behind him, Goss behind them, and Erickson as the final line of defense.

"We lined it up different because teams were able to look at what we did the year before and then we gave them a little bit different look initially," Goodrich said. "But once the ball was in, the rotation became the same and it was the same press."

UCLA entered the season widely expected to contend for a second consecutive national title, but the Bruins certainly didn't look like champions in their opener, a 110–83 loss to Illinois. "It's not a misprint," Goodrich said when reminded of the 27-point margin of defeat. "It was a wakeup call. That was the first game of the year, it was a wakeup call. It really told us that this is a new team, that this was not the same team we were in '64."

The Bruins also lost 87–82 to Iowa in late January at Chicago Stadium after going a week without practice because of the semester break. The team hit its stride after that, going 14–0 in the Athletic Association of Western Universities and beating rival USC on back-to-back days to conclude the regular season.

The Bruins were at their best in the NCAA tournament, opening the postseason with a 100–76 rout of Brigham Young before facing San Francisco in the regional final for a second consecutive season. The Dons had given UCLA trouble the previous year before wilting, and this time would be no different, with the Bruins rallying on their way to a 101–93 victory.

A relatively uneventful 108–89 victory over Wichita State in a national semifinal set up a championship showdown against top-ranked Michigan. The Wolverines, winners of a Big Ten Conference whose teams had handed UCLA its only two defeats, were favored in part because of a size advantage and in part because of the presence of star forward Cazzie Russell. UCLA considered its opponent and shrugged, knowing it had routed Michigan by 18 points the previous season. "There was never a doubt going into the game that we would win," Goodrich said. "Our team was a confident team."

Michigan took an early lead, but had no answer for the Bruins' quickness or Goodrich's game-long brilliance. The UCLA guard scored 42 points, setting a record for a championship game, largely on the strength of repeatedly driving to the basket and getting fouled. He made 18 of 20 free throws and 12 of 22 shots from

91

the field to go with four rebounds in an undeniable display of dominance that led UCLA to a 91–80 triumph. "Even the diehard Michigan backers acknowledged Gail's greatness and joined with the others in the rafter-rocking salute," Don McLeod wrote in *The Oregonian*.

UCLA had won a second consecutive title while becoming the first team to average 100 points per game in the tournament, but Princeton's Bill Bradley was selected Most Outstanding Player of the Final Four despite not even reaching the title game. Voters were awed by Bradley's having scored 29 points in a semifinal loss to Michigan and then 58 points during a consolation victory over Wichita State.

The Bruins had the satisfaction of being champions. "We figured if we played the game the way we were capable of playing and the way we were taught," Goodrich said, "that at the end of the day we would come out champions, and that's exactly what we did."

26 Lucius Allen

He was considered a pest, his two older brothers constantly trying to shoo him away from the basketball court whenever they played. They might have succeeded had their single mother, a garment factory supervisor, not intervened on behalf of little Lucius. "Let him play with you," she would insist.

They were words that set Lucius Allen on a course to stardom, with an assist from those same brothers who came to embrace their younger siblings' skills. "They told me always to play with people better than I," Lucius told the *Long Beach Press-Telegram*. "I've always tried to do that."

Teaming with Lew Alcindor was a pretty good starting point, even if the idea initially caused some hesitation about Allen's college choice. Allen picked UCLA over Kansas, Kansas State, and Northwestern, which had been among 75 suitors who pursued the star guard from Wyandotte High in Kansas City, Kansas. He liked the Westwood campus, the people, and the weather, but was especially smitten with John Wooden after the venerable coach stopped in Kansas City for a visit with the widely coveted high school prospect and his mother.

"I had seen UCLA on TV when it won the national championship in Portland and had gotten interested at that time," Allen told the *Press-Telegram*, referring to the Bruins' title in 1965. "And I made up my mind after we had our luncheon visit with Coach Wooden."

Allen almost backed out when he read that the celebrated Alcindor, who would later change his name to Kareem Abdul-Jabbar, was also headed to Westwood. "I had been the big gun in high school and it was kind of a childish reaction," Allen said. "I thought it over for a week and decided to stick to my original choice."

It was a decision he would not regret. Only a few months after he started college classes, Allen became the answer to a trivia question. He scored the first basket in the history of Pauley Pavilion, on a 15-foot jumper, just 51 seconds into the freshman team's game against the two-time defending national champion varsity team in November 1965. It was a sign of things to come as the freshmen routed the upperclassmen, 75–60. Allen contributed 16 points and eight rebounds in a victory that could hardly be considered an upset given the freshman roster was also graced by Alcindor, the rainbow-shooting Lynn Shackelford, and defensive specialist Kenny Heitz.

Allen possessed fast hands, a quick burst toward the basket, and precise passing skills. He was also a more-than-capable rebounder for someone who stood 6'2" and his style was perfectly suited to the up-tempo running game favored by Wooden. Allen would average 22.4 points per game for the freshman team, which went 21–0 playing against junior college and other freshman teams. Included in the unbeaten run was a 103-point victory over MiraCosta College of Oceanside.

Not everything was as pleasurable as a game decided in the opening minutes, however. Allen would later acknowledge that the early portion of his time at UCLA was a struggle. "I couldn't even eat the food; I wasn't used to food like that," Allen told the *Milwaukee Journal* after reaching the NBA. "Kareem and I actually had to threaten to leave when we were freshmen, just to get food we liked."

Staying worked out for the best. Allen became the varsity team's second-leading scorer, behind only Alcindor, averaging 15.5 points per game, during his sophomore season in 1966–67. Playing in the backcourt alongside Mike Warren, Allen helped the Bruins go 30–0 to capture Wooden's third NCAA championship. But in the spring, Allen was pulled over for speeding and the cops found a small bag of marijuana in his pocket and another in his glove compartment. UCLA booster Sam Gilbert bailed Allen out of jail and arranged for a criminal lawyer who got the charges dropped for insufficient evidence.

Allen's junior season served as a salve for the headline-grabbing incident. He averaged 15.1 points per game to help UCLA repeat as national champions, the Bruins avenging a loss to Houston in emphatic fashion in a national semifinal when they overwhelmed the Cougars 101–69 on the way to a championship matchup against North Carolina. Allen then scored 11 points during the Bruins' breezy 78–55 victory over the Tar Heels. Allen was selected a first-team All-American as a junior after helping the Bruins go 59–1 during his first two varsity seasons.

There would not be a third. Allen departed UCLA before what would have been his senior season because of academic issues and another arrest for marijuana possession that was later dismissed in court. The Bruins went on to win a third consecutive national championship and Allen later acknowledged he had some growing up to do. "I should have had more sense," he would say. "I should have had more discretion. I won't make the same mistake again."

Allen went on to a 10-year NBA career in which he was reunited with Abdul-Jabbar. The former Bruins teamed to win the 1971 NBA championship with Milwaukee, and Allen averaged 13.4 points, 4.5 assists, and 3.1 rebounds during his career with the Bucks, Seattle SuperSonics, Los Angeles Lakers, and Kansas City Royals. He was inducted into the UCLA Athletic Hall of Fame in 2000.

27 The 1966–67 National Championship

UCLA made some history during the 1966–67 season. The Bruins became the first team to win a national basketball championship that was upstaged by their own exhibition triumph the previous season.

It came against a team that returned three starters from the two-time defending national champions, not to mention key reserve Kenny Washington.

The game pitted a freshman team featuring Lew Alcindor, Lucius Allen, Lynn Shackelford, and Kenny Heitz against a far more seasoned group of upperclassmen. It was the first game ever played in Pauley Pavilion, the Bruins' new basketball palace that opened in November 1965. It was a mismatch indeed.

Allen sank a 15-foot jumper only 51 seconds into the game and the freshmen were on their way. Alcindor overwhelmed his more experienced counterparts by making 13 of 22 shots and finished with

31 points and 21 rebounds. Allen collected 16 points and eight assists while harassing sophomore Mike Warren into a 2-for-14 shooting performance. That wasn't as harrowing for Warren as what came after the freshmen completed their 75–60 victory, with the reserves playing the final minutes after the outcome had been decided.

"I remember going into the locker room and not really knowing what to think," Warren told the *Los Angeles Times*. "It was my first experience up on the varsity. I'd been a freshman [the year before] and we'd gotten killed by the varsity, so it was a very strange feeling to lose. I remember sitting there with head bowed, not knowing where to look, and all of a sudden, what sounded like 2,000 feet came running past our locker room yelling, 'We're No. 1! We're No. 1!'

"It was the frosh."

Those freshmen became equally dominant as sophomores. They played with a sense of redemption even though they weren't part of the team that failed to make the NCAA tournament the previous season after losing to the freshmen. The 1966–67 Bruins featured four sophomores in their starting lineup with Alcindor, Allen, Shackelford, and Heitz joining Warren, a junior.

Alcindor, who later became Kareem Abdul-Jabbar, was just as dominant in his first varsity game as he had been in his freshman debut. He broke the school record with 56 points during a 105–90 victory over rival USC and topped that later in the season with a 61-point outburst against Washington State.

The 7'1" Alcindor proved nearly unstoppable, averaging 29 points per game for the season and setting an NCAA record by making 66.7 percent of his shots. Allen (15.5 points per game), Warren (12.7), and Shackelford (11.4) provided a strong supporting cast for a team that went 30–0, winning every game by at least five points.

UCLA's romp through the NCAA tournament lacked drama, the Bruins winning their four games by a combined 95 points.

Houston tried to counter Alcindor in the national semifinal by constantly attacking him around the basket with an array of six players who were at least 6'6". "All week we just said, 'Go to him,'" Cougars coach Guy Lewis told reporters. "All week that was it."

Houston held a one-point lead midway through the first half as part of a crisp opening salvo in which it held its own on the boards and routinely broke the Bruins' press. But the margin of that advantage was telling. If the Cougars couldn't pull away while playing a nearly flawless game, they had no chance. Alcindor blocked four shots early in the game, forcing Houston star Elvin Hayes to abandon attack mode in favor of outside jump shots. It wasn't a winning formula and UCLA pulled away for a 73–58 victory.

The championship game against unranked Dayton was even more anticlimactic. Coming off an upset over North Carolina in the other semifinal, the Flyers were riding high, but completely outmanned against UCLA. Dayton had to use the 6'6" Dan Sadlier against Alcindor, one of several mismatches that worked heavily in the Bruins' favor. The Flyers didn't score for the game's first 5½ minutes and soon found themselves trailing 20–4. Wooden mercifully removed Alcindor and Warren with more than five minutes left in an eventual 79–64 triumph that gave UCLA its third national championship in four seasons, making the Bruins universally envied outside Westwood.

"We're not very popular, are we?" Heitz sighed to reporters afterward.

Actually, opinion was shifting in their favor, at least internally. Those freshmen-turned-sophomores had been fully embraced by the upperclassmen and there was a feeling that collectively, with Alcindor eligible for two more seasons, the Bruins were just getting started.

28 A Rainy Night in Westwood

Dick Enberg called eight national championships in his nine years as the television voice of UCLA basketball. Only once did he run out of things to say.

The Bruins were up big over Oregon almost midway through the first half of a game on January 9, 1970, at Pauley Pavilion when UCLA coach John Wooden ordered his players to go into a stall against the Ducks' zone defense. The lack of action at a time when there was no shot clock in college basketball presented quite the dilemma for Enberg, particularly since he worked by himself on the KTLA-Channel 5 broadcast without a color analyst.

So he matched the Bruins' stall with one of his own. First, he ticked off the team's upcoming schedule. "I started talking about, 'Coming up, you know, they're going to Cal and Stanford and then Washington and Washington State [come] here,'" Enberg recalled. "That killed a minute. And then I go, 'Look at the banners, the national championships.' That borrowed me another minute." It wasn't long before Enberg ran out of topics. He admitted as much to his audience.

But something kept running through Enberg's head during this rainy night in Westwood. It was the theme song from the recently released *Butch Cassidy and the Sundance Kid*, Burt Bacharach's "Raindrops Keep Falling on My Head." Enberg didn't know the words but began to hum the tune to fill some of the dead air of top-ranked UCLA's eventual 75–58 victory.

The following day, when Enberg returned to Pauley Pavilion to prepare for a game against Oregon State, a handful of students were waiting for him at his perch in the second deck of the arena. They presented him with the lyrics to the song, apparently having heard the previous night's broadcast. Enberg promised on the air that night that he would sing the song at center court if and when the Bruins won what was then the Pacific-8 Conference championship.

Sure enough, UCLA won the title on what turned out to be another rainy night in Westwood. Enberg briefly delayed after wrapping up his broadcast, hoping fans would leave, before stepping out to midcourt and warbling his way through "Raindrops Keep Falling on My Head." As he started to sing, scores of students opened umbrellas they had toted inside the arena as a tribute to the broadcaster who had kept his word.

Enberg would go on to work 28 Wimbledons and 10 Super Bowls, as well as becoming the voice of the Anaheim Angels, Los Angeles Rams, and San Diego Padres during a Hall of Fame career that ended in October 2016 on the same day that Dodgers counterpart Vin Scully completed his final broadcast.

UCLA honored Enberg by naming its media room inside Pauley Pavilion after the 14-time Emmy Award winner during a ceremony in February 2017. Enberg openly wondered what he had done to deserve such an honor after having being hired at UCLA from his job teaching and coaching baseball at San Fernando Valley State College (now Cal State Northridge). The Bruins lost a total of 12 games during his time on campus, including only two defeats inside Pauley Pavilion.

"You talk about the good fortune, the intersections of life and being at the right place at the right time," Enberg said. "Here's a guy just a year out of teaching and coaching who's able to settle in his seat, didn't have a color man. In the nine years that I called UCLA games, they won eight national titles. I mean, who was looking over me at that time to be able to come in and ride the Wooden wave and watch the Bruin ballet?"

Enberg provided the soundtrack, his most famous call coming on the night he hummed his way through the latter part of the first half. About a month after he sang the same song at midcourt,

Enberg received a letter on UCLA stationary from a professor in the music department. "Someday, when you're on the Westwood campus, would you mind stopping by my office?" the professor asked. "In all my studies, you hit some notes I've never heard in my life."

Years later, at a party with Bacharach in La Hoya, Enberg asked the famed singer and composer if he had heard him croon his tune. "He nodded, yes," recalled Enberg, who died in December 2017, "and I said, 'Well, what did you think of it?' and he didn't answer, which seemed really appropriate."

29 The 1967–68 National Championship

One game on UCLA's basketball schedule loomed larger than the rest, like the 7'1" Lew Alcindor strolling past classmates on campus. It would be dubbed "The Game of the Century," even though it was played in the middle of the 1967–68 season and had no bearing on whether the Bruins could repeat as national champions.

All this would decide—for the moment, anyway—was the best team in the nation in a matchup between top-ranked UCLA and second-ranked Houston. The game was expected to be a spectacle, considering it would be staged in Houston's Astrodome, a slab of wood doubling as the court placed in the middle of a dirt floor and situated far from the seats inside a stadium built for Major League Baseball. More significant, the game would be broadcast to the masses via national television, syndicated by Eddie Einhorn on TVS for 120 stations in 49 states.

"It was the first time ever that a college or pro game was televised in prime time, a non-playoff game," recalled broadcaster Dick

Enberg, who was in his second season as the television voice of the Bruins and got to work the game thanks to the insistence of UCLA athletic director J.D. Morgan. "I contend that it was the most important game in college basketball history in terms of catapulting college basketball interest into the stratosphere. That was the rocket ship."

UCLA didn't just bring every key player back from the previous season; the Bruins fortified themselves with the return of forwards Edgar Lacey and Mike Lynn. Lacey had been a starting forward on UCLA's 1964–65 championship team who missed the 1966–67 season because of a broken kneecap. Lynn had been suspended for that same season after being charged with and later convicted of illegal use of a stolen credit card.

Houston featured star forward Elvin Hayes, who had claimed when the teams met the previous season in an NCAA tournament national semifinal that Alcindor, UCLA's hulking center, was overrated. There were fears that Alcindor (who later became Kareem Abdul-Jabbar) would not be able to play in the rematch on January 20, 1968, after suffering a scratched cornea against California eight days earlier.

Doctors told Bruins coach John Wooden that Alcindor would have to sit out because he was suffering from vertical double vision, but the big man tried to play anyway to help extend his team's 47-game winning streak. Alcindor was a nonfactor from the start, having three of his shots blocked by the 6'9" Hayes even though the players were not matched against one another.

UCLA tried to counter Hayes with Lacey, who gave up 10 points while defending his Cougars counterpart before being taken out of the game with 11 minutes to play in the first half. Lacey would not return, Wooden later explaining that Lacey did not look like he wanted to go back into the game.

Hayes scored 29 of his 39 points in the first half during what Wooden would call "one of the great individual performances in a game I ever saw." Alcindor played what was easily his worst college game, missing 14 of 18 shots on the way to 15 points.

Nevertheless, UCLA hung tough. Bruins guard Lucius Allen tied the score at 69–69 on two free throws before Hayes, a 60 percent free-throw shooter, went to the line with 28 seconds left and sank two shots. A few UCLA turnovers later, Houston emerged with a 71–69 victory that prompted some from the record crowd of 52,693 to storm the court.

The Bruins lost more than a game and their winning streak. Lacey quit the team three days later, telling the *Los Angeles Times* that he "never enjoyed playing for" Wooden and that getting benched against Houston "was the last straw." Wooden later said he regretted his comments about Lacey and wished that he would have returned to the team.

The remaining Wooden soldiers pressed on toward what felt like an inevitable rematch with Houston in the NCAA tournament. It happened in a national semifinal at the Los Angeles Sports Arena (and incidentally on the same court, which had been trucked to Houston for the first meeting). The Bruins were more than ready.

Wooden installed a diamond-and-one defense that put Shackelford on Hayes, whose struggles were reminiscent of Alcindor's when the teams met earlier in the season. Hayes had difficulty getting the ball and made only three of 10 shots on the way to 10 points. Alcindor made seven of 14 shots and finished with 19 points and 18 rebounds.

UCLA raced to a 22-point halftime advantage and prevailed 101–69, before easily handling North Carolina in the championship game. The Bruins used a 2-2-1 zone defense that befuddled the Tar Heels and Alcindor was dominant across the board with 34 points, 16 rebounds, and nine blocked shots.

Wooden later was quoted as saying that it would be hard to pick any of his championship teams over this one, which featured "the most valuable player of all time" in Alcindor, in addition to the savvy Warren, quick and skilled Allen, shooting savant Shackelford, and finesse-oriented Lynn.

"I will say it would be the most difficult team to prepare for and play against offensively and defensively," Wooden said. "It created so many problems. It had such great balance."

It also knew how to get redemption.

30 Sidney Wicks

Sidney Wicks lost only four games in three seasons while winning three national championships at UCLA, so of course he remembers the defeats.

"We lost to USC, Oregon…" Wicks said before a long pause. "Shoot, who did we lose to?"

Okay, maybe this won't be so easy. Wicks tries again.

"Senior year was Notre Dame," Wicks said. "We also lost to USC and Oregon."

Wicks is informed there was another loss to USC, during his sophomore season.

"I lost my sophomore year to USC, yes," Wicks said. "And I lost to USC again?"

Yes, he did, a one-point setback against the Trojans during the Bruins' final home game of his junior season in 1969–70. Perhaps it should come as no surprise that Wicks couldn't recall a blip on his continuum of collegiate success. UCLA went 86–4 with Wicks on the roster while winning three consecutive NCAA titles, Nos. 3, 4, and 5 in its record-breaking run of seven in a row. Wicks also was part of the start of the Bruins' record 88-game winning streak that began with a triumph over UC Santa Barbara midway through his senior season.

Wicks became a prototype for the modern power forward, a powerfully built 6'8", 230-pound scorer who could handle the ball, find an open teammate, dominate around the basket, and shoot mid-range jumpers. "I was one of the first big guys that was quick like they are now and had range," Wicks said.

He had starred at Hamilton High in Los Angeles and was intrigued by the possibility of following fellow prep stars from the area to UCLA to play for coach John Wooden, who had already won four national championships before Wicks' arrival. "I said, 'Wow, if a local guy can go there and do well, be of color and everything was cool'… It really made a lot of sense [to go there], if you know what I mean."

Wicks came off the bench as a sophomore, which was a doubly jarring transition because most games were already blowouts by the time he checked in. "For me, sometimes I made mistakes trying to catch up," Wicks said. "I was so in a hurry to play well and fit in and join in in the success the team was having. That's when Coach Wooden, his phrases started to come in to play—'Be quick but don't hurry.'"

Despite his reserve status, Wicks became an integral part of the team, averaging 7.5 points per game. He was the one who took a shot that could have tied the score against USC in the final seconds of a 46–44 loss, UCLA's first defeat in the history of Pauley Pavilion after a 51–0 start. Then the Bruins went back to winning, notching four consecutive victories in the NCAA tournament to capture a third consecutive national title.

With Lew Alcindor (now Kareem Adbul-Jabbar) gone the following season, it was widely believed that UCLA would experience a significant dip in stature. But with Wicks and fellow juniors Curtis Rowe and Steve Patterson manning the frontcourt and senior John Vallely and sophomore Henry Bibby in the backcourt, the Bruins got off to a 21–0 start. "We had a very, very good team," Wicks said, "and we always had that mind-set of playing as a team and it was like magical, basically."

Wicks was the team's leading scorer (18.6 points per game) and rebounder (11.9) as well as its grittiest defender. In the championship game against Jacksonville, Wicks outplayed Artis Gilmore, forcing his 7'2" counterpart to miss 20 of 29 shots and blocking five of his shots. Wicks scored 17 points and outrebounded Gilmore 18–16 while proving all the doubters wrong. "It was like a justification that the Bruins are still there, they're still on top of it," said Wicks, who was selected Most Outstanding Player of the tournament.

There wasn't much drama during Wicks' senior season as UCLA went 29–1, losing only to Notre Dame. Wicks again was the team's leading scorer (21.3 points per game) and rebounder (12.8) while becoming United States Basketball Writers Association and *The Sporting News* National Player of the Year as well as a first-team Associated Press and United Press International All-American.

Wicks was the second overall pick of the 1971 Draft by the Portland Trail Blazers and also played with the Boston Celtics and San Diego Clippers during a 10-year NBA career in which he was the league's Rookie of the Year during the 1971–72 season. Wicks later returned to UCLA as a volunteer assistant for four years under coach Walt Hazzard, helping the team capture the National Invitation Tournament championship in 1985.

No UCLA season felt complete to Wicks unless it ended with a victory. His four losses as a Bruin still stick with him in the worst way. "I'm upset because I wanted to be undefeated, to show you how crazy I am," said Wicks, who splits his retirement between residences in Los Angeles and Wilmington, North Carolina, and regularly attends games at Pauley Pavilion. "I mean, we lost games I wanted to win and if that sounds selfish or egotistical, it wasn't. I just thought we had a great team and I didn't think anybody could beat us. That was the attitude I had on the court and that's the attitude I have now. I don't think we should have lost a game. That's just me."

31 The 1968–69 National Championship

With nemesis Elvin Hayes off to the NBA before the 1968–69 season, UCLA center Lew Alcindor and the Bruins might have felt like a congressman running unopposed in an election. Who was possibly going to stop them?

UCLA rolled through its schedule with the expected ease, starting the season 25–0 while seeking an unprecedented third consecutive national championship.

It took 3½ months to find out that the only way to slow this team was to bring the game to a grinding halt.

The unbeaten Bruins had persevered through a stuck-in-mud 61–55 victory over rival USC in double overtime at the Los Angeles Memorial Sports Arena the night before their regular-season finale back inside the friendlier confines of Pauley Pavilion.

Rather than abandon the slowdown tactics, Trojans coach Bob Boyd doubled down.

Bruins fans might have been more prepared for the rematch than the players, toting a sign that read "Stalls are for Horses." USC's strategy was unsightly but effective. The Trojans took only 20 shots but made 12, including eight of nine in the second half. They also denied Alcindor his usual array of touches, holding him to four shots. He made three and finished with 10 points.

USC's Ernie Powell made the go-ahead shot with six seconds left, providing the Trojans with a history-making 46–44 triumph that ended four UCLA winning streaks. It was the Bruins' first defeat inside Pauley Pavilion, where they had started 51–0, and ended the team's 41-game winning streak that began after a setback against Hayes' Houston Cougars at the Astrodome some 14 months earlier. UCLA also bid farewell to streaks that involved 45 consecutive victories in conference play and 17 straight wins over USC.

Hardly devastated by the defeat, Alcindor shrugged it off to the tedium of so much winning.

March 22, 1969, Louisville, Kentucky: Coach Wooden is flanked by Sidney Wicks (right) and Kareem Abdul-Jabbar (then known as Lew Alcindor, left) after UCLA beat Purdue to win the national championship. (AP Photo, File)

"We all had a plain case of the blahs," Alcindor wrote after the season in a first-person story for *Sports Illustrated*. "The game meant nothing, and we weren't sharp. It was bound to happen. We had lost one game in three years, and all that winning was bound to come down on us. When you're expected to win every game, you lose a lot of your energy and your inspiration, and you lose your edge. So we lost a game. No big deal."

It was the first and only time the Bruins would taste defeat that season. They played the first two games of the NCAA tournament on their home court after the West Regional was placed in Pauley Pavilion, an advantage UCLA probably didn't need in routing New Mexico State and Santa Clara.

Those triumphs propelled the Bruins to the Final Four in Louisville's Freedom Hall, where they would face a plucky upstart in Drake, the Midwest Regional champion that had finally cracked the Associated Press poll in the final week of the season. The Bulldogs were as tenacious as their nickname suggests, putting the 6'5" Al Williams on Alcindor while hounding the Bruins with such ferocity that they had trouble getting the ball to their primary scorer.

UCLA needed every one of guard John Vallely's 29 points to prevail in an 85–82 victory in which they withstood a late 8–0 blitz by Drake, Bruins forward Lynn Shackelford's two free throws in the final moments setting the final score.

Purdue was a team built in the mold of Drake but could not mount a similar challenge in the championship game. Alcindor made his final college game memorable, collecting 37 points and 20 rebounds to lead the Bruins to a 92–72 runaway victory. Just as significant as Alcindor's output was the defensive might of guard Kenny Heitz, who helped limit Purdue's Rick Mount to 28 points on 12-for-36 shooting. Most of Mount's points came in the second half when the outcome was already secure.

UCLA's record third consecutive title was a tribute to the coach and his center who would tower over the college game like no others. Alcindor had completed his UCLA career having led the Bruins to an 88–2 record while becoming the only player in history to be named Most Outstanding Player of the Final Four three times.

"It was not as easy an era as it might have seemed to outsiders," UCLA coach John Wooden would say afterward by way of exhaling. "But it's been a tremendous era, I think. I've heard it said that any coach would have won championships with Lewis. That might be true, it really might. But they'll never know. I do."

32 Henry Bibby

When the 12-hour workdays were over, all the tobacco, corn, and soybeans either tended or picked, Henry Bibby girded himself for more punishment. It was delivered by his older brothers on a dusty basketball court with a white wooden backboard that his father, Charlie, had put up behind the family farmhouse in tiny Franklinton, North Carolina.

Games involving Henry and siblings Jim and Fred would sometimes stretch deep into the night, illuminated by a single light bulb on the outside of their house. It was here that little Henry developed the outside shot that would lead him to stardom at UCLA and a nearly decade-long NBA career despite not being gifted with natural athletic talent.

"He had to shoot from out there," Jim told *Sports Illustrated*, "because if he came inside he got no pity."

Henry took his game indoors when he wasn't hoisting long jumpers, sitting on his bed and tossing wads of paper into a hat, envisioning himself playing in Boston Garden. He averaged 33 points a game at Person-Albion, an all-black public school with 120 students in Grades 1 through 12, and it appeared as if he was bound to play for a college in North Carolina.

One night after a game against a rival high school, a woman approached Bibby and introduced herself as a teacher at the school. She asked if he would be interested in attending UCLA. "She said she had gone there and knew some people in the athletic department," Bibby told the *Los Angeles Times*.

Bibby told her the idea intrigued him but didn't think much of it until he received a phone call a few weeks later from Jay Carty, an assistant coach for the Bruins. UCLA rarely recruited so far from Westwood back then but was in desperate need of a guard. Carty had planned to stay only one night but Person-Albion's opponent was so underwhelming that Carty didn't feel he had gotten an adequate feel for Bibby's talents even though he had scored 25 points.

Carty stayed an extra night and Bibby poured in 37 points against a much tougher opponent. Carty told Bibby after the game that he was welcome in Westwood. Bibby eventually picked UCLA over Guilford College, his other finalist, but he didn't initially find life on the West Coast welcoming for someone who had never ventured west of North Carolina or even boarded a plane, for that matter.

Bibby lived with a white family upon his arrival at UCLA. The biggest adjustment might have been at the breakfast table, where Bibby found the lighter fare significantly less satisfying than what he had enjoyed back on the farm. "Right after breakfast I had to sneak off to a restaurant and eat again," he told *SI*. Bibby also struggled socially and academically while living in a heavily integrated setting for the first time in his life.

Bibby found comfort in the same place he always did—on the basketball court. Standing 6'1" and weighing 180 pounds, he led the Bruins freshman team by averaging 26 points per game and distinguished himself with his outside shooting, often spotting up from beyond 18–20 feet. "I don't believe I've ever had a player with more range than Bibby," John Wooden told the *Times*.

There was more to Bibby's game than shooting. He eagerly accepted Wooden's tenets of discipline and selflessness as a pass-first guard and tenacious defender. It was a perfect fit for what the Bruins needed.

Bibby was also a kindhearted teammate, nursing center Bill Walton back to health inside Bibby's apartment after Walton had come down with the flu as a sophomore.

His value on the court was every bit as vital to the Bruins' fortunes. Bibby was the starting guard on three consecutive NCAA championship teams from 1970 to '72 that went a combined 87–3 and was selected to two All–Final Four teams. He was an All-American and captain in 1972, when the Bruins went 30–0.

He played in the NBA for nine seasons in New York, New Orleans, Philadelphia, and San Diego, winning a championship with the Knicks in 1973 as an important contributor off the bench. He averaged 8.6 points per game before going into a lengthy career coaching at the college and pro levels, guiding USC to an NCAA tournament regional final in 2001.

Jim Bibby would go on to pitch in the major leagues, throwing a scoreless inning in the 1980 All-Star Game, but not before helping to shape the fortunes of the brother four inches shorter and 20 pounds lighter. "We had some brawls," Jim told the *Times*. "That's why Henry learned to shoot from outside… he had to shoot before we got to him and knocked him down."

33 The 1969–70 National Championship

UCLA became the first three-time-defending national champion in the history of college basketball to inspire a touch of sympathy when it opened practice prior to the 1969–70 season.

The Bruins returned starters Curtis Rowe and John Vallely from the team that had whipped Purdue by 20 points in the championship game the previous season, but all anyone seemed to care about was the departure of celebrated center Lew Alcindor.

"They said, 'Okay, now that he's gone, they don't have that anymore. So now they should be vulnerable,'" recalled Bruins forward Sidney Wicks, capturing the prevailing sentiment among the 224 other college teams trying to unseat UCLA as champions. "'So we can take out our wrath on them because he's gone.'"

Then the weeks passed… and the months… and UCLA was still unbeaten. The Bruins started the season 21–0, showing that there was indeed life after Lew. Wicks had capably moved into the starting forward spot vacated by Lynn Shackelford, Steve Patterson manned center, and sophomore guard Henry Bibby played with maturity beyond his years. All five starters would average double figures in scoring.

UCLA was cohesive and explosive, setting a school record for points during a 133–84 throttling of Pete Maravich and Louisiana State and moving into the No. 1 spot in the Associated Press ranking after a 31-point dismantling of No. 13 Notre Dame. The Bruins didn't lose until a 78–65 setback against Oregon in late February. UCLA coach John Wooden conceded defeat during a timeout with two minutes to play, walking over to the Ducks bench and shaking counterpart Steve Belko's hand. "It's going to be a little wild at the end, Steve," Wooden said, anticipating the celebration about to unfold in Eugene. "So I thought I'd say congratulations now."

The Bruins would lose only once more before the postseason, an 87–86 setback against USC at Pauley Pavilion unable to keep UCLA from clinching its fourth consecutive Pac-8 Conference championship. UCLA opened the NCAA tournament with quick-work victories over Long Beach State and Utah State before encountering New Mexico State, a familiar foe. The Bruins and Aggies had met the previous two years in the West Regional, with UCLA advancing.

New Mexico figured things might finally be tilting in its favor after circumventing UCLA in the early rounds by way of the Midwest Regional. But the Aggies couldn't match the quickness of the Bruins' frontcourt.

"Last year, we played UCLA [and] they had the big man, Lew Alcindor," New Mexico State coach Lou Henson said after his team's 93–77 defeat. "And so this year, we felt we had a better chance of beating them. But after Thursday evening's ballgame, we found out they not only had one big man, they had five. They used balance, speed, and quickness to defeat us handily."

UCLA seemed at ease heading into its championship matchup against Jacksonville even though the Dolphins featured two incredibly skilled 7-footers in Artis Gilmore and Pembroke Burrows III. At a practice the day before the game, Wooden passed out jelly beans to sportswriters and alluded to Alcindor having prepared the teammates he left behind for this moment when the coach cracked to Patterson, "Steve, you ever have any practice against a 7-footer?"

The initial defensive plan on Gilmore was to have the 6'8" Wicks, who was giving up six inches to his counterpart, front him while help came from the backside. But after repeated lobs over Wicks allowed Gilmore to score three times from point-blank range, helping Jacksonville take a 14–6 lead, changes were contemplated in UCLA's timeout huddle. "I went to coach and said,

'Coach I've got to play behind this guy because this way he's getting uncontested shots; at least I could try to contest him if I'm playing behind him,'" Wicks recalled.

Wicks moved behind Gilmore, with Patterson leaving the high post for double teams whenever the ball was thrown to the Jacksonville star. The switch allowed Wicks to get in position to block five of Gilmore's shots, with some of the blocks triggering UCLA fast-breaks. The Dolphins didn't make a field goal over the final three minutes of the first half, and a give-and-go basket by Bibby gave the Bruins their first lead with 1:16 left before halftime.

UCLA's 41–36 advantage at the game's midpoint swelled in the opening minutes of the second half. The Bruins dominated the game at the free-throw line, outscoring the Dolphins 24–7 in that department, and held Gilmore and Burrows to seven points in the second half after the tandem had combined for 22 points in the first half.

The closing minutes lacked drama, as UCLA emerged with an 80–69 triumph that gave the Bruins their fourth consecutive title and sixth in seven years. In a jubilant locker room afterward, Rowe revealed that the Bruins were among those who were fine with Alcindor having left because it allowed them a chance at their own legacy. "Everybody was looking forward to playing without Lew," Rowe told *Sports Illustrated*. "Right now if Alcindor was on the team who would the reporters be talking to? Look around the room—the reporters are with five people and that's beautiful. Every time somebody mentions the three in a row they say Lew did it. Now we just proved that four other men from that team could play basketball—with the best of them."

34 The 1970–71 National Championship

Winning had become so routine for UCLA's basketball team entering the 1970–71 season that the Bruins' biggest challenge might have been finding a worthy foil.

They had won four consecutive national titles, going a combined 126–4. Even the championship games produced little drama, the Bruins winning by an average of 17 points per game.

With its entire frontcourt of Sidney Wicks, Curtis Rowe, and Steve Patterson returning, UCLA seemed destined to let the good times roll on like an endless Southern California summer.

But the top-ranked Bruins would find a surprising number of irritants in the coming months. The first was Notre Dame shooting guard Austin Carr, who poured in 15 of his team's final 17 points and 46 overall during the Fighting Irish's 89–82 upset of the unbeaten Bruins during a late January game in South Bend, Indiana.

The defeat was doubly annoying because it thrust rival USC into the top spot in the rankings two weeks before the Trojans were scheduled to face the Bruins at the Los Angeles Memorial Sports Arena.

"We hated those guys," said UCLA guard Henry Bibby, who had supplanted the departed John Vallely as the Bruins' primary playmaker. "We hated Paul Westphal. We hated Mo Layton and people like that. I hated Ron Riley and these were good guys, but the competition at that time was to beat USC. Never let USC beat you; they can't even come close to beating you. That was our mentality."

The Trojans made the Bruins hate them even more, taking a 59–50 lead midway through the second half at a sold-out Sports

Arena. But USC went cold for an extended stretch and UCLA guard Kenny Booker, Bibby's starting backcourt mate, produced a steal and layup that gave the Bruins a 61–59 lead with 5½ minutes left, prompting a rare stall by coach John Wooden.

UCLA held on for a 64–60 triumph that restored it to the top of the polls, but there would be other narrow escapes for a team that considered any victory by less than double digits too close for comfort.

Bibby provided a heart-thumping victory over Oregon when he stole the ball with the Bruins trailing by one point with less than a minute to go and drove for the winning basket. Wicks drained a 20-foot jumper in the final seconds to edge Oregon State. The Bruins needed two free throws with seven seconds left to beat Washington State. Rowe made a jumper with less than a minute left to beat Washington. And UCLA rallied from 11 points down to beat Long Beach State by two points in the NCAA West Regionals.

And still, a fifth consecutive championship was considered such a foregone conclusion that UCLA fans arrived at Houston's Astrodome for the Final Four wearing buttons reading "Gimme Five" and the school's student newspaper, the *Daily Bruin*, had already budgeted an eight-page color supplement chronicling the title.

A 68–60 triumph over Kansas in a national semifinal was memorable mostly for the Bruins' sideline squabbling. Wooden and assistant Denny Crum engaged in disagreements over strategy and substitutions, with Wooden reportedly threatening to send Crum to the end of the bench and telling his subordinate at one point: "I'm the coach of this team, and don't tell me how to coach my team."

UCLA's championship matchup against Villanova, a team with six losses that went only nine players deep, seemed as flimsy as the four-foot-high platform that served as the court plunked in the middle of the Astrodome. But even while playing from behind, the

Wildcats flummoxed the Bruins in the first half with a 2-3 zone and in the second half with a man-to-man defense after Wooden ordered his team to go into a stall.

Villanova's Howard Porter twice made jumpers that pulled the Wildcats to within three points in the game's final minutes. But with Wicks slowed by a sore big toe and Rowe struggling to find his usual scoring touch, Patterson continually dazzled. He went in for a layup that counted thanks to a goaltending call, giving the Bruins a 66–60 lead with only 38 seconds left.

Patterson finished with a career-high 29 points and UCLA emerged with a 68–62 victory. The *Daily Bruin* special section could go to press as planned. *Sports Illustrated* might have captured the essence of the moment best with its headline, "A Close One At Last." The only thing the Bruins were counting was titles, not margins of victory.

Wicks, Rowe, and Patterson had combined to average 51.8 points and 32.6 rebounds per game, eclipsing the production of any starting frontcourt including legendary Bruins center Lew Alcindor. All that mattered to Wicks was that he had matched Alcindor in the title department.

"Lew said he came to win three," Wicks said. "And I did, too."

35 Keith Wilkes

Just because Keith Wilkes and his fellow UCLA freshmen couldn't participate in varsity games during the 1970–71 season didn't mean they couldn't wow those who got to see them play.

A group of UCLA students regularly congregated on the side of Pauley Pavilion where the freshmen practiced behind a curtain to get a look at Wilkes and the other Bruins newcomers. One day Wilkes made a slick move and thought little of it until he was eating alongside his teammates in the dining hall. Along came Oliver Trigg, an engineering student who played in the band and liked to trumpet things that captivated him.

"This fella came by and he started yelling and talking real loud, he was just so excited," Wilkes recalled. "He just blurted out, 'Silk! Keith, man, that move you made was smooth as silk.'" Freshman players Bill Walton, Greg Lee, Vince Carson, and Gary Franklin all heard the exchange and started ribbing their freshly anointed teammate about it. The next year, when Wilkes was a sophomore, Bruins broadcaster Dick Enberg heard a couple of UCLA players call the 6'6" forward "Silk" and used the same expression on the air. A nickname was born.

"I loved it," Wilkes said. "I wore it like a badge of honor. It was better than my high school nickname in Santa Barbara, which was 'Spider.'"

The new nickname came with a touch of irony considering the curious form on Wilkes' jump shot. He would hold the ball high off to the right side of his head before releasing it with a side-winding motion. He had developed this approach as a boy while competing with older players at a time when he was still shooting on a 9-foot hoop. Holding the ball in this way and releasing it at the last moment helped keep Wilkes from getting his shot blocked.

No one mentioned anything about the way the shot looked until Wilkes' first UCLA practice. That's when coach John Wooden called him over. Wilkes was worried, wondering what he had done wrong. Wooden asked Wilkes to take a series of shots around the court while the coach rebounded and fed him passes. Wilkes made almost every shot, figuring that would be the end of the conversation. Not quite.

"He says, 'Okay, now how did you shoot that?'" Wilkes said of Wooden. "And I'm like really confused because he just saw me not just shoot a lot of shots but make a lot of shots." Wooden went on to ask Wilkes about his release and the way the ball left his fingertips before relenting. "Okay, you're dismissed," the coach finally told him. It was not until years later that Wilkes and Wooden joked about the exchange, Wooden acknowledging that he had considered changing Wilkes' shot. Instead, the coach gave the budding star the green light to do it his way while thinking about the nuances of his technique.

Accuracy was never an issue for Wilkes over the next three seasons. He made 51.4 percent of his shots and 75.0 percent of his free throws as a Bruin while averaging 15.0 points and 7.4 rebounds per game. He teamed with Bill Walton to lead UCLA to back-to-back NCAA championships and undefeated seasons in 1972 and '73 before losing to North Carolina State in a national semifinal as a senior in '74. Wilkes was also part of UCLA's record 88-game winning streak, starting his collegiate career 73–0 before the Bruins fell to Notre Dame in January 1974.

The two-time All-American might have been an even better student, earning first-team Academic All-American honors three times. His dedication to his studies resulted from an edict he received from his mother in the seventh grade after bringing home a report card featuring A's and C's. "She looked me dead in the eye and says, 'Do you like playing basketball?' and I almost laughed, the question was so ridiculous at the time," Wilkes recalled. "Then I could see she was being very serious. I said, 'Well, yeah, of course.' And she said, 'Well, you're going to have to do better with your grades.'"

Wilkes complied, allowing him to keep playing long after his UCLA career ended. The Golden State Warriors selected him 11th overall in the first round of the 1974 Draft and he became the NBA's Rookie of the Year during the 1974–75 season while helping his team win the league title. A three-time All-Star, Wilkes also won championships with the Los Angeles Lakers in 1980, '82, and '85 during his 12-year professional career. Both the Lakers and UCLA retired his No. 52 jersey and he was enshrined in the Naismith Memorial Basketball Hall of Fame in 2012. He changed his name to Jamaal Abdul-Lateef in 1975 upon converting to the Muslim faith but remained Jamaal Wilkes for purposes of public recognition.

He never did change the shot that Lakers coach Paul Westhead once said was "like snow falling softly on a bamboo leaf. One minute it's there, the next it's not. Unfortunately, people don't get into falling snow." Wooden was indisputably into Wilkes, singling him out in multiple interviews when asked to describe his ideal player. "I would have the player be a good student, polite, courteous, a good team player, a good defensive player, and rebounder, a good inside player, and outside shooter," Wooden once said. "Why not just take Jamaal Wilkes and let it go at that?"

36 1971–72 National Basketball Championship

UCLA's streak of consecutive national championships in basketball might have ended at five were it not for the scoring and rebounding of Bill Walton, the smooth moves of Keith Wilkes… and the poetry of John Wooden. It's true.

Wooden's verse was needed before the season even started. Wilkes, feeling overwhelmed as part of a group of sophomores ascending to the varsity level with great expectations following the departures of Sidney Wicks, Curtis Rowe, and Steve Patterson, walked into Wooden's office with intentions of leaving the team. "I was going to quit and go home," Wilkes recalled. "It was just too intense for me. It was really off the charts of the anticipation and the tradition, the expectations, plus trying to stay in school. It was heavy."

Soon the only thing weighty were Wooden's words. "What I remember, it was like he didn't even hear me and I don't even know how he transitioned to it, but he would just start rattling off these poems, poems he had written, his favorite poems, and I would just get so caught up in it; I mean, it was like magic," Wilkes said. "And then I forgot why I even went to his office in the first place and I left there just feeling so refreshed and so renewed."

Basketball would provide another respite for Wilkes and the Bruins, whose roster overhaul led to familiar results. Senior guard Henry Bibby was the only returning starter, though junior Larry Farmer was an easy pick to fill one of the vacated starting forward spots after having been a star reserve the previous season. They were joined in the starting lineup by Walton, the wunderkind sophomore big man; Greg Lee, a skilled sophomore point guard who was a natural running the fast-break; and Wilkes, whose initial skepticism about meeting expectations after being part of a freshman team that had gone 20–0 was quelled by a series of blowout victories.

Sports Illustrated was so intrigued by the super sophomores that it inquired about doing a story on their replacing Wicks, Rowe, et al. "Bill and I just kind of looked at each other and we were stunned," Wilkes said. "We said, 'Well, we haven't done anything yet.' And so we passed on it."

UCLA opened the season by scoring 100 points in its first seven games, setting the stage for what was to come. The Bruins would win their games by an average of 30.3 points that season, an NCAA record. Part of their prowess was attributable to a quality bench that featured Larry Hollyfield, Tommy Curtis, and Swen Nater, who would go on to be selected in the first round of the NBA draft despite never starting a college game.

The blowout victories seemed to impress everyone but the Bruins. "We were glad we won, don't misunderstand me," Wilkes said, "but we weren't really focused on what the margin was." The Bruins took a 26–0 record into the NCAA tournament, coming no closer to defeat than a 78–72 triumph over Oregon State to start Pac-8 Conference play.

They opened postseason play with a 32-point victory over Weber State and a 16-point win over Long Beach State to make the Final Four against a recognizable opponent in familiar environs—the Los Angeles Memorial Sports Arena, their former home arena. UCLA's semifinal foe was Louisville and coach Denny Crum, the former Bruins assistant who had served under Wooden, recruited Wilkes, and was known by pretty much every other player on the roster.

In a corridor before the game, *SI* noted, Walton jokingly asked Crum, "Coach, where's the money you promised me last year under the table?" Walton proved worthy of a significant payoff, scoring 16 of UCLA's first 20 points and rendering several of Louisville's top players essentially useless. Walton finished with 33 points and 21 rebounds and Farmer scored 15 points in the second half, leading to a runaway 96–77 victory.

There would be far more drama in the championship game. Florida State made seven consecutive shots during one stretch to take a 21–14 lead, signaling the only time all season that UCLA had trailed by more than four points. Just like the other deficits, this one wouldn't last. Bibby and Walton sparked a Bruins run that forged a tie and then a 50–39 halftime lead with considerable help from Curtis.

The Seminoles paid so much attention to Walton—who nevertheless finished with 24 points and 20 rebounds—that it gave Wilkes free passage to roam and finish them off. Wilkes helped force a turnover, controlled a jump ball with 65 seconds left, and made the layup that secured UCLA's 81–76 triumph. Wilkes had gone from overwhelmed to overpowering, writing his own poetic ending.

He would go on to help the Bruins complete a second consecutive 30–0 season while extending their winning streak to 45 games. The national championship was UCLA's sixth in a row and eighth in ninth years, a new cast of players proving that they were every bit as worthy as their predecessors. "We really felt like we belonged," Wilkes said. "We had contributed, we didn't let the guys down [who had come] before us and it was just great."

37 The 88-Game Winning Streak

Sidney Wicks was sitting curbside at Los Angeles International Airport on January 24, 1971, one day after UCLA had lost to Notre Dame in South Bend, Indiana. His body and his baggage were home but his mind was elsewhere.

The Bruins' defeat snapped a 19-game winning streak that dated to the previous season, when they had won a fourth consecutive NCAA championship, and sent Wicks into a mild depression as he sat there waiting for his parents to pick him up. As cars whirred past on the arrivals level, coach John Wooden walked up to the senior forward. He noticed the dejected look on Wilkes' face and asked him what was wrong.

"I said, 'Coach, I don't feel good. I don't like this losing,'" Wicks recalled. "And he said, 'Well, I suggest you don't do it again.' That was his suggestion. And I said, 'Touché, my good brother. I won't do it again.'"

Wicks lived up to his words, winning the balance of his games as a Bruin. The players who succeeded him kept winning. UCLA went 30–0 during the 1971–72 season and matched that perfect record the following season. The Bruins opened the 1973–74 season with a 75-game winning streak… and kept winning.

By the time the streak ended, UCLA had won a record 88 consecutive games, more than doubling the NBA record of 33 consecutive victories that the Los Angeles Lakers established during the 1971–72 season. The Bruins' streak encompassed three national championships, nine NCAA tournament victories, a few dozen players, and parts of four seasons.

Making UCLA's barrage of success even more amazing were all the close calls along the way. What came to be known as "The Streak" nearly ended at one, following a rote triumph over UC Santa Barbara that came a week after the Notre Dame loss. The Bruins trailed top-ranked and unbeaten USC by nine points with 9½ minutes left before pulling out an improbable 64–60 victory.

UCLA's next two games were equally harrowing. The Bruins trailed Oregon by five with 2½ minutes left and by one with 43 seconds to go. UCLA guard Henry Bibby then stole the ball from Bill Drozdiak and went in for a layup that gave his team the lead. The Ducks still had a chance to win, but Len Jackson's 20-foot jumper from the left corner bounced off the rim. Game over.

The next day, Oregon State held a 64–58 lead with 3:17 to play. The Bruins seemed sunk for a third consecutive game. But the ending would also become familiar. They rallied furiously, tying the score with 28 seconds left and benefiting from Oregon State guard Freddie Boyd dribbling the ball off his foot. Wicks made an 18-foot jumper with two seconds remaining, giving UCLA a 67–65 victory.

The Bruins rolled into the NCAA tournament before facing Long Beach State and coach Jerry Tarkanian in a regional final. The 49ers' 2-3 zone befuddled Bibby, Kenny Booker, and Steve Patterson, who missed all 17 of their shots in the first half. Long Beach State held a 44–33 lead and Wooden would later acknowledge that he figured he was bound for the Final Four as a spectator.

Nope. He was back on the job after UCLA came back to win 57–55.

The Streak started to become big news when it reached 40 games in March 1972, as newspaper headline writers finally began acknowledging its presence. But there didn't seem to be much danger of it ending during a season in which the Bruins won their games by an average of 30 points, an 81–76 victory over Florida State in the championship game representing their narrowest margin of triumph.

The Streak was at 45 games heading into the 1972–73 season. It was becoming an unavoidable topic. "As I reflect back on it," said former UCLA forward Keith Wilkes (now Jamaal Wilkes), "when we got to around 50 [games], that's when it really started to pick

January 19, 1974, South Bend, Indiana: Coach Wooden (center) during the last timeout against Notre Dame. With 21 seconds remaining, UCLA had the ball but was unable to score, ending the Streak. (AP Photo/File)

up momentum because the [record] streak had been 60 games with Bill Russell and USF [the University of San Francisco]. Everyone's talking about it, we're aware of it, but because of Coach's way of teaching and way of doing things, it wasn't something we talked about a lot amongst ourselves."

One streak did end when Wooden missed a game against UC Santa Barbara after suffering a heart attack—concluding a stretch in which he had coached 679 consecutive games since taking over at UCLA in 1948—but the Bruins easily beat the Gauchos with assistant coach Gary Cunningham guiding the team.

San Francisco had a chance to preserve its record, but instead became consecutive win No. 58 for UCLA, which throttled the Dons by 28 points. The Bruins tied the record by beating Loyola of Chicago six days later and then topped it by getting past the last team that had vanquished them, an 82–63 triumph over Notre Dame on January 27, 1973, in South Bend giving them the longest winning streak in college basketball history.

"We knew it was a big achievement and there was a bit of a sigh of relief," Wilkes said, "but that wasn't our primary goal, which was to try and win another championship."

UCLA won that as well, extending its national title streak to seven by beating Memphis State behind Bill Walton's 44 points. The winning streak stood at 75 games. The Bruins kept winning, pulling out a 65–64 victory over Maryland for consecutive win No. 77 and prevailing in three consecutive games with Walton sidelined by a back injury to reach No. 88.

Two days later, against Notre Dame in South Bend, Walton put on a corset and declared himself ready to go. It looked like another routine UCLA victory when the Bruins led by 11 points with 3½ minutes to go. They wouldn't score again. Notre Dame ran off a game-ending 12–0 run that gave the Irish a 71–70 victory after the Bruins missed five shots in the final 20 seconds.

The Streak that seemed like it might go on forever was over. "We had won so much that it [losing] just never entered our minds," Wilkes said. "So we were devastated. It's hard for people to believe that."

38 | The 1972–73 National Championship

UCLA was hardly a one-man show going into the 1972–73 season. The Bruins had Bill Walton, the center who hovered over college basketball like the North Star, but they continued to be known as the Walton Gang because one player, no matter how gifted, cannot win championships alone.

UCLA's roster was almost identical to the one that had won the school's sixth consecutive national championship the previous season. Surrounding Walton were guard Greg Lee and forwards Keith Wilkes and Larry Farmer, all returning starters. Rounding out the starting lineup was senior guard Larry Hollyfield, who took over for the departed Henry Bibby, and the Bruins also featured excellent bench depth with Tommy Curtis, Dave Meyers, Swen Nater, and Pete Trgovich.

All of those supporting players needed to do very little during the Bruins' championship game against Memphis State at St. Louis Arena besides throw the ball to their best player. The Bruins were more like a Walton Boomerang because everything kept coming back to him.

In the first NCAA championship game played in prime time on network television, on March 26, 1973, Walton was more than ready for his closeup. He scored in almost every way imaginable, on jump hooks, layups, tip-ins, and bank shots. He also dunked four times for baskets that were disallowed because that shot was not legal at the time.

Memphis State publicity man Bill Grogan might have quickly come to regret the slogan he had devised months earlier that read "Meet me in St. Louis, Wooden," tempting fate as well as the potential wrath of a team coached by legendary coach John Wooden. Gene Bartow, Wooden's Memphis counterpart who would go on to succeed him at UCLA two years later, did manage to momentarily slow Walton with a zone defense that, combined with foul trouble on the big man, powered a Memphis State surge late in the first half.

After trailing by nine points, the Tigers pulled into a 39–39 halftime tie and even briefly took a lead early in the second half. None of it mattered once Walton began to have his way again. Repeatedly snatching lobs from Lee around the basket, Walton scored and scored and scored.

UCLA built a 57–47 lead with 12 minutes left and the onslaught was back on, Walton shrugging off his fourth foul to remain on the court for another 9½ minutes. Something eventually did stop Walton: a sprained ankle. Memphis State's Billy Buford helped Walton off the court with 2:51 left as the crowd of 19,301 stood and roared in appreciation for the historic effort it had witnessed.

Walton made 21 of 22 shots—25 of 26, if you include the disallowed dunks—on the way to 44 points, edging former Bruins great Gail Goodrich's previous championship-game record of 42 points set in 1965 against Michigan. Walton also grabbed 13 rebounds during his team's 87–66 victory. *Sports Illustrated* would later rank Walton's performance as the ninth-greatest college sports feat in history.

The Bruins finished the season 30–0, becoming Wooden's fourth unbeaten team, while stretching their winning streak to

75 games as part of an unprecedented seventh straight national championship.

Walton told the *San Diego Union-Tribune* in 2016 that he never watched a replay of his scoring outburst that still stands as the championship-game standard, but he did recall his only miss on what he described as a wide-open shot directly in front of the basket. He also remembered what happened next: "I got the rebound and put it back in," he said.

Walton would resist strong overtures from professional teams to return for his senior season, helping the Bruins extend their winning streak to 88 games. But first, he was able to enjoy some ribbing from his coach over the only blemish from his historic night.

"Coach Wooden looked at me and said, 'Walton, I used to think you were a good player,'" Walton told the *Union-Tribune*, "'until you missed that one shot.'"

39 Marques Johnson

It's no exaggeration to say that Marques Johnson was born to go to UCLA. His mother wrote "UCLA-bound" under an infant photo. His father also favored his only son becoming a Bruin and had a premonition about him becoming a star basketball player while his wife was pregnant.

"When I found out he was a boy," Jeff Johnson told the *Los Angeles Times*.

A high school basketball coach in Louisiana, Jeff decided upon his son's first name after driving to Shreveport to watch Marques Haynes, the Harlem Globetrotter who could dribble a basketball while seated. Marques Johnson was 22 inches long at birth and the delivering physician, Robert Sillis, predicted that he would stand 6'6" as an adult. He was close; Marques reached 6'7".

Marques' basketball education began inside the home, where he would roll the ball through the house. At age two, he started dribbling—"dibbling," he called it. By four, he became an instant crowd-pleaser at his father's games by dribbling the length of the court and back during timeouts and between quarters.

The Johnsons moved to Los Angeles when Marques was seven, his father entering him into a league for nine- and 10-year-olds at Sportsman's Park. He made the All-Star team every year.

But there was one place where Marques couldn't win: his own backyard. He estimated that his father beat him 1,000 consecutive times in one-on-one games before he finally prevailed. "You better believe," his mother, Baasha Johnson, told the *Times*, "that he came in the house slapping hands that day and telling everybody."

Like his parents, Johnson had long wanted to attend UCLA. He had watched coach John Wooden's Bruins since the 1960s, becoming enamored with the play of their powerful forward, Sidney Wicks. Johnson even wore Wicks' No. 35 at Crenshaw High. UCLA's interest in Johnson was initially lukewarm until he scored 36 and 29 points in back-to-back games at Pauley Pavilion to lead Crenshaw to the L.A. City title. That was enough for UCLA to intentsify its pursuit and offer a scholarship.

Johnson became the first true freshman to start for Wooden since the early 1950s when he stepped onto the court for tipoff of a game against Notre Dame on January 26, 1974, inside Pauley Pavilion. It was a surprise to most, coming exactly one week after the Fighting Irish had snapped the Bruins' 88-game winning streak in South Bend. He would call it one of the greatest thrills of his life.

"A freshman at UCLA, starting with Bill Walton and Keith Wilkes," he told the *Daily Bruin*, the student newspaper, somewhat incredulously. Johnson proved he belonged, collecting 16 points and four rebounds during the Bruins' 94–75 victory over the Fighting Irish. He went on to average 7.2 points and 3.3 rebounds per game.

Johnson enjoyed other pursuits besides basketball as a film and television major, once even making his own movie in which he wrote, filmed, and edited the project while adding the soundtrack. It was called *Living for the Weekend* and featured a construction worker played by Rick Walker from the football team.

As a sophomore, Johnson overcame a preseason bout of hepatitis that caused him to lose 10 pounds to average 11.6 points per game. He helped UCLA edge Louisville, 75–74, in overtime in the national semifinal by scoring 10 points and grabbing a team-high 11 rebounds. He contributed across the board during the Bruins' 92–85 victory over Kentucky in the championship, getting six points, seven rebounds, three blocked shots, one assist, and one steal. It was the last game Wooden would ever coach.

Johnson moved into an even more prominent role as a junior, becoming UCLA's second-leading scorer by averaging 17.3 points per game while leading the team with 9.4 rebounds per game. The Bruins reached the Final Four but lost to Indiana in a semifinal.

It was very nearly Johnson's final UCLA game. The Denver Nuggets of the American Basketball Association offered Johnson a five-year, $1-million contract, triggering another lucrative offer from the NBA's Detroit Pistons, who appeared likely to draft him. But Denver eventually withdrew its offer as part of wrangling over the ABA-NBA merger, prompting Detroit to slice its offer roughly in half.

Johnson decided to return to UCLA for one more season, saying he wanted to show he was worth more than what he considered a lowball offer for a player that one pro scout told *Sports Illustrated* was a bigger, quicker, and stronger version of NBA star Elgin Baylor. "How do you stop Marques Johnson?"

then–Washington State coach George Raveling mused at the time. "With the 82nd Airborne."

Johnson was UCLA's captain as a senior, leading the team in scoring (21.4 points per game) and rebounding (11.1 rebounds per game) as the Bruins won the Pac-10 Conference for an 11th consecutive season and reached the second round of the NCAA tournament before losing to Idaho State.

Johnson was selected a consensus first-team All-American and National Player of the Year as well as the first recipient of the John R. Wooden Award, given annually to the nation's top player. At the time his UCLA career ended, Johnson's 1,659 points were the most by any forward in school history, surpassing Wicks, Keith Wilkes, David Meyers, and Richard Washington.

Johnson was the third overall pick in the 1977 NBA Draft by the Milwaukee Bucks and went on to an 11-year career in which he was a five-time All-Star while averaging 20.1 points and 7.0 rebounds per game. UCLA retired Johnson's No. 54 jersey during a ceremony on February 1, 1996. His son Kris was a forward on the UCLA team that won the 1995 national title, making Marques and Kris the only father and son to win the college championship at the same school. It almost felt like destiny.

40 The 1974–75 National Basketball Championship

Opinion was split among UCLA's basketball players as to whether the 1975 NCAA tournament would be John Wooden's last.

The venerable coach had guided the Bruins to nine national championships over the previous 11 years and it appeared as if the end of his career might be imminent. He had suffered a heart attack two years earlier and planned to retire after the 1973–74 season, only for his wife, Nell, to talk him out of it.

Senior guard Pete Trgovich said he figured Wooden might be on the way out because he had stopped promising recruits he would stay around for the entirety of their careers beginning with his class. But sophomore forward Richard Washington said he dismissed teammate Dave Meyers' chatter about Wooden possibly retiring as a motivational ploy.

"I thought he was just saying that to fire me up," Washington said of the late Meyers, then a senior forward, "because he really wanted to win the championship that year for Wooden."

The Bruins were seeking redemption after having lost to North Carolina State in a 1974 national semifinal, ending their run of seven straight national championships. Also gone were stars Bill Walton and Jamaal Wilkes, both off to the NBA after having been first-round draft picks.

All doubt about Wooden's status was removed only minutes after Washington buried a 10-foot turnaround jumper with two seconds left in overtime against Louisville in the 1975 semifinal, nudging the Bruins into the championship game against Kentucky. Wooden entered the locker room inside the San Diego Sports Arena and told his players he was retiring, leaving the underclassmen in a daze.

"I don't remember him even mentioning the game other than saying he thought we had played well or something like that," Washington said. "And then he made the announcement that kind of shocked everybody. I really don't remember too much of what happened after he made the announcement. I don't remember getting on the bus and going back to the hotel or much of anything after that."

Wooden then repeated his announcement in front of the media, causing Kentucky coach Joe B. Hall, seated in the audience, to fall out of his chair. "He knew what he was doing by announcing his retirement," Hall said. "He was a crafty guy."

Wooden's players didn't feel they needed any extra incentive to beat a youthful Wildcats team featuring four freshmen known as the "Super Kittens." "If you need Coach Wooden to retire to get motivated for a national championship," Trgovich said, "you're doing something wrong."

UCLA trailed by six points early amid a flurry of missed shots before Trgovich started sinking jumpers against Kentucky's zone defense. The Bruins were also bolstered by 7'1" center Ralph Drollinger, the team's only reserve who would play in the game. Drollinger controlled the interior after two Kentucky starters got into foul trouble.

It appeared the game might be tilting in the Wildcats' direction with about 6½ minutes left when Meyers was called for an offensive foul after colliding with Kentucky's Kevin Grevey while rising for a jumper. Meyers earned a technical foul for banging the hardwood with his hand in disgust, prompting Wooden to rush onto the court.

"He was upset with the rough play that Kentucky brought," Trgovich said. "They were a big, strong, physical team and he was sending a message. It's a national championship game, you already gave us a technical foul. Are you going to give Coach Wooden a technical foul? I don't think so. I can guarantee you this: He used no swear words when he talked to the officials."

As a referee tried to pull Wooden by the elbow back to the bench, Hall walked to the scorer's table, where he said he was admonished by another official to return to the bench with his team trailing by a point.

The next sequence proved pivotal. Kentucky missed the technical free throw, the front end of a one-on-one opportunity, and committed a turnover on an inbounds pass. "It so disrupted Grevey he couldn't even see the basket," Hall said of Wooden coming onto the court.

UCLA finished off the Wildcats 92–85, with Bruins sophomore forward Marques Johnson flinging the ball toward the rafters in celebration at the final buzzer. Wooden hugged Johnson and shook hands with Meyers before being applauded by some of the 200 reporters on hand for the conclusion of a 27-year career at the school that included 767 games, 620 victories, and 10 national titles.

"In the locker room," Washington said, "he said he never had a team that he enjoyed coaching more than us."

Wooden told reporters he was sad. "Sad that I'm leaving the youngsters and all the wonderful associations I've made… you men, my coaches, other players and coaches," Wooden said. "I haven't agreed with you on everything, but we all agree on our love for this game."

41 David Greenwood

David Greenwood came to UCLA largely because of John Wooden. He just never got to play for John Wooden.

The revered Bruins coach caught many by surprise when he announced his retirement prior to UCLA's 1975 NCAA tournament championship game against Kentucky. That left Greenwood and fellow recruit Roy Hamilton, teammates at Verbum Dei High in Los Angeles, to ponder college life without the man who had enticed them to spend their college years in Westwood.

Greenwood remained sold on UCLA because of a challenge issued by Wooden. The coach told him if he went to Nevada Las

Vegas or Notre Dame—two of the 300 or so colleges Greenwood said were recruiting him—he would become an All-American. But if he went to UCLA, Wooden asserted, Greenwood would be able to test himself against 12 other high school All-Americans every day in practice. "It was kind of like, 'Come here and test your mettle,'" Greenwood told the *Los Angeles Times*.

The 6'9", 240-pound forward did that from his first day on campus. He came off the bench initially until coach Gene Bartow, Wooden's successor, decided to make a change against USC on January 31, 1976. Greenwood moved into the starting lineup, replacing Ralph Drollinger, and the Bruins won 12 of their next 13 games. "We started moving better, we started playing together," Greenwood recalled. "We just got up and down the court a lot faster." Greenwood credited his having played against former Bruins stars Sidney Wicks and Curtis Rowe since he was 15 with preparing him for college basketball's big time.

Greenwood didn't lack for confidence heading into the NCAA tournament even though the defending champion Bruins faced a field that included Indiana, which had knocked off the Bruins, 84–64, in the season opener. Greenwood openly coveted a rematch in a national semifinal. "We just wanted a little payback," Greenwood said. UCLA got its chance against the Hoosiers but fell short, 65–51.

Greenwood started 28 of 29 games as a sophomore, finishing second to Marques Johnson in both scoring (Greenwood averaged 16.7 points per game) and rebounding (9.7). The Bruins went 24–5 but were upset 76–75 by Idaho State in the second round of the NCAA tournament. By then it had become painfully clear that voracious UCLA fans would be satisfied by nothing less than national championships in the wake of Wooden's glorious run. The first casualty was Bartow, who resigned after two seasons, two conference titles, and a 52–9 record.

The pressure was also palpable among the players. "For a while the whole idea that people were so hung up on winning really depressed me," Greenwood said during his senior season, "but I've matured now and it doesn't bother me as much. That's the way it is here, and you have to live with it. It comes with the territory and you realize it when you sign your letter of intent."

Not every moment was pressure-filled. A music lover, Greenwood started a side business using his vocal gifts to record cassettes for friends who brought him poems they had written for girlfriends, mixing smooth jazz into the background. He only charged a nominal fee. Greenwood also appeared on the *Richard Pryor Show* in a minor role as a Swahili warrior.

Greenwood's legion of basketball admirers included Wilt Chamberlain, who passed along his compliments one day while on campus to use UCLA's handball courts. "You guys were awesome the other night," Chamberlain told Greenwood, shaking his hand.

His shooting style was unusual, Greenwood leaning forward as he elevated into his jumper and releasing the ball while holding it in front of his body instead of over his head. He reasoned that it helped him draw more fouls. Greenwood developed a reputation as consistent but not flashy. He averaged 17.5 points per game as a junior, dipping into single digits only once. His 11.4 rebounds per game that season were the most by a UCLA player since Bill Walton. "My only goals for each game," Greenwood said at the time, "are to get 12 rebounds and stop my man defensively. The points will come."

Sometimes they came with unexpected ferocity. Against Washington State, Greenwood grabbed an offensive rebound with five seconds left and slammed the ball through the basket, giving UCLA a 60–59 victory. He also blocked Arkansas star Sidney Moncrief's two-handed dunk in the final seconds of UCLA's season-ending 74–70 loss to the Razorbacks in an NCAA tournament semifinal.

The mission for Greenwood's senior season was making sure he didn't leave campus without winning the first national title since Wooden's departure. "The older guys told us we'd be the first seniors in 12 or 13 years that hadn't played on a national championship team," Greenwood said midway through the season. "I thought, 'Wow! I don't want to go down in the books for that. I don't want to be the guy that didn't win one.' So that's No. 1 on my agenda. I get home every night picturing me in Utah," the site of the Final Four.

Alas, the top-seeded Bruins fell to second-seeded DePaul, 95–91, in a regional final, but Greenwood's legacy was secure. A three-time all-conference selection and two-time All-American, Greenwood was the second overall pick in the 1979 NBA Draft by the Chicago Bulls. He spent 12 years in the NBA, also playing with the San Antonio Spurs, Denver Nuggets, and Detroit Pistons.

42 The Pyramid of Success

In and around Pauley Pavilion, it's as ubiquitous as Blue and Gold and every bit as meaningful. A version of it can be found in the tunnel leading from the UCLA men's basketball locker room to the court, inside the women's basketball locker room, inside the Pavilion Club that hosts donors before games, inside a display case on the concourse above the court, inside the school's nearby Athletic Hall of Fame, and on the desk of men's basketball coach Steve Alford.

John Wooden's Pyramid of Success is a constant reminder of the values he held dear long before the legendary basketball coach guided the Bruins to a record 10 national championships. It includes 17 tenets and three tiers of building blocks, all aimed at fulfilling one's capabilities. Across the bottom are industriousness, friendship, loyalty, cooperation, and enthusiasm. The second level includes self-control, alertness, initiative, and intentness. The third level is formed by condition, skill, and team spirit. The fourth level includes poise and confidence and on the top, all alone, rests competitive greatness. But what Wooden cherished most abuts the top sides of the pyramid: faith and patience.

"I say to you, in whatever you're doing, you must be patient," Wooden said during a public appearance after his retirement. "You have to have patience. We want things to happen. We talk about our youth being impatient a lot, and they are. They want to change everything; they think all change is progress and we get a little older, we sort of let things go and we forget that there is no progress without change. So you must have patience, and I believe that we must have faith. I believe that we must really believe—not just give it word service—but believe that things will work out as they should, providing we do as we should. I think our tendency is to hope that things will turn out the way we want them to much of the time, but we don't do the things that are necessary to make those things become a reality."

The precursor to Wooden's pyramid was a definition of success that can be heard during a video featuring his voice that's played before men's basketball games inside Pauley Pavilion. "Success is peace of mind," Wooden says, "which is a direct result of self-satisfaction in knowing you made the effort to do your best to become the best that you are capable of becoming." Eventually considering his definition inadequate in encompassing his beliefs, Wooden spent the next 14 years while he worked as an English teacher and coach building his pyramid as a way to guide his students and players, leading to its completion in 1948. It became a model for personal and team excellence in all facets of life.

Just like the pyramids of Egypt, Wooden's pyramid has become an enduring symbol. It's been studied, memorized, and applied by scores of athletes, leading businessmen, a Navy SEAL, and even elementary school students in South Dakota who built their own pyramid in 2013. Wooden helped spread the word about the pyramid before his death in 2010 by mailing thousands of copies to fans. The pyramids have taken many forms, with a massive custom-built wooden version resting on "Wooden Way" inside the Pauley Pavilion concourse. Many of Wooden's coaching peers said they were inspired by his beliefs. "My Pyramid of Success," famed Connecticut women's basketball Coach Geno Auriemma once said, "is the same as his."

43 The O'Bannon Brothers

Charles O'Bannon's dream was to star for two seasons at UCLA alongside older brother Ed, the siblings raising championship banners together inside Pauley Pavilion before going on to the NBA. Part of his hopes came true, though Charles probably never envisioned the brand of brotherly love he would experience along the way.

Midway through Charles' sophomore year, with fans streaming out of Pauley Pavilion late in a loss to California, Ed lit into Charles in the timeout huddle, contending he wasn't playing up to his ability level amid a seven-point, three-turnover performance in which Charles made three of nine shots. The big brother's tirade brought his little brother to tears.

"It was showing how much Charles did care," Steve Lavin, then a Bruins assistant coach, recalled, "but I think also there was this other element of siblings and respect for the older brother and letting him down. I still get kind of goose bumps on the back of my neck or whatever when I think about it."

That the brothers would experience that moment together at UCLA seemed unlikely only a few years earlier. Ed had intended to play for Nevada Las Vegas as the nation's top recruit out of Artesia High in Lakewood before switching his allegiance to UCLA after the Rebels were placed on probation. Charles, who was three years younger than his brother, followed him to UCLA, but initially figured he would get to play with Ed in college for only one year. Then Ed suffered a career-threatening left knee injury during a preseason pickup game that wiped out what was expected to be his freshman year, forcing him to redshirt.

Ed spent much of the next three seasons trying to regain his dominant form while proving to himself that he was fully recovered. He returned in January of his second year at UCLA and played sparingly for a team that won the Pac-10 Conference title and advanced to a West Regional final before getting blown out by Indiana. "When I first started playing [again]," Ed told the *Los Angeles Times*, "I had that big old brace and I could hardly straighten my leg. There were times I felt, 'Man, I'm just out here to fill the roster.'"

He would be more than filler the next two seasons, making the All-Pac-10 first team twice while averaging 16.7 points and seven rebounds as a sophomore and 18.2 points and 8.8 rebounds as a junior. His senior year, Ed became an entirely different animal. "He was anointed the Papa Bear of this Bruin team and he took the mantle, he took the reins and just ran with it," Lavin said. "Before, because he's a humble, unassuming, thoughtful, really caring individual, that sometimes that would interfere with his ability just to take the reins and be the kick-ass kind of leader that we knew he was capable of. Now he was doing everything in this wonderful way because there's this regal kind of quality to Ed where he just has this unique kind of grace and energy field around him. It's like an old Indian chief where he looks at you and it's like, wow."

Ed could be fiery with opponents as well as with his brother, running the length of the court to deliver a retaliatory shove to Notre Dame's Derek Manner in February 1995 after the Irish forward had landed hard on Bruins point guard Tyus Edney's shoulder while trying to block a fast-break layup. "I guess I shouldn't have done it," Ed said afterward of a gesture that triggered a 38–13 run by the Bruins, "but I was just sticking up for a friend."

The O'Bannons were often double trouble during their two years together as Bruins. A hanging jumper from Charles and a three-pointer by Ed on back-to-back baskets in overtime powered UCLA to an 82–77 victory over Arizona State about two weeks after the Notre Dame game. With the 6'8" Ed the undisputed leader and the 6'6" Charles an important complementary piece, the Bruins got to hang one of those championship banners in Pauley after going on to beat Arkansas in the championship game. Ed scored 30 points and grabbed 17 rebounds against the Razorbacks, becoming the Final Four's Most Outstanding Player.

The New Jersey Nets selected Ed ninth overall in the 1995 NBA Draft after a senior season in which he led UCLA in scoring (20.4 points per game) and rebounding (8.3), becoming the Pac-10 co-Player of the Year. Ed finished his career with 1,815 points, fifth all-time at UCLA, and later had his jersey (No. 31) retired.

Ed's departure allowed Charles to go from supporting cast to starring role. He boosted his scoring in each of his four seasons, averaging 14.3 points per game as a junior and 17.7 points as a senior, making the All-Pac–10 first team the latter year. "Charles was channeling Ed from two years prior in terms of taking on that leadership role and thriving in it," said Lavin, who would take over as UCLA's head coach during Charles' senior season.

The O'Bannons never did reunite in the NBA. Ed's career lasted just two seasons before he spent the next seven years playing professionally in five different countries, retiring at age 30. Charles was a second-round draft pick of the Detroit Pistons whose NBA career also lasted only two seasons. But they'll forever cherish the one shining moment they spent together as Bruins, two brothers hoisting the last banner to be raised inside the building that John Wooden's teams made famous. "He just said, 'Great job,'" Ed said that day, recalling what Wooden told the Bruins, "'and now you guys know what it feels like.'"

44 The 1994–95 National Basketball Championship

Ed O'Bannon's voice could be heard through the locker room door, not to mention the sound of various items bouncing off the walls. "I'm sick of this bullshit!" the UCLA forward yelled. "It's not happening anymore!"

As his coaches listened to the minutes-long rant from the safety of the other side of those walls following the Bruins' 112–102 loss to Tulsa in the first round of the 1994 NCAA tournament, they also heard O'Bannon deliver a nod toward the future. "It starts now!" he said. "It starts here!"

The challenge resonated among players and a coach who felt they had plenty to prove. UCLA coach Jim Harrick had guided his teams to 20 wins in each of his first six seasons in Westwood, but the Bruins had never made the Final Four and had twice lost in the first round of the NCAA tournament, including the embarrassment against Tulsa in which they yielded 63 points in the first half alone. Senior point guard Tyus Edney was seeking to silence the doubters who felt that at 5'10" he was too small to dominate on college basketball's highest level. Senior center George Zidek was eager to show he was more than a plodding 7-footer. And O'Bannon was only four years removed from a career-threatening knee injury that forced him to miss an entire season, making the 1994–95 campaign his last at UCLA.

The Bruins entered the season with four returning starters, three senior leaders, and four heralded freshmen, but questions about toughness and defense persisted after what had unfolded the previous year. Players wore T-shirts in practices and game warmups reading "Bruin Defense," "Masterlock," and "Red Zone" that had been made by assistant coach Steve Lavin, a constant reminder of the strides they intended to make. Some initial progress was displayed against third-ranked Kentucky in the second game of the season, when UCLA's pressure forced a turnover that gave the ball back to the Bruins while trailing by one point with 16.5 seconds left. Freshman forward J.R. Henderson sank two free throws with six-tenths of a second left to give UCLA what it hoped would be a tone-setting 82–81 triumph over the Wildcats.

The team won its first six games before blowing a 13-point lead during an 82–72 loss to Oregon in its Pac-10 Conference opener, which ended with Harrick getting ejected in the final minute after receiving back-to-back technical fouls for disputing a traveling violation on Edney. UCLA rebounded with another six-game winning streak that included a 71–61 victory over Arizona that represented what was then the Wildcats' worst home conference loss of coach Lute Olson's era in Tucson.

Next came one of the season's most bizarre moments, when California coach Todd Bozeman said his team's 100–93 upset of UCLA (later forfeited because of NCAA violations) was sparked by Bruins players and coaches wandering into Pauley Pavilion and heckling Golden Bears players shooting free throws toward the end of a practice the previous day. UCLA players denied the allegations and the loss didn't seem to bother them, the Bruins rattling off 13 consecutive victories to take the nation's longest winning streak into the NCAA tournament.

By then, UCLA had shown it could win with big lineups featuring Zidek, who had developed a sweeping hook shot he could shoot with either hand, or the 6'9" Henderson and 6'8" O'Bannon manning the frontcourt as part of a small-ball lineup that harassed teams into turnovers leading to easy baskets. "When you had five guys who could pass, catch, run, put the ball on the deck, create, and make decisions and finish," Lavin recalled of the latter alignment, "it was quite a thing to behold and entertaining."

The top-seeded Bruins easily outclassed Florida International in their West regional opener before needing Edney's length-of-the-court dash and buzzer-beating layup to edge Missouri in the second round. UCLA's improved defense was on display again during an 86–67 victory over Mississippi State in which Zidek held Bulldogs counterpart Erick Dampier to only four shots and 11 points. Connecticut then made the mistake of thinking it could run with the Bruins in the regional final, only to get trampled during UCLA's 102–96 triumph that sent it to the Final Four for the first time since 1980.

The tiny Edney came up big against Oklahoma State in a national semifinal, outmaneuvering Cowboys point guard Andre Owens for two layups and two additional plays in which the Bruins were fouled and made four free throws over the final 3½ minutes of UCLA's 74–61 victory. But Edney sprained his wrist against the Cowboys, putting his status into doubt for the national title game against Arkansas, the defending national champion. Privately, Harrick worried his team might be sunk without Edney against a counterpart that liked to constantly press. His assistants were more upbeat when it came to contemplating their chances with Cameron Dollar, who had led the team to a victory over USC earlier in the season with Edney sidelined by the flu.

Ed O'Bannon stands on a ladder and uses a video camera to record the victory celebration after UCLA defeated the Arkansas Razorbacks in Seattle for the NCAA national championship on April 3, 1995. (AP Photo/Eric Draper)

"It was kind of like a Steve Young and [Joe] Montana deal, where Montana got hurt and you're bringing in Steve Young," Lavin said, referring to the former San Francisco 49ers quarterbacks. "It felt like we're fine here; we might even present some problems because they're preparing in terms of game film for Tyus Edney and suddenly you've got a quarterback stepping in that they haven't schemed for."

With Edney able to play only 2½ minutes because of his sore wrist, Dollar stepped in and remained steady, finishing with six points, eight assists, and three turnovers. Freshman guard Toby Bailey broke through with 26 points and nine rebounds and O'Bannon fulfilled the pledge he had made in the locker room a year earlier with 30 points and 17 rebounds. Meanwhile, Zidek limited the effectiveness of Arkansas' Corliss Williamson, who went scoreless for a 33-minute stretch and made three of 16 shots.

After the buzzer sounded on UCLA's 89–78 triumph, the Bruins convened at halfcourt and knelt around O'Bannon, the Most Outstanding Player of the Final Four. The moment mostly belonged to the coach and the three seniors who had helped the program win its first national title since coach John Wooden's last in 1975. "The three of them being together for that to happen and to be the only championship other than Wooden's 10," Lavin said, "does make you believe a little bit in terms of the stars aligning for UCLA in that particular season."

45 Henry Russell "Red" Sanders

John Peterson remembers the headline in a local newspaper after Henry Russell "Red" Sanders had been hired as UCLA's football coach before the 1949 season. "RED SANDERS WHO?" read the large block type, speaking for legions of fans and players unfamiliar with the coach who had spent his career in the South.

"Nobody knew anything about him," said Peterson, who would play center and linebacker under Sanders for the Bruins. Sanders largely remained an enigma until the day he shockingly died of a heart attack after nine seasons with the Bruins, all of them winning and one securing the only national championship in the program's history.

He came to be known as a master tactician who formulated a smothering 4-4 defense that was widely copied and a reliable if predictable single-wing offense that benefited from the dominance of its defense. The coach made no secret of his preference for running the football. "He thought the pass was the most dangerous offensive way in football," Peterson said. "We'd maybe pass six times, seven times in a game."

Sanders had been hired not long after John Wooden arrived to coach the basketball team. The men couldn't have been more different—Wooden the stoic, buttoned-down nondrinker and Sanders the reveler who enjoyed the Hollywood scene and a glass of Jack Daniel's. It was Sanders, and not Wooden, who was the darling of Los Angeles sportswriters in the 1950s after he guided UCLA to three Pacific Coast Conference titles, two Rose Bowl appearances, one national title, and a 6–3 record against rival USC.

"Sanders fielded smart, fast, well-drilled, admirably-schooled teams that managed to make the Trojans look like clumsy Elks on a convention," Jim Murray wrote in the *Los Angeles Times*. "Sanders beat them six out of eight [sic] tries, sometimes by 39–0 and 34–0. For Red, it was like playing poker with your grandmother."

One similarity between Sanders and Wooden was their love of details, down to the precise footwork of their players. "You'd take so many steps here and they're this long, and he would demonstrate these things," Peterson said of Sanders' edicts. "So he was a real perfectionist when it came to execution of plays."

Sanders could be prickly with his players. He once told his linemen they ran "like a bunch of Easter bunnies" and admonished one player for running up to an opponent "like you were trying to borrow money from him." Things changed for Sanders' players only after they became his former players.

"He wasn't your buddy until you graduated," Peterson said. "Then the day you graduated and you weren't on his team anymore, he called me in the office and he said, 'Oh, I just always wanted to talk to you, John.' He was interested in what I was going to do and that sort of thing. Prior to that, he'd be there to criticize you. If you screwed up in a game or did something wrong, he'd tell you about it—in a constructive way, I must say, not just to be derogatory toward you."

Sanders was quick with a quip, including two of the most iconic quotes in college football history. "Beating 'SC is not a matter of life and death," Sanders said, "it's more important than that." Sanders also coined a phrase erroneously attributed to legendary Green Bay Packers coach Vince Lombardi, saying, "Winning isn't everything; it's the only thing."

Sanders did plenty of that. His 1954 team finished 9–0 while earning a share of the national championship. He went 66–19–1 at UCLA, a .773 winning percentage that remains the best for a Bruins football coach. His success earned him a 10-year contract paying $20,000 per season the year before he died, helping him remain committed to UCLA despite lucrative overtures from Texas A&M and Florida.

Sanders continued to win despite PCC sanctions that included a three-year Rose Bowl ban and the loss of some eligibility for every implicated player on the 1955 varsity and freshman teams, ending the careers of 11 players. The sanctions were the result of under-the-table payments to players exceeding the conference limit of $75 per month. Sanders shrugged and continued coaching his undermanned teams; his 1956 team finished 7–3 and his 1957 team—the last he ever coached—went 8–2.

Even Sanders' death, at age 53 in August 1958, came with a Hollywood flair when he was found dead in a second-floor room of the Lafayette Hotel on Beverly Boulevard near downtown L.A. The *Times* was initially duped by the account of W.T. Grimes, a convicted panderer who said he was an old friend of the coach and claimed he "came to talk baseball and football" with Sanders.

It was soon discovered that the married Sanders was at the hotel for a rendezvous with Ernestine Drake, a blond woman of about 30 in a flowered dress and high spiked heels who said she was a fashion model from Vienna. She said she had been introduced to the coach by Grimes, the registered occupant of the room, and was unaware Sanders was a football coach. Grimes was not present when Sanders was stricken after complaining of heat and humidity upon his arrival, removing his shirt and tie and sending Drake to fetch soft drinks.

While making small talk, Drake said she told Sanders she didn't follow his sport. "Football is a great game," Drake said Sanders had replied. "You should come out this fall and see a few games." Those were Sanders' last words before he clutched his chest and rolled over on one side of the bed. Drake told authorities she ran for help and found the coach on the floor when she returned.

By the time a police ambulance arrived about an hour later, Sanders was long dead. The autopsy revealed he had an enlarged heart, scar tissue indicating the presence of advanced coronary heart disease. UCLA made Sanders a charter member of its Athletic Hall of Fame and presents the Henry R. "Red" Sanders Award to its most valuable offensive player each season, keeping alive the memory of a man who took the program where no one else has before or since.

46 The 1954 National Football Championship

UCLA knew its bowl fate even before the opening kickoff of the 1954 season. The Bruins couldn't play in the Rose Bowl because they had gone the previous season and there was a "no-repeat rule" in place that forbade teams from appearing in that game in two consecutive years.

Funny thing was, the entire season felt like it was stuck on repeat—one drubbing of an opponent after another on the way to a perfect 9–0 record. The Bruins led the nation in scoring thanks to a predictable but powerful single-wing offense, averaging 40.8 points per game. They also happened to lead it in scoring defense, allowing only 4.4 points per game while logging five shutouts. UCLA won games by scores of 61–0 and 67–0. "If this sort of thing keeps up," the *Los Angeles Times'* Jack Geyer wrote after UCLA's 41–0 rout of Oregon, "the district attorney will charge the Bruins with murder."

During a particularly monotonous 72–0 thrashing of Stanford in which UCLA intercepted eight passes and its offense rushed for 418 yards, an Indians tackle turned to Bruins linebacker John Peterson and voiced his frustration. "He looked at me in about the fourth quarter and he said, 'This is really the shits,'" Peterson recalled more than 60 years later, laughing. "I said, 'Yeah. When are we going to get this thing over with?'"

UCLA had a pretty good idea it was going to be good long before the season. The Bruins had gone 8–1 in 1952 and 8–2 in 1953, the latter season concluding with a 28–20 loss to Michigan State in the Rose Bowl. UCLA returned all of its primary starters in 1954, including linemen Jack Ellena and Jim Salsbury, fullback Bob Davenport, and tailback Primo Villanueva—all of whom became first-team All-Americans. Even with the Rose Bowl off the table, players had a clear mandate. "Our goal," Peterson said, "was to go undefeated from spring practice."

There were two close calls. UCLA pulled out a 12–7 victory over Maryland, the defending national champion, in the third week of the season after Davenport rushed for two touchdowns. The Bruins then built a 21–0 halftime lead over Washington in Seattle that was anything but safe. Substitution rules in place at the time because of a shortage of players during the recently concluded Korean War necessitated that UCLA's second-stringers play in the third quarter, Peterson said. The Huskies scored three touchdowns but missed an extra point. The Bruins prevailed, 21–20, only after Villanueva, one of the team's many two-way players, deflected a late pass.

The near-miss reawakened UCLA's dominance. The Bruins outscored their last five opponents by an aggregate score of 235–6. The season-ending rivalry game against USC before 102,548 at the Los Angeles Memorial Coliseum looked like anything but a rout for three quarters. USC was trailing only 7–0 in the third quarter, with the ball deep in UCLA territory, when the Bruins' Jim Decker intercepted a pass. That was the turning point, as UCLA scored 27 points in the fourth quarter on the way to a 34–0 victory.

All that was left was to await the judgment of the pollsters. The vote was ultimately split, with UCLA ranked No. 1 by United Press International and Ohio State getting the top spot by Associated Press.

"Sure there was frustration," Ellena told the *Times*. "We were a hell of a football team. What I remember so well is that we went into the games with so much confidence that we came up to the line of scrimmage with smiles on our faces. We just knew that we were in complete control."

The Bruins celebrated as best as they could. At the team banquet at the Moulin Rouge in Hollywood, a hot spot for movie stars, Peterson and Ellena—who finished seventh in voting for the Heisman Trophy—bounded onto a stage on the back of an elephant. The team still holds school records for points in a season (367), points in a game (72), touchdowns in a season (55), rushing defense (659 yards), total defense (1,708 yards), and scoring defense (40 points). "All I know," UCLA Coach Henry "Red" Sanders told reporters of the only Bruins team to win a share of the national championship, "is that I wouldn't trade this team for any other."

47 Tommy Prothro

Tommy Prothro was always direct. If you were a better team, he told his players, you should win. If you executed and played to your abilities under those conditions, you would prevail. And if Prothro felt he had been outcoached, his UCLA players would be the first to know.

That's how he came to stand in front of the Bruins in September 1965 and deliver a mea culpa following a season-opening loss to Michigan State, which had gone 4–5 the previous year.

"He walked in and very quickly said, 'Look, you didn't lose this game, we did—we, the coaching staff,'" Gary Beban, the UCLA quarterback who would go on to win the Heisman Trophy in 1967, recalled Prothro saying that day. "'We did not think that this team was that good and we probably weren't prepared and we did not prepare you. We didn't prepare you well enough to win this game and that will never happen again.'

"I remember reflecting in the years later that it never happened again. I think all of us were confident every game that our game plan was better, stronger, and had more tweaks in it and it always did and they always worked."

A chain smoker and Coca-Cola guzzler, Prothro was a man of many quirks. He liked to carry a briefcase, clutching it even when his players hoisted him onto their shoulders after beating those same Michigan State Spartans four months later in the 1966 Rose Bowl. He was just as guarded about everything else as the contents of that briefcase. "He was just the opposite of John McKay," Beban said of the gregarious USC coach, "who of course was a laugh a minute."

Prothro kept late hours in his den scheming ways to beat his next opponent during his six years as UCLA's head coach. It was there that he devised the famous "Z streak" before a game against Washington midway through the 1965 season. The play called for a UCLA end to break the huddle early and jog toward the sideline but remain in bounds by a foot. Washington was particularly susceptible to the deception because its defenders broke the huddle in perfect sync, with each player's bowed head rising in unison.

Prothro called for the play in the third quarter with his team trailing the Huskies, 24–21. UCLA end Dick Witcher watched the Washington players, waiting for their heads to go down in the huddle. Then he broke for the sideline, staying on the field. He was wide open when the ball was snapped, taking a pass from Beban for a 60-yard touchdown, the decisive points in UCLA's 28–24 triumph. "The Z streak is legal," Prothro would say later. "But if you were to put it on the ballot, I would vote against it. Deception should happen after the ball is snapped, not before."

Prothro was strongly disliked by some who thought his methods were unethical. Penn State's alumni secretary contended that the Bruins sent signals to Beban's helmet after a traffic director in the parking lot claimed to have intercepted plays from UCLA coaches in the press box that were relayed via walkie-talkie. Prothro denied the accusation after the Bruins upset the Nittany Lions 24–22, quipping that if Penn State knew the plays and still lost, "I would say it did a sorry job with an advantage like that."

Prothro also dismissed a series of photos in the *Santa Monica Outlook* that appeared to show his assistant coaches signaling plays from the sideline against Stanford, a tactic that was not allowed at the time. Responded Prothro: "If you take pictures of any coach during a game, you are apt to find him in unusual positions."

Standing 6'2½" and weighing 255 pounds, Prothro was a commanding presence wherever he went. He first came to UCLA in 1949 as backfield coach under the legendary Red Sanders, remaining for six years and one national championship as part of the Bruins' undefeated season in 1954.

Prothro became the head coach at Oregon State the following year, going 63–37–2 in 10 seasons while leading the Beavers to two Rose Bowls before UCLA hired him back to take over its program before the 1965 season. "I watched what he did with inferior material at Oregon State," UCLA athletic director J.D. Morgan told *Sports Illustrated*. "… I felt I had to get him. In our larger setup he would be a knockout."

He was indeed, engineering UCLA's 14–12 upset of top-ranked Michigan State in the 1966 Rose Bowl that represented perhaps the greatest victory in the history of the program. Prothro went 41–18–3 with the Bruins before leaving in 1971 for NFL jobs coaching the Los Angeles Rams and San Diego Chargers. Prothro was unable to repeat his success at the professional level, going 35–51–2 in six seasons before retiring to become a world-class bridge player and dying from cancer in 1995.

His tactical brilliance as UCLA's coach was cemented in Dick Vermeil's mind while Vermeil served as an assistant at Stanford who was responsible for scouting the Bruins. "He said, 'I'd watch you guys and grade you guys and you guys never got better than a "C" and yet you kept winning,'" Beban recalled Vermeil, who would later coach under Prothro before becoming UCLA's head coach, telling him. "[Vermeil] said, 'Then the light bulb went on. It was Prothro.' So I think that reflects the genius of the man."

48 1966 Rose Bowl

The phrase "gutty little Bruins" has long characterized UCLA's fighting spirit amid challenging circumstances, more of a nod to the school's underdog mentality than a literal lack of size.

But the Bruins really were dwarfed in the game that best symbolized the popular expression. UCLA was taking on a giant in every sense in the 1966 Rose Bowl when it faced top-ranked and two-touchdown favorite Michigan State, whose unbeaten record included a 13–3 triumph over the Bruins in the season opener.

"I remember running past Bubba Smith and he was about 7-foot tall and I was looking into his belt buckle," UCLA linebacker Wade Pearson told the *Los Angeles Times*. "I thought, 'That's the biggest man I've ever seen.'"

Not even Bruins coach Tommy Prothro thought his team had a chance, a sentiment he shared with his players in the locker room before the game. "I don't think we have a prayer today," quarterback Gary Beban recalled Prothro saying. "Every one of you can play their best football, all at the same time—which would never happen—and we can't win. So let's make sure we go out there and don't embarrass ourselves."

Prothro liked to gamble when he considered his team lesser in talent than its opponent, and that was certainly the case when he contemplated how to beat Michigan State. Fortunately for the Bruins, Spartans coach Duffy Daugherty had provided a tip-off in the days before the game, saying his team would stick to what had helped it go 10–0 before the Rose Bowl.

That convinced Prothro to formulate his defense to stifle Michigan State's staple plays, especially when needing short yardage on third down. The plan worked perfectly. Six times during the game, UCLA stopped the Spartans in those situations. It helped that Prothro had instructed his players on what to look for in certain situations. If a Spartans running back changed the positioning of his feet, for instance, it meant that the play was designed to go to the left side. "They had it all down," Beban said of UCLA's defensive players, "and that's all coaching."

Prothro also made sure his offense was as unpredictable as possible. On UCLA's first play from scrimmage, he ordered Beban to fake a handoff to Mel Farr and circle around the right end. Prothro didn't tell anyone but the quarterback and the running back, ensuring no one tipped off the play. It worked, with Beban rambling for 27 yards. "It was worth more than 27 yards," Prothro would tell *Sports Illustrated* afterward. "We wanted Michigan State players to ask themselves, 'What will those lunatics do next?'"

Prothro also decided before the game that he would try to shake Michigan State's confidence by attempting an onside kick should the Bruins score first prior to halftime. He put the plan into motion after UCLA scored a touchdown early in the second quarter on Beban's one-yard run. The Bruins tried the onside kick and recovered it, with Beban eventually scoring again on another one-yard touchdown run to give his team a 14–0 lead that energized the crowd of 100,087.

Having held the Spartans scoreless for more than three quarters, UCLA's defense began to tire in the fourth quarter. Michigan State fullback Bob Apisa took a lateral and ran for a 38-yard touchdown, but the score remained 14–6 after a surprise two-point conversion attempt failed.

The drama heightened when the Spartans partially blocked a UCLA punt and took over at the Bruins' 49-yard line. Michigan State converted three fourth downs on the way to the 1-yard line, where quarterback Steve Juday scored on a quarterback sneak with 31 seconds left in the game to shave UCLA's lead to 14–12.

Needing the two-point conversion to tie the score, Michigan State lined up on the left hash mark and pitched the ball to Apisa. He fought off contact from defenders Dallas Grider and Jim Colletto, though the latter's pursuit forced Apisa to run parallel to the goal line instead of cutting inside for the tying points. That's when Bob Stiles, a 5'8", 175-pound junior, hurled himself into Apisa's upper body and brought him down.

As the Bruins began to celebrate their first Rose Bowl triumph, Prothro walked over to Beban and draped an arm around him as they walked off the field. It wasn't exactly a warmhearted exchange. The coach informed his quarterback of his failure to burn enough seconds off the play clock by lingering in the huddle between snaps.

"He says, 'Gary, if you had used up all the time in the huddle, Michigan State would have not had time to run that last series of plays where they scored, and they certainly would not have had time to go for two points,'" Beban recalled. "He didn't say, 'Congratulations.' It was a learning moment."

The biggest lesson was to never count out the Bruins or risk being gutted. "If we had played them 100 times," Beban said of the Spartans, "we would have lost by 100 points 99 times except that one day."

49 Ann Meyers

Dave Meyers brought something besides his laundry home from college one weekend. The standout forward on UCLA's basketball team was accompanied by his roommate, Kenny Washington, who had been a member of legendary coach John Wooden's first two national championship teams and was now coach of the Bruins women's basketball team.

Together they made a pitch to Ann Meyers, Dave's younger sister and a player so gifted at basketball that, as a senior at Sonora High in La Habra, California, she became the first high school player to make a United States national team. Meyers was a 5'9" dynamo who could play all five positions and lettered in seven sports at Sonora—basketball, track and field, softball, field hockey, badminton, tennis, and volleyball. She had dreamed of becoming an Olympian in track after reading a book on Babe Didrikson Zaharias, who had won two gold medals in the 1932 Summer Olympics.

Ann hailed from a basketball family. Her father, Bob, had played guard for Marquette and her older sister Patty had starred at center for Cal State Fullerton's 1970 national championship women's team. The assumption among most in Southern California was that Ann would follow her sister's path to Cal State Fullerton, which was only about 15 minutes from the Meyers' home.

Everything changed when her older brother and his roommate asked Ann whether she would like to go to UCLA on scholarship. "I had no idea where I was going to go to college," Ann recalled. "And then when my brother came home that weekend and said, 'Well, UCLA would like to offer you a scholarship,' I was in seventh heaven."

Ann accepted the offer, becoming the first woman to attend UCLA on a full athletic scholarship. The media descended on Westwood upon her arrival to chronicle the dynamic brother-sister tandem, featuring Dave, star of Wooden's final national championship team in 1974–75, and Ann, the face of a fledgling women's team that played its games on a side court inside Pauley Pavilion.

Ann continued her diverse athletic pursuits in college, competing in volleyball as well as track and field in the high jump and pentathlon. She tried out for the tennis team and played a little rugby before being asked to stop for fear of injury. But there was no doubt in which sport she was most skilled after having competed against—and often dominated—players a decade older than herself since she began playing AAU basketball at 13.

She was a gritty defender who clogged the passing lanes, anticipated an opponent's release of a shot to make the block, and out-toughed others for rebounds. She could be tenacious to a fault. Angry about a call in her very first college game, Meyers hurled a basketball at official Rosie Adams, who happened to be a former college teammate of her sister Patty's. "It knocked the wind out of her and I felt so bad because it was Rosie and I had lost my temper and so they called a 'T' on me," Meyers said, "but I had fouled out and Kenny put me down on the bench right after that. Lesson learned. I just learned to control my temper."

Meyers largely channeled her energy into winning. The Bruins advanced to the Association for Intercollegiate Athletics for Women tournament in each of her final three seasons, winning the national championship in 1978 with a nationally televised 90–74 victory over Maryland in which Meyers was strong across the board with 20 points, 10 rebounds, nine assists, and eight steals. Her stat line was not unusual for someone who had become the first college player—male or female—to record a quadruple-double when she logged 20 points, 14 rebounds, 10 assists, and 10 steals during a game against Stephen F. Austin on February 18, 1978. "You can't achieve something like that without your teammates, there's no question, especially on the assists," Meyers said. "People have to finish shots for you. But yeah, even today I look back and think, 'Wow, I was able to do that?'"

Meyers finished her career with averages of 17.4 points, 8.4 rebounds, and 5.6 assists per game and still holds school records for career steals (403) and blocks (101). She became the first four-time women's All-American basketball player and won a silver medal while competing for the U.S. women's team in the 1976 Olympics. Meyers made more history by earning a tryout with the NBA's Indiana Pacers in 1979, failing to make the team but earning a legion of admirers nationwide. "Annie was one of the best basketball players ever," Hall of Fame center Bill Russell, who won 11 NBA titles with the Boston Celtics, once said. "I didn't say male or female. I said ever."

She was selected No. 1 overall by the New Jersey Gems of the Women's Professional Basketball League, where she spent three seasons. Meyers went on to become a longtime television analyst for various networks before serving as vice president of the Phoenix Suns and vice president and general manager of the WNBA's Phoenix Mercury, as well as a member of the Suns' broadcast team. She was married to Don Drysdale before the former Los Angeles Dodgers pitcher and Hall of Famer died of a heart attack at age 56 in 1993.

Widely regarded as the pioneer of women's college basketball, Meyers has left a permanent legacy—the women's basketball court inside UCLA's new Mo Ostin Basketball Center was named in her honor. "That," Meyers said, "is pretty cool."

50 The 1978 AIAW National Championship

The biggest issue confronting women's college basketball in its infancy wasn't that the game was being played below the rim, but under the radar. Immaculata, a small Catholic school in Pennsylvania, won the first three titles in the tournament run by the Association for Intercollegiate Athletics for Women, starting in 1972. Immaculata was finally dethroned in 1975 by Delta State (enrollment 3,200) of Cleveland, Mississippi, which won the next three championships.

Women's college basketball finally went national—if not viral—in 1978, thanks to a nationally televised championship game between UCLA and Maryland. It was the first time that two traditional men's college basketball powers had met for the women's title, and nobody associated with the sport seemed to mind that NBC had acquired the television rights to the game for a sum *Sports Illustrated* reported to be "considerably less than $25,000."

The championship was a rematch between teams that had met during the regular season, with Maryland prevailing 92–88 on its home court. UCLA had lost three of five games on an East Coast swing that involved the game against the Terrapins, its only setbacks in the regular season. Rather than demoralize her team, first-year Bruins coach Billie Moore told reporters the defeats had galvanized her players by helping them better assess their strengths and weaknesses. "Billie said she didn't care if we went 5–0 or 0–5 as long as we learned something," UCLA center Heidi Nestor told *SI*.

The Bruins rolled through the rest of their schedule unbeaten, but stared defeat in the face during an AIAW tournament regional game against Long Beach State. Trailing by a point in overtime, UCLA was saved when forward Anita Ortega stole a pass and went in for a layup at the buzzer, giving the Bruins a 79–78 triumph. "Once we got through that Long Beach State game," Bruins guard Ann Meyers said, "we felt pretty confident."

UCLA had ample reason to believe in itself. The Bruins featured a starting lineup with five players averaging double figures in scoring, led by the versatile Meyers and prolific freshman Denise Curry, who averaged 20.3 points and 9.1 rebounds per game. *SI*'s Bruce Newman described Meyers as "a four-time All-America who is probably the best UCLA basketball player with a girl's name since Gail Goodrich." Moore added a winning pedigree, having guided Cal State Fullerton to what was recognized as the national championship in 1970 when the Titans captured the national women's invitational tournament.

UCLA certainly had the crowd behind it in its final two games. The national semifinal and final were played at Pauley Pavilion, where the Bruins withstood a 40-point outburst from Montclair State's Carol "The Blaze" Blazejowski on the way to an 85–77 victory in the semifinal round. The championship game was played before what was then a record crowd of 9,351, which included Meyers' father, Bob, a former standout guard at Marquette who would yell, "Attaboy, Annie!" whenever his daughter delighted him.

That was often in the early going, as the scrappy Meyers shut down Tara Heiss, Maryland's leading scorer who had thrashed the Bruins only a few months earlier. This time, Meyers held Heiss to one field goal over the game's first 25 minutes as UCLA built a 43–33 halftime lead. "She had a pretty good second half," Meyers said of Heiss, who finished with 12 points and nine assists, "but it was too late; we had already taken them out of their offense." Meanwhile, Maryland forward Jane Zivalich, who was supposed to guard Meyers, could only watch from the bench after injuring her knee two days earlier. Meyers rendered the other Terrapins defenseless, collecting 20 points and 10 rebounds to go along with nine assists and eight steals.

UCLA never trailed and led by as many as 19 points on the way to a 90–74 triumph. Players received championship watches afterward, but not rings, until the school honored the team in 2008 on the 30th anniversary of its only national title in the sport. Women's college basketball could trace its explosion in popularity back to the first championship game played on a national stage. *SI*'s Newman, contemplating the implications of the game, wrote that "Ann Meyers is still out there somewhere, signing autographs for dozens of little girls who want to grow up someday to be just like her."

51 Cade McNown

It was going to be the last drive of a lost season, UCLA just trying to make the score respectable while trailing USC by two touchdowns with only a handful of minutes left at the Rose Bowl.

"I remember getting in the huddle and just telling everybody, 'Hey, guys, let's end the season on a great note,'" Bruins quarterback Cade McNown recalled of the 1996 crosstown rivalry game. "'It's our last drive of the year, let's get a touchdown and finish strong.'"

Did they ever on a day most everything had been tilting in the Trojans' direction. UCLA trailed 38–21 early in the fourth quarter after USC receiver R. Jay Soward scored on a 78-yard touchdown pass. When the ABC broadcast returned from a commercial break, Soward spotted a cameraman behind him, leaped to his feet from the bench, whirled around, and looked into the lens. "Hey!" Soward said before referencing UCLA's winning streak in the series. "Five years? It's over." As he uttered the last two words, Soward made a throat-slashing gesture with his right hand.

Soward would not have the final say. The Bruins scored 10 unanswered points, but an onside kick failed and the Trojans had a first down with 1:37 to play. Ballgame? Hardly. UCLA linebacker Danjuan Magee ripped the ball away from USC's LaVale Woods and the Bruins recovered to give themselves one last chance.

"I remember, the butterflies went in my stomach because I realized, oh my gosh, they're putting this on a silver platter for us," McNown said. "We could actually win this game. This is unbelievable."

Bruins tailback Skip Hicks made the most of the opportunity, running for an 11-yard touchdown to tie the score with 39 seconds left. USC put together a frantic drive and UCLA needed Travis Kirschke to block a field goal to force the first overtime in the history of the rivalry. The teams traded field goals in the first overtime before Hicks sprinted 25 yards for a touchdown on the first play of the second overtime.

After Soward dropped a third-down pass and UCLA's Anthony Cobbs made a game-ending interception, the Bruins emerged with a most improbable 48–41 victory. "While it didn't matter at all on the national stage," McNown said, alluding to the fact that both teams would finish with .500 or worse records, "it was such an amazing game where so many things had to go right."

That was the story of McNown's career against USC. He would finish 4–0 against the Trojans, becoming the only starting quarterback from either team to do so in the history of a rivalry that dates to 1929.

It all started after McNown had become UCLA's full-time starting quarterback only five games into his freshman season after beating out concussion-plagued counterpart Ryan Fien. UCLA was not expected to put up much of a fight against the Trojans when the teams met on November 18, 1995. USC had already secured a spot in the Rose Bowl and the Bruins were playing without star running back Karim Abdul-Jabbar, who was sidelined by a sprained ankle.

None of that mattered as McNown's opportunistic play helped UCLA pull out a 24–20 victory. McNown completed only eight of 17 passes for 131 yards with two interceptions, but his 21-yard scramble on third-and-13 from the Bruins' 29-yard line helped seal UCLA's fifth consecutive triumph in the series and sent the Bruins to the Aloha Bowl.

McNown was more efficient against the Trojans during his junior season in 1997, completing 15 of 24 passes for 213 yards and three touchdowns while also rushing for 48 yards during UCLA's 31–24 victory that was a prelude to a comeback victory over Texas A&M in the Cotton Bowl. The rivalry game his senior season was a 34–17 romp in the Bruins' favor. McNown's final act against USC was to jump into the arms of guard Andy Meyers before flipping the ball into the air and walking to the sideline to embrace offensive coordinator Al Borges. UCLA's eight-game winning streak against the Trojans was the longest by either team in the history of the rivalry.

McNown finished his UCLA career as the school's all-time leading passer with 10,708 yards, while going 30–14 as a starter and leading the Bruins to a school-record 20 consecutive victories during his junior and senior years. An All-American as a senior, McNown was selected No. 12 in the first round of the 1999 NFL Draft by the Chicago Bears before also gracing the rosters of the Miami Dolphins and San Francisco 49ers during his four-year professional career.

USC fans might want to avoid getting too cheeky during any encounters with McNown, who returned to Los Angeles after his playing career ended to work in asset management, because he'll always have the ultimate comeback.

"Every now and again if I get a really overzealous Trojan fan, I might give them my four-fingered handshake—just collapse the thumb and say, 'Oh, I'm sorry, I'm sorry,'" McNown said with a laugh, referring to going 4–0 against USC. "But those are only with the aggressive guys."

McNown said he didn't realize the significance of his achievement until he attended a UCLA basketball game a couple of years after his final college season and was introduced as the only quarterback to have beaten the Trojans all four years.

"People went crazy and I thought, 'Oh, wow, I guess that was going to be an important distinguishing fact going forward,'" McNown said. "Until then, I didn't really give it any thought. You just want to beat them, right?"

52 20-Game Winning Streak

The pointed radio show questions and fan negativity hovered like a thick marine layer over Westwood after UCLA dropped its first two games of the 1997 season.

The Bruins had fallen to Washington State in the final minutes of their opener after running back Jermaine Lewis missed a hole on the left side of the offensive line on fourth-and-goal at the 1. Then they lost a heartbreaker against Tennessee when quarterback Cade McNown's fourth-down pass flew over the head of receiver Eric Scott inside the Volunteer 20-yard line with 27 seconds left.

Some self-soothing was in order because no one else around the players was doing any consoling.

"I remember going on a radio show with Jim Rome and a lot of the boo birds were coming out and questioning this and questioning that," McNown said, "and I just remember thinking, people don't realize we're a good team and I think we'll prove it in short order."

What no one knew at the time was that Washington State would go on to appear in the Rose Bowl that season as the co-Pac-10 Conference champion, while Peyton Manning–led Tennessee was bound for the Orange Bowl after winning the Southeastern Conference.

The Bruins quickly showed they weren't too bad either. They parlayed eight Texas turnovers into a 66–3 rout of the Longhorns, in which McNown set a UCLA record with five touchdown passes in a game—all in the first half. *Los Angeles Times* writer Jim Hodges described it as "Texas' worst home loss since the Alamo." For UCLA, it was a momentary reprieve but hardly vindication given the Bruins' record stood at 1–2.

"We had a huge chip on our shoulder following losing those two games by close margins and feeling like we had a lot to prove," McNown said, "so the rest of that year we spent trying to prove that we were a good team."

UCLA stormed through the balance of its schedule like an Olympic distance runner competing with 10-minute milers, winning the next eight games by an average of 21 points. The Bruins earned an invitation to the Cotton Bowl and promptly spotted Texas A&M a 16–0 lead, stirring reminders of the slow starts and failed comebacks against Washington State and Tennessee. But the Bruins came all the way back this time, securing a 29–23 victory after Ryan Neufeld scored on a five-yard reverse.

UCLA took a 10-game winning streak into the 1998 season and didn't expect any letup. Star running back Skip Hicks had exhausted his eligibility, but the rest of the offense returned and prized running back recruit DeShaun Foster was set to make his collegiate debut.

The Bruins turned Texas into toast again during the season opener and rolled over Houston in the second game, though receiver Freddie Mitchell was lost to a season-ending injury when his femur snapped against the Cougars. "It sounded like a shotgun blast," McNown said. "It was quite a noise."

Consecutive matchups against unbeaten Pac-10 rivals would prove pivotal. First up was Arizona, which held a nine-game

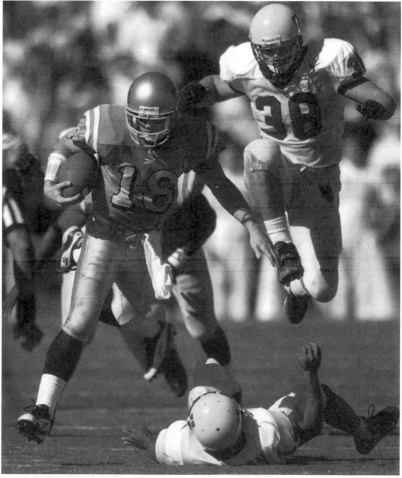

Cade McNown runs upfield, dodging Oregon defenders Terry Miller (leaping) and Rashad Bauman (laying) to gain 25 yards during the fourth quarter of this Pac-10 matchup. (AP Photo/Michael Caulfield)

winning streak dating to the previous season. UCLA had several players battling injuries and was without Lewis because of a suspension. But a team meeting the night before gave the Bruins an unexpected edge.

UCLA Coach Bob Toledo trotted his embattled defensive linemen in front of the team and challenged them individually. When he reached Vae Tata, a senior reserve who had been seriously injured in a car accident the previous year, the fiery coach choked up. So did many of his players. The moment galvanized the Bruins, who outscored the Wildcats 21–0 in the fourth quarter to run away with a 52–28 victory.

UCLA brought its 14-game winning streak back to the Rose Bowl the following week to face Oregon, which was 5–0 and ranked No. 11 in the country. Passes weren't the only thing that McNown would heave on a memorable afternoon. The quarterback didn't like eating before 12:30 PM starts, though he always drank plenty to stay hydrated. On this day, that combination left him nauseous after a quarterback scramble in the third quarter.

"As I was walking back to the huddle," McNown recalled, "I could feel like I was not going to be in good shape. But you don't call a timeout because your stomach hurts, right? So I went into the huddle and called the play and got out and I could feel everything coming up, but I just kind of put the guy in motion and tried to get the second call of the signal out and I couldn't and something else came out instead."

McNown vomited, forcing a stoppage of play. He was practically unstoppable from there, completing nine of 12 passes for 202 yards and a touchdown—just in the fourth quarter. "My post-vomit statistics," McNown cracked, "were much better than my pre-vomit statistics." UCLA ultimately prevailed in overtime, 41–38, on Chris Sailer's 24-yard field goal, which made up for his missing a 21-yarder on the final play of regulation.

UCLA's flair for the dramatic would continue two weeks later with a 28–24 victory over Stanford in which Foster scored the winning touchdown from eight yards out midway through the fourth quarter, culminating the Bruins' comeback from a 24–14 deficit. The heroics had become routine by the time McNown fired a 61-yard touchdown pass to Brad Melsby with 21 seconds left against Oregon State the following week, giving UCLA a 41–34 triumph and an 18th consecutive victory.

Relatively routine victories over Washington and USC followed, stretching the streak to a school-record 20 games. The Bruins typically finished the season against the Trojans, but a makeup game against Miami loomed on December 5 after Hurricane Georges had forced the postponement of the previously scheduled game in September. UCLA was decimated by another Hurricane—tailback Edgerrin James—during the 49–45 loss that ensued, his 299 yards and three touchdowns ending UCLA's dreams of an unbeaten season and a berth in the inaugural Bowl Championship Series title game. Looking back, McNown didn't have any regrets about the inability to sustain the streak any further. "It was a phenomenal experience," McNown said. "We had a fantastic run and it was really, really fun those two years."

53 The Hurricane Bowl

The game was played in warm and dry conditions on December 5, 1998, at the Orange Bowl, with a temperature of 80 degrees at kickoff that was accompanied by partly cloudy skies and gusty winds.

UCLA and Miami were supposed to have faced one another on the same field 2½ months earlier, but the game was called off over concerns about the approaching Hurricane Georges, which eventually skirted Miami without inflicting any serious damage on the city.

UCLA athletic director Peter Dalis acknowledged that the decision whether to reschedule the game was his alone, but players were canvassed about their feelings. Quarterback Cade McNown voiced some reluctance about the potential impact of a makeup game on his undefeated team, which was vying to appear in the Fiesta Bowl that would decide the national championship in the first year of the Bowl Championship Series.

"I just remember standing up—I wanted to address the team—and I said, 'Well, look, for what it's worth, the way I see it, there are three possible outcomes,'" McNown recalled. "'We can play them and beat them and go to the national championship. We can play them and lose to them and not go to the national championship. Or we can not play the game and go to the national championship. The way I see it, not playing assures us of going to the national championship.'

"The reality is, it was never our choice. Let's be honest. We were still going to play. There was far too much at stake. We had to play the game."

Dalis said he felt an obligation to play the game that UCLA coach Bob Toledo would dub the "Hurricane Bowl" because the Bruins had agreed to it in the first place. But there were probably other factors in play as well, including a fear that the Bruins could be punished for playing only 10 games and bypassed by other contenders for the inaugural BCS title game.

UCLA versus Miami seemed like a classic mismatch. The third-ranked Bruins were 10–0, No. 2 in the BCS ratings, and owners of a school-record 20-game winning streak; unranked Miami was 7–3 and had just allowed Syracuse to hang 66 points on it the previous week.

Of course, UCLA was dealing with some turmoil of its own, including a controversy in which Toledo refused to allow players to wear black armbands in support of a protest over a decrease in minority enrollments among University of California schools. The Bruins were also saddled with significant defensive shortcomings that had been offset all season by one of the nation's most dynamic offenses.

For much of the game, it seemed like that formula would work once more. Even with Miami tailback Edgerrin James stomping all over the UCLA defense, the Bruins took a 38–21 lead late in the third quarter on a 59-yard touchdown pass from McNown to Brad Melsby. Miami answered with a touchdown, but UCLA appeared on its way to restoring a comfortable cushion early in the fourth quarter when Brian Poli-Dixon caught a long pass for a first down… only to fumble the ball.

It was the first of two mistakes that would prove decisive. The Hurricanes had pulled to within 45–42 when the Bruins were driving for a score that would put the game out of reach. Melsby caught a pass for a first down but fumbled as he hit the ground. Replays showed his right knee was down before the ball came out, but referees called it a turnover and their mistake could not be overturned because there was no instant replay in college football at the time.

James scored the go-ahead touchdown on a one-yard run with 50 seconds left, his final carry during a performance in which he finished with 299 rushing yards, a record for a UCLA opponent. McNown could not engineer any last-second magic on the day he set one school record with 513 passing yards and tied another with five touchdown passes, his final pass sailing out the back of the end zone. Game over. National championship hopes gone.

UCLA's 49–45 defeat sent it to the Rose Bowl, suddenly the granddaddy of all consolation prizes. "Definitely some of the air had come out," McNown conceded. "As great of a situation as the

Rose Bowl was and as great of a venue and as great of a game as that is, it was still a consolation game, which was disappointing."

The letdown continued against Wisconsin on January 1 inside UCLA's home stadium, which was largely overrun by Badgers fans and tailback Ron Dayne. UCLA's defense was as vulnerable against Wisconsin as it had been against Miami, allowing Dayne to roll up 246 yards rushing and four touchdowns. Wisconsin fans also caused problems by making so much noise that UCLA tailback DeShaun Foster couldn't hear an audible that changed his carry from a handoff to a pitch, resulting in a fumble after the Bruins had first-and-goal from the Badgers' 6-yard line.

Another chance was squandered early in the fourth quarter when miscommunication between McNown and Foster resulted in an interception that Wisconsin returned 46 yards for a touchdown. The Badgers' 38–31 triumph saddled UCLA with a second consecutive loss to end its season and led many to wonder what might have been had the Bruins not agreed to reschedule their game with Miami.

"I was never crying in my soup that we had to play the game," McNown said. "The moment they decided we were playing it, we were fired up. I think it was the best game we ever played offensively as a team. They just outgunned us on the other side."

54 Chris Chambliss

As he ran down the first-base line on that October night in 1976, thrusting his arms into the air, Chris Chambliss never could have imagined that what would come next would prove more challenging than what had already transpired, that rounding the bases would be harder than launching a pitch over the wall in right-center field inside Yankee Stadium.

The New York Yankees were headed to the World Series after Chambliss' walk-off homer in the ninth inning provided the go-ahead run in a 7–6 victory over the Kansas City Royals in Game 5 of the American League Championship Series—if only Chambliss could touch home plate.

His path was clear all the way to second base, even as thousands of fans began swarming onto the field in celebration. Chambliss low-fived one fan before momentarily being knocked to the infield dirt by another fan who had moved into his way. He was surrounded by a horde of humanity as he neared third base, abandoning his pursuit of anything resembling a traditional home run trot.

"It was just a mob of people, so I headed straight for the dugout; I didn't even come close to home plate," Chambliss recalled more than four decades later. "I went into the clubhouse."

Asked whether he had touched home plate with the most important run of the Yankees' season, Chambliss acknowledged he had not. So he pulled on a jacket, found a couple of New York policemen to accompany him and trudged back toward home plate, only to find it was no longer there. Chambliss touched the area where the plate had been and retreated once more into the clubhouse to resume the revelry. The chaos resulted in what came to be known as "The Chris Chambliss Rule," providing an exception to the regulation that a batter must touch home plate in order for his run to count whenever fan obstruction makes that physically impossible.

The first baseman who clubbed one of the most storied homers in Yankees history had previously gone down in UCLA lore as the star of the Bruins' first College World Series team in 1969. He arrived in Westwood the previous summer after two seasons at MiraCosta College in Oceanside, California, where he played both football and baseball, spurning what he considered to be paltry bonus offers after twice being drafted by the Cincinnati Reds. UCLA baseball coach Art Reichle offered Chambliss a scholarship after watching him complete batting practice, the slugger showing the hand-eye coordination he had developed while whacking bottle caps with a broomstick in the backyard with his three brothers.

The Bruins' baseball team didn't have much tradition before Chambliss' arrival, never having played on the sport's biggest stage. The influx of Chambliss and relief pitcher Jim York, another junior college transfer, would change that. A late-season surge in which UCLA won 15 of 17 games put the Bruins in position to reach the NCAA tournament if they could beat rival USC once during a two-game series to forge a tie for the Pac-8 Conference championship.

The Bruins won both games handily against the defending national champions, rocking undefeated pitcher Brent Strom in the series opener and then scoring 12 runs off future major leaguer Jim Barr during a 14–5 triumph in the second game. Next up was a best-of-three District 8 series against Santa Clara, which had won nine of 12 games against Pac-8 opponents that season. UCLA rallied from a 3–0 deficit to win the opener 7–5, and prevailed in the next game thanks to a single, an error, and a sacrifice fly that provided the winning run in the 10th inning. It was on to the College World Series for the Bruins.

"That was a thrill and a half," Chambliss said of becoming the first team in school history to make the trip to Omaha.

Unfortunately for the Bruins, the thrill would be short-lived. UCLA held 4–0 and 5–2 leads it could not hold in its opener against Tulsa thanks in large part to six errors that led to four unearned runs. Tulsa won 6–5 in the 10th inning on a walk, an error, and a single. Another blunder proved pivotal the next day against Arizona State, when York fielded a potential double-play grounder in the 11th inning and threw the ball into center field, allowing the winning run to score from second base during the Sun Devils' 2–1 victory.

"Arizona State didn't lose the rest of the tournament," Chambliss said of the eventual champions. "And I heard a lot of their quotes saying we were one of the better teams that they played. It was rough for us. That was really disappointing for us. We had a good team, we felt."

Reichle had expected Chambliss to return for his senior season after having batted .340 with 45 runs batted in and what was then a school-record 15 home runs. But after starring for the Anchorage Glacier Pilots, who would win the National Baseball Congress Championship with Chambliss being selected the Most Valuable Player of the tournament, he decided to make himself available for the Major League Baseball Draft, a move that necessitated dropping out of UCLA.

"Art Reichle, I know I hurt him bad on that one," Chambliss said. "He understood later—we talked later—because he meant to sign me for the last two years."

No one could argue with Chambliss' decision after the Cleveland Indians made him the No. 1 overall pick in the 1970 Draft and he quickly rose through the organization, becoming American League Rookie of the Year in 1971. He was an All-Star with the Yankees in 1976 and developed a reputation as a reliable contact hitter, batting .279 with 185 home runs and 972 RBIs during his 17-year career. "He isn't the type of hitter who swings from his ass all the time to try to hit the ball out of the park," Yankees closer Sparky Lyle wrote of Chambliss in *The Bronx Zoo*. "He takes his time and swings at good pitches. He's the only guy who rarely gets in a slump."

After his playing career ended, Chambliss became hitting coach for the Yankees, helping them win four World Series titles, before also working for a variety of other major league organizations preceding his retirement.

55 Do the Frisbee Cheer

It's a routine that's nearly as old as Pauley Pavilion, performed before every UCLA basketball game and considered as much a part of the school's athletic culture as the eight clap. It starts with a student holding up a basketball and yelling, "Is this a basketball?"

The student section immediately takes the cue: "Yes, that's a basketball!"

"Is this a court?" the student leader continues.

His or her classmates shout back: "Yes, that's a court!"

The student leader then gestures with a waving arm toward the opponents warming up on the court. "Is that the loooooosing team?"

"Yes, that's the loooooosing team!" students roar while repeating the gesture.

No Bruins basketball game would be complete without the Frisbee Cheer, named for creator Larry "Frisbee" Davis. He was a UCLA undergraduate majoring in biochemistry when he introduced the chant during the 1976–77 season as part of his efforts to revive interest in the school's basketball team after the departure of legendary coach John Wooden.

"That cheer can be a very good motivator for the team," Davis said. "It's almost like an all-Pauley eight-clap but extended for one minute. It can be really, really powerful." Davis led the cheer for roughly a quarter of a century, first as a student and then as a devoted alumnus. He liked to directly face the students and enjoyed the freedom to roam the court, sidling up to Larry Brown on the sideline the night Brown made his debut as Bruins coach in November 1979. Davis pointed at Brown before unleashing a routine that played off the coach's charm. "Is this Larry Brown? Is he our new coach? Does he have charisma?"

The origins of the Frisbee Cheer can be traced to one of UCLA's Southern California rivals. Davis was watching Pepperdine water polo players perform a similar cheer in support of their school's volleyball team during a match against UCLA when he decided to make it his own. He later learned it had been performed previously at a Pepperdine swim meet, where a student stood up and asked, "Are those the starting blocks? Is that a diving board?"

The cheer officially belonged to Davis once he copyrighted it. It got off to a modest start at UCLA, with Davis engaging a small group of students before it quickly mushroomed to the entire student section. "First it was 10 or 20 people doing it, then it was 100 people doing it, and then it was 1,000 people doing it," Davis said. "A very simple, elegant cheer that took off." Davis was soon given access to the court, allowing him to engage the whole crowd whenever he had the microphone. "Every once in a while," Davis said, "I was able to get the alumni into it and that made it really fun when you could get 10,000 or 12,000 people doing it."

Davis took his cheer to football and baseball games as well as track meets. He made use of various props, dressing in a robe and wheeling a 5-foot-tall oil derrick into Pauley Pavilion for a game against the rival Trojans during the 1979–80 season after the Shah of Iran had given millions of dollars to USC. Bruins star David Greenwood, whose final college season was in 1978–79, told Davis that his antics represented the first time he had ever stopped warming up before a game to watch a cheer. "That made me feel good that the team was paying attention and they were getting excited about it," Davis said.

Davis earned his nickname by continually toting a Frisbee along to pass the time during the long wait to acquire student tickets. He said he possesses student ticket No. 1 for Wooden's final game in the NCAA tournament championship in 1975 in

San Diego. He never got to ask Wooden what he thought of his cheer but can guess what the mannerly coach would have told him. "I suspect when you start pointing to the losing team," Davis said, "he'd probably say something like, 'That's not too cool.'"

Over the years, Davis said, the school increasingly placed restrictions on his routine that pushed him away. He stopped doing it around the time the Den, a student athletics group, was formed in 2003. That's when a different student was designated to perform the cheer each game.

Regardless of who's leading the cheer, its legacy seemed secure, until Frisbee asked UCLA to stop conducting it before the final two home games of the 2017–18 season, apparently upset over what it had become.

"It's terrible, absolutely terrible," Davis told the *Los Angeles Times* in 2017. "Now the way they perform it, it's an afterthought. It's really an embarrassment. It's nothing compared to what I started and what it became."

Davis received permission to lead the cheer one last time in 2011, when his oldest son was a UCLA junior. It was the first time his son had seen him perform the routine as an adult after helping him carry it out as a four-year-old.

"I walked back to my son and I said, 'Well, so, what do you think? How do you think your old man did?'" Davis recalled. "And he said, 'That was pretty good, Dad.' Two girls behind him said, 'Frisbee's your father?' I don't know if he got any dates out of it, but it was pretty funny."

56 Visit the Athletic Hall of Fame

There is a place where UCLA sports are celebrated year-round, even when Pauley Pavilion is empty and the Rose Bowl grass bears the weight of just its groundskeepers. It can be found at the UCLA Athletic Hall of Fame, a treasure trove of athletic memorabilia nestled inside the J.D. Morgan Center on campus.

Want to see Gary Beban's Heisman Trophy from the 1967 season? It's here. Jackie Robinson's ring from the College Baseball Hall of Fame? That can also be found. There's even a full-size re-creation of coach John Wooden's den from his condominium as well as more whimsical items such as a Maui Invitational surfboard and a vintage Joe Bruin costume.

The 8,000-square-foot Hall of Fame opened in 2001 after its directors toured other athletic museums throughout the country to collect ideas and incorporate their favorite features. A two-story foyer welcomes visitors with giant banners featuring the logos of the school's 24 intercollegiate sports, as well as a wall of televisions and displays featuring Bruins athletes in the current Hall of Fame induction class.

The first thing you see when you step toward the interior of the building is a massive UCLA emblem commemorating the school being the first university to reach 100 NCAA championships, a feat secured in 2007 by the men's water polo team. Each of the Bruins' 116 titles is listed on a wall across from a timeline display showing significant events in school history starting with its formation in 1919 as "the Southern Branch of the University of California." The timeline puts those events in context by listing them next to significant world occurrences from the same years. The bottom of the display case is lined by artifacts, including a pair of ice hockey skates from 1927 when the university sponsored the sport.

Scores of items inside the building are dated, but the feel of the place is not. "We're always trying to design some new displays," said Emily S. Knox, senior art director and curator of the Hall of Fame. "The idea is that if you come back every six months, there would be something new and different to look at." One constant are replica jerseys from the various eras of Bruins athletics that hang above the exhibits.

Each sport is exhibited in its own display case, featuring pictures of players and coaches on the current team as well as a schedule, team picture, and list of Olympians, professional players, and All-Americans. "We try to hit all of the information you could want to know about these sports," Knox said. There are extra-large sections for football and men's basketball, including the 1947 college All-Star uniform worn by end Burr Baldwin, UCLA's first consensus All-American in football. Highlight videos from recently completed seasons are shown in the 34-seat UCLA Spirit Theater, where Bruins fans can also learn about campus life, the school's Olympians and the Centennial Campaign fundraising efforts.

Other displays include one for Robinson that includes photos from different stages of his career as well as "The Women of Westwood," featuring greats such as softball pitcher Lisa Fernandez and track standout Jackie Joyner-Kersee. UCLA's most recent Olympians are featured in a 2016 Rio de Janeiro display bearing the bright colors of the event. The display lists participants from the school as well as every medal winner and photos of the athletes competing.

One of the more unique exhibits shows what the lockers of Robinson, Wooden, Joyner-Kersee, and quarterback Troy Aikman would have looked like back in their respective eras, complete with letterman's jackets and the various shoes they would have worn. Robinson has dark wood lockers for football, basketball, baseball,

Furnishings and items in the "John Wooden—The Den" exhibit in the UCLA Athletic Hall of Fame as seen on Tuesday, October 26, 2010. (AP Photo/Reed Saxon)

and track, because he played all four sports. The lockers rest above a section of the original court from the men's gym where UCLA once played under Wooden.

The Bruins' athletic prowess is acknowledged by a giant photo and blurb from *Sports Illustrated* in 1997 that proclaimed UCLA as the nation's No. 1 sports college. The photo shows athletes from a variety of sports, including third baseman Troy Glaus and guard Toby Bailey from the 1995 national championship men's basketball team.

The crystal Sears trophy from that title—the most recent of UCLA's 11 national championships in men's basketball—can be found inside the Hall of Champions, which Knox calls "our most awe-inspiring room." It features all 116 national championship trophies in chronological order starting with men's tennis in 1950. There are so many trophies that the original display case ran out of room, necessitating the creation of a new case to house every one starting with No. 113. The room also includes watches, rings, and other championship memorabilia either on loan or donated by coaches and players.

The final display as visitors head back toward the entrance is a list of each of UCLA's Hall of Fame inductees, including their signatures on individual black-and-white glass plates that are backlit, creating a visually appealing look. Some of the signatures from athletes who have passed away were acquired by creative means. Their spouses donated canceled checks that included their signatures, allowing Knox and her colleagues to scan the images and create outlines that were transferred to the plates. It's one of many little details that make UCLA's Athletic Hall of Fame a must-see for anyone who loves Bruins athletics.

57 Sinjin Smith

Sinjin Smith came to UCLA almost by accident. A highly skilled but unknown player at Los Angeles Loyola High, Smith was spotted by Bruins men's volleyball coach Al Scates while competing against one of Scates' top recruits, Greg Giovanazzi of Culver City High. Smith fully understood why Scates was there to scout his counterpart. "He was a monster of a player," Smith said of Giovanazzi.

Scates could see that Smith was also a star in the making, having already developed the ability to pass, set, and hit at a high level while playing on the beach and in the backyard with his three brothers. Scates approached Smith after watching him play and asked if he wanted to come to UCLA. "I said, 'Heck, yeah. Sure I do,'" Smith recalled.

It wasn't as easy as that. Scates didn't have any scholarships left for the following season but promised to give Smith whatever financial assistance became available once he arrived on campus. Smith came as promised and helped lead the Bruins to an NCAA championship in 1976 as a freshman, but not before a very humbling demotion.

Smith was practicing alongside UCLA's top players on the No. 1 court when he let a ball drop near him without making an effort to go for it in front of his coach. "I yelled over to the coach on the second court, 'Send me an outside hitter!' and I sent Sinjin down," Scates said. "So he sent me the best outside hitter from the last few days or maybe from that day and I kept that guy on the court for three weeks instead of Sinjin."

Smith had to prove himself anew during what he said felt like "an eternity" before making it back, but he returned with a new determination. "Without saying a word to me, Al taught me a very valuable lesson about always being ready and going for every ball and I never forgot it for the rest of my career," Smith said. "I just knew how important it was always to be ready to play and go after everything. I made sure there was never a ball that was going to drop without me making the effort to go after that ball."

Smith's leadership skills never needed any tweaking. He was a natural at galvanizing his teammates and making them feel like their mistakes were no big deal. "We had great players and if for some reason they were having trouble, if I could take the pressure off them somehow, some way, to allow them to play at their best, then I would try to do that," Smith said. "For instance, if a guy was having hitting trouble or he just got blocked, I would say, 'Hey, my fault. I'll get you off the net a little bit more.'

"So he knows he's going to have another shot at it and he's not going to take the full blame for it. I can take the blame for it, it's not a problem. And I can help him out too by giving him a set that's going to make him look good. If he puts that ball away, he looks good, but not only does he look good, I look good in a secondary way. Everybody remembers the hit, they don't remember the set. But that was okay for me. I wanted to win."

Ultimate success eluded Smith the next two years, a back injury as a sophomore hurting the Bruins' chances to repeat as national champions and the Bruins falling to Pepperdine in five sets during the NCAA tournament to end Smith's junior season. Then the arrival of another talented freshman changed everything. Karch Kiraly teamed with Smith to give the Bruins perhaps the most impressive duo in college volleyball history.

Scates altered the way his team played, utilizing a 6-2 offense that featured Smith and Kiraly as alternating setters who would give their team an extra attacker near the net. The freshman and the senior became as competitive with each other as they were with their opponents, facing off in one-on-one battles before practice on a truncated court. "We would push pretty hard and compete against each other in everything we did—every drill, every aspect of practice," Smith said. "We would keep pushing each other farther. 'Okay, let's see if you can do this.' It would just keep going."

The result was UCLA's first undefeated volleyball season—after the Bruins knocked off rival USC to finish 30–0—and another national championship in 1979 to bookend Smith's college career. The two-time All-American was selected as the NCAA tournament's Most Outstanding Player and finished his career as part of teams that went 85–9. Smith and Kiraly competed together for two years on the pro beach volleyball tour, winning 21 tournaments while compiling a winning percentage that still ranks among the best in the history of the sport, before Smith teamed with Randy Stoklos to win a record 114 open beach tournaments together.

Smith's departure wasn't the end of his UCLA legacy. His No. 22 was unretired and the old 6-2 offense revived upon the arrival of his oldest son, Hagen, on the Bruins' volleyball team in 2014. "It was really awesome to watch him play at UCLA," the elder Smith said.

58 Chase Utley

Chase Utley once spent hours behind the counter at the Lakewood Batting Cages, sweeping the floors and selling popcorn. He didn't work there. At least not officially.

The budding baseball star would barter his services for extra sessions in the cages after his money ran out, which was often. His parents would drop him off and leave him for long stretches to work on every aspect of his swing. "There were times," David

Utley, Chase's father, told Philadelphia.CBSlocal.com, "we were afraid, me and my wife, that we'd be accused of abandoning him."

They were actually doing him a favor, allowing the infielder from Long Beach Poly High to develop the skills that would make him such a feared hitter that he was once intentionally walked with the bases loaded during an American Legion game. Utley's potential compelled the Los Angeles Dodgers to select him in the second round of the 1997 Draft.

But Utley had other plans. He turned down a $1-million signing bonus to attend UCLA, only to experience a somewhat jarring introduction to college baseball that had nothing to do with his ability to put the bat on the ball. Utley continued his hitting tear, smashing 15 home runs to break Bob Hamelin's school freshman record of 13 and finishing the 1998 season with an 11-game hitting streak. But his play at shortstop was lacking. He struggled to reach ground balls that flew off aluminum bats and didn't possess enough arm strength to beat runners with his throws to first base. As a result of constantly rushing himself, he committed 24 errors.

Bruins coach Gary Adams devised a simple solution: move Utley to second base. The switch had a secondary benefit in that it allowed co-captain Jack Santora to play shortstop. Utley asked Adams to hit him ground ball after ground ball to master his new position. Just when he thought they were done, Adams would be asked to hit even more ground balls. The extra work allowed Utley to lower his error total to 13 as a sophomore.

Utley was developing a reputation as an ironman, starting all 62 games during the 1999 season and becoming the only player on the team to appear in every single inning. He talked Adams into letting him play through calf and foot injuries as a freshman and by the time his college career was over, he had played in 126 consecutive games, a rarity in college baseball.

UCLA advanced to the NCAA tournament during Utley's sophomore season, blasting Oklahoma State 12–6 in the opener of the Wichita regional. The Bruins were eliminated after dropping their next two games—a 4–2 setback against Wichita State and a 17–10 defeat in a rematch with Oklahoma State—but Utley had starred for the first time on a big stage. He batted .412 with two doubles, two homers, and four runs in the three regional games.

The Bruins got back to the NCAA tournament during Utley's junior season in 2000 after tying Stanford and Arizona State for the Pac-10 Conference title. This time, they rolled through the Oklahoma City regional, edging Delaware 13–12 in the opener before posting back-to-back victories over Oklahoma, 10–5 and 11–3, respectively. That advanced UCLA into the Baton Rouge super regional, where it faced top-seeded Louisiana State in the Bruins' first-ever appearance in a super regional after the NCAA tournament field had expanded to 64 teams the previous year.

It wasn't a long stay, however. LSU ousted the Bruins in a two-game sweep, winning 8–2 in the opener and 14–8 in the second game. The Tigers went on to win the College World Series with an undefeated run through the NCAA tournament. Utley finished his junior season hitting .382 with 22 homers, 69 runs batted in, and a team-high 15 stolen bases in 16 attempts. He also committed only 12 errors, continuing his improvement in the field.

Baseball America rated Utley as the best college hitter in the 2000 Draft after he completed his UCLA career with a .342 batting average that helped him twice earn All-Pac-10 honors. The Philadelphia Phillies selected Utley with the 15th pick in the first round and he went on to become a six-time All-Star who won a World Series in 2008 before being traded to his hometown Dodgers late in the 2015 season. Phillies Manager Charlie Manuel once said Utley's quick hands and compact swing reminded him of Hall of Famers Billy Williams, Stan Musial, and Wade Boggs. It all started with the unofficial part-time job that would lead to much more lucrative things.

59 J.D. Morgan

He remains at the center of UCLA athletics more than a quarter century after his death, hundreds of Bruins athletes and coaches coursing through the building named in his honor every day.

J.D. Morgan was the essence of UCLA athletics from the day he first stepped onto campus in the fall of 1938 until his death in December 1980, a little more than a year after he retired as athletic director because of a persistent heart ailment. He helped make UCLA an athletic juggernaut, the Pac-10 Conference a power player on a national scale, and was renowned across the country for ushering in the era of college sports being widely televised.

Morgan had a golden touch, being dubbed "J.D. Midas" after a 1966–67 school year in which the Bruins went a combined 47–1 in football, men's basketball, and track. The record reflected one of his mantras, that "Winners attract winners." He was involved with 37 of UCLA's first 38 NCAA champions, either as an assistant coach, coach, or athletic director. He coached the Bruins men's tennis team for 16 seasons—the last three while also serving as athletic director—winning eight NCAA championships and finishing as runner-up four times. He coached eight NCAA singles or doubles champions, including Arthur Ashe.

UCLA was thriving in the revenue sports as well. The Bruins won their first 10 basketball titles while he was athletic director and Morgan presided over UCLA's first Rose Bowl victory, over top-ranked Michigan State in 1966, as well as a triumph over No. 1 Ohio State in the 1976 Rose Bowl.

Morgan had come to Westwood as a single-wing tailback but couldn't play football because of a back injury, forcing him to confine his athletic career to tennis as a four-year letterwinner and captain of the 1941 team. After serving in World War II as a torpedo boat commander, Morgan returned to UCLA as an accountant before becoming an assistant business manager and eventually associate business manager while serving as assistant and then head tennis coach.

He was instrumental in the construction of the UCLA residence halls and chaired the finance committee that secured the construction of the $5.5-million William C. Ackerman Student Union. Largely as a result of his business savvy, Chancellor Dr. Franklin D. Murphy appointed Morgan as UCLA athletic director on July 1, 1963.

His tenure was auspicious from the start. Basketball coach John Wooden won his first national title in Morgan's debut year as athletic director after Morgan had freed the coach of his bothersome administrative duties. Morgan helped obliterate a $136,000 athletic department deficit in his first two years on the job while doubling the budget. He did so by quadrupling income from radio and television, which also allowed him to reduce the need for collecting student fees to help fund athletic programs.

It probably helped that Morgan wasn't a big spender himself. "He hired really good coaches and he paid them very little and somehow he was able to hold onto them," said former UCLA volleyball coach Al Scates, who was making only $14,000 per year before finally being made full-time in 1979, bumping him up to $22,000 a year. "He paid John Wooden his last year $32,000 and basketball coaches were already making six figures back in those days. It shows you he had some uncanny ability to keep talented coaches."

Morgan helped the athletic department move into permanent quarters and oversaw the completion of Pauley Pavilion, the opening of a new boathouse for crew in Marina del Rey, and the opening of Drake Stadium, considered one of the top track and field facilities in the country.

Morgan helped turn the NCAA tournament into a huge moneymaker through a lucrative rights deal with NBC and helped get the TVS network started. He was instrumental in a nationwide TV audience savoring an epic battle between UCLA and Houston on January 20, 1968, at the Astrodome, the Cougars snapping the Bruins' 47-game winning streak. The event was widely seen as helping to sell college basketball to the masses through the power of television.

Morgan was known for working 12- to 16-hour days, though his coaches sometimes wondered what he was doing behind closed doors. "Whenever you went to see him he would usually make you sit on your butt waiting for about 10, 15 minutes and then he would look busy when you came in," Scates said. "One time, I was there on my lunch hour and I had to get back to school, I didn't have time to wait out there, so I just burst past [his secretary]. He was sitting there with his feet on the desk reading the paper."

No one could quibble with the results. Over his 17 years as athletic director, UCLA won 30 NCAA team championships and 48 conference titles. The building that houses the Bruins' athletic department was named in his honor in 1983, three years after his death.

60 Dave Roberts

The joyful hubbub coming from the dugout didn't jibe with the scoreboard at Jackie Robinson Stadium. UCLA was in the midst of a meltdown during the 1992 season when Bruins coach Gary Adams heard laughter from two of his players, Kris and Kurt Schwengel.

Before Adams could take a step toward the perpetrators, Dave Roberts, a young outfielder, raced over to the brothers and got in their faces. "He said, 'Schwengels, you guys get your heads in the ballgame!'" Adams recalled at an event to celebrate Roberts becoming the Los Angeles Dodgers manager in 2016. "'I bet you don't even know the score!'"

Quiet fell over the dugout. The Bruins had never seen Roberts angry before and here he was, challenging two upperclassmen. After some jabbering between Roberts and Kris Schwengel, the latter player acknowledged his mistake by turning toward his teammates. "What's the score?" Schwengel said rhetorically. "How would I know? I don't even know who we're playing." Everyone waited for a cue from Roberts. His face lit up with a big smile, prompting laughter all around.

Almost a quarter of a century before he would become the first black manager in Dodgers history, Roberts was already leading the way. "That's D.R.," Adams said, referring to the initials Roberts went by while playing for UCLA. "I've never coached a player who showed so much passion and love for the game of baseball and how it should be played and yet he still possessed the rare quality of showing his teammates how much he cared for them, not just as players, not just as teammates, even, but he cared for and treated them like they were his best friend."

Roberts arrived at UCLA without much fanfare. A quarterback on the football team at Rancho Buena Vista High, he had dreamed of football stardom before tearing a knee ligament during spring practice before his junior season. After sitting out a year, his interest in the sport waned despite an appointment to play football for the Air Force Academy. During the summer after his senior year, his high school baseball coach called Adams and pitched Roberts as a fast young outfielder who could help win games. Adams agreed to bring Roberts on board without a scholarship and he played sparingly as a freshman, mostly as a pinch-runner.

But Roberts' speed was evident immediately and he worked his way into the lineup as a center fielder on scholarship his sophomore season. Major League Baseball executives didn't believe that Roberts was a top-level prospect. He wasn't drafted until the 47th round after his junior season, prompting him to return for one more college season after a heartfelt conversation with Adams. "Coach Adams was very forthright, upfront with me, and told me what I needed to do to get better," Roberts said. "It was just continuing to get better at all facets of my game—arm strength, charging the ball, continuing to be a better defender."

He improved across the board as a senior, setting the school single-season record with 45 stolen bases while notching career highs in batting average (.353), on-base percentage (.445), and slugging percentage (.468). He also finished his career as UCLA's all-time leader with 109 stolen bases. His draft stock soared, and the Detroit Tigers took him in the 28th round in 1994.

Roberts made his major league debut with the Cleveland Indians in 1999, became the Dodgers' starting center fielder in 2002, and logged the most famous stolen base in Boston Red Sox history in 2004, sparking the team's comeback from a three-games-to-none deficit to defeat the New York Yankees in the American League Championship Series on the way to a World Series title. He returned to the Dodgers in 2016 as a groundbreaking manager for the forward-thinking franchise that had also played a key role in allowing former UCLA great Jackie Robinson to break baseball's color barrier.

Roberts credited his formative years as a Bruin for playing a crucial role in his success. His Dodgers reached the World Series in 2017, ending a 29-year drought for the franchise. "Without my time at UCLA and Coach Adams' influence," Roberts said while sitting in his office inside Dodger Stadium, "I wouldn't be a major league player, let alone a major league manager right now."

61 Brett Hundley

The footage delights Brett Hundley every time he watches it. He's standing on top of a rain-slickened table next to teammate Joseph Fauria inside the Rose Bowl, leading UCLA fans in an eight-clap toward the end of the 2012 season after having guided the Bruins to their first victory over USC in six years.

Not even a year earlier, inside the Los Angeles Memorial Coliseum, the scene had been very different. Hundley could only stand on the sideline, forced to absorb UCLA's 50–0 loss to the Trojans as a spectator at the conclusion of a redshirt season in which he never played. He figured that might be the case after a spring game in which he took only a handful of snaps, leading to an outpouring of emotions.

"That was essentially saying, 'You're not going to play this year,'" said Hundley, the dual-threat quarterback who had graduated early from Chandler (AZ) High to join the Bruins as a 17-year-old. "I went to the sideline and just broke down, man, I'm not going to lie." Hundley held out hope that Bruins coach Rick Neuheisel might change his mind, especially with the highly coveted prospect lobbying to compete as a true freshman. "I was pressing this guy every day to play," Hundley said.

Hundley reckoned he might get his chance in the fourth game of the 2011 season, against Oregon State, after Bruins quarterback Kevin Prince had struggled mightily the previous week against Texas. But Neuheisel went with Richard Brehaut instead of Hundley and it became clear that the coach intended to preserve his star recruit for 2012, even with Neuheisel's job on such shaky ground that he would be fired two days after the USC shellacking. Though the competitor in him was aching to participate, Hundley understood. "I just wasn't ready," Hundley said. "It wasn't anything more or less."

Hundley showed he was worth the wait on the first play of his college career. He had told Bruins running back Johnathan Franklin beforehand that he was going to hand off the ball to Franklin no matter what Rice did on that opening play of the 2012 season. But as the Owls' defensive end sprinted toward Hundley, instinct kicked in. The quarterback kept the ball and took off, picking up a key block from receiver Shaq Evans on the way to a 72-yard touchdown run. "It sort of sparked our season," Hundley said.

UCLA beat 16th-ranked Nebraska the following week and was 8–2 heading into its rivalry game against USC. The Trojans had won five consecutive games against the Bruins, and featured senior quarterback Matt Barkley, who had been the Heisman Trophy frontrunner going into the season. Most expected the Trojans to easily stamp out another victory. "It was like USC was the big dog, the powerhouse, and on the field they started walking around like it and everybody sort of just got tired of it," Hundley said in explaining his mind-set. "I always said, 'When I get my opportunity, it will be different.'"

Was it ever. Hundley hurt the Trojans with his arm and his feet, completing 22 of 30 passes for 234 yards and a touchdown while running for two touchdowns against a ferocious pass rush. He also outplayed Barkley during a wild game in which the Bruins rolled up a big lead and held on for a 38–28 victory that Hundley would call the most meaningful of his college career. "I was proud of everything that happened in that game," Hundley said. "It was my favorite."

There would be lots of contenders for that title. Hundley led the Bruins to victories over Virginia Tech in the Sun Bowl and Kansas State in the Alamo Bowl, not to mention an emotional comeback triumph over Nebraska in 2013 shortly after the death of

Brett Hundley runs for a touchdown during the 2012 Pac-12 championship game against the Stanford Cardinal. (Cal Sport Media via AP Images)

teammate Nick Pasquale. Hundley finished his career 3–0 against USC, including a 35–14 victory in 2013 and a 38–20 triumph in 2014. UCLA went 9–5, 10–3, and 10–3 during Hundley's three seasons, his 28 wins trailing only Cade McNown's 30 for most by a Bruins quarterback.

Hundley finished his career ranked first on the all-time school lists for touchdown passes (75), completions (837), and total yardage (11,713), as well as second for passing yards (9,966) and rushing yards by a quarterback (1,747). He threw for or rushed for a touchdown in all but one of his 40 games, the exception coming when he left a game against Texas in the first quarter after getting hurt.

The Bruins didn't win a Pac-12 Conference title, appear in a Rose Bowl game, or participate in the College Football Playoffs during Hundley's three seasons, but they certainly fulfilled Hundley's intentions of reviving the program. He also led one memorable celebration in the rain at the Rose Bowl. "Those memories are what I remember," Hundley said. "I don't care about the records; it was those times."

62 See a Game at the Rose Bowl

The San Gabriel Mountains jut over the rim of the Rose Bowl, giving the stadium one of the most breathtaking views in all of college football. A moment marinating in that view can make UCLA fans feel like winners even before kickoff.

Of course, the Bruins might never have called the Rose Bowl home had they not suffered what initially felt like a devastating setback involving their previous football residence. UCLA had shared the Los Angeles Memorial Coliseum with USC since the 1920s and with the NFL's Los Angeles Rams from 1946 until 1979, when the Rams relocated to Anaheim.

In the summer of 1982, the Oakland Raiders were preparing to replace the Rams as the Coliseum's NFL tenant upon their move to Los Angeles. The Raiders demanded scheduling priority, control of locker rooms, and all the revenue from proposed luxury boxes, relegating the Bruins to second-class citizens in the stadium they had occupied for more than a half century.

Rebuffed in his appeals to the Coliseum Commission for more hospitable terms, UCLA chancellor Charles E. Young engaged officials from the City of Pasadena about moving the Bruins' football games to the Rose Bowl. The massive stadium nestled in the Arroyo Seco, a ravine of parkland and natural vegetation on the west side of Pasadena, had regularly accommodated crowds topping 100,000 while hosting the Rose Bowl game that was dubbed "The Granddaddy of Them All." Despite concerns that UCLA would be abandoning Los Angeles and forcing job losses among low-income families, Young remained steadfast, receiving support from the university's Board of Regents, who left the decision with him.

Young formally announced UCLA's move to the Rose Bowl on July 23, 1982, with football coach Terry Donahue predicting upon a tour of the stadium the following month that the Bruins would not only begin their season there but also end it on the same field on January 1, 1983, in the Rose Bowl game. That's exactly what happened, with UCLA capping a 10–1–1 season with a 24–14 triumph over Michigan on New Year's Day before a crowd of 104,991. The Bruins would go on to appear in three of the first four Rose Bowl games after their move, winning on each occasion.

By the mid-1980s, the Rose Bowl looked vastly different than the nameless horseshoe-shaped stadium that had been completed in 1922 with a construction cost of $272,198 and seating capacity of 57,000. The south end of the stadium was enclosed in 1928, adding 19,000 seats and bringing capacity to 76,000. Capacity was further increased throughout the years until the stadium could hold as many as 104,594 fans by 1972, though crowds even larger occasionally jammed their way into the facility.

The Rose Bowl twice staged events for the Olympic Summer Games, hosting cycling in 1932 and soccer in 1984. The stadium also hosted Super Bowls in 1977, 1980, 1983, 1987, and 1993; the World Cup in 1994; the Women's World Cup in 1999; the Los Angeles Galaxy from 1996 to 2003; Bowl Championship Series title games in 2002, 2006, 2010, and 2014; College Football Playoff semifinals in 2015 and 2018; as well as numerous concerts and other events. UCLA has appeared in 12 Rose Bowl games, most recently on January 1, 1999.

A $170-million renovation was unveiled in 2013 that included new press boxes, broadcast booths, and luxury suites dedicated as the Terry Donahue Pavilion, among other upgrades, vastly enhancing the stadium that *Sports Illustrated* had named the best venue in college sports only six years earlier. Seating capacity has been reduced to 90,888 for football games, eliminating the availability of thousands of seats with bad views. UCLA has settled in for the foreseeable future, committing to the Rose Bowl at its home through 2042. And why not, given those views?

"It's an amazing scene," said Randy Cross, a former UCLA All-American offensive lineman whose son Brendan, a backup quarterback, got to call the Rose Bowl home during the 2013 season. "I just hope everybody appreciates how special the Rose Bowl is because you had to earn the right to play there when I was in college. When I was at UCLA, you played all your home games in the Coliseum. It's a fantastic experience for the team and the fans and they do an amazing job as far as the game-day experience. I mean, it's unbelievable."

63 John Sciarra and Mark Harmon

The bond between John Sciarra and Mark Harmon started to solidify during Sciarra's first college workouts in the summer of 1972. The hotshot freshman might have been UCLA's most athletic quarterback, but he lagged behind counterparts Harmon and Rob Scribner in terms of footwork and learning the nuances of the offense. Harmon, a junior, and Scribner, a senior, had mastered those concepts while participating in spring practice while Sciarra completed his high school studies.

Sciarra confided in Harmon after one practice that he was having problems with his feet and getting his technique down as well as his positioning coming away from center. "Mark was like, 'Oh, let me show you how to do this. I was watching and I think I can help you here,'" Sciarra remembered his teammate telling him. "It wasn't like, 'Hey, we're competing, you figure it out,' it was like, 'Yeah, let me show you how to do this.' I said, 'Wow, this guy's a pretty cool guy.' I mean, he didn't have to do this."

And so began a friendship that has spanned more than four decades. Sciarra (pronounced "SHAR-ah") and Harmon would eat together, double date together, and even live together, except for their final season as college teammates in 1973 when they decided it would be best to separate while splitting time at quarterback. But living apart never diminished their fondness for one another.

Harmon had been the full-time starter the previous season, engineering an upset of top-ranked Nebraska in the opener that ended the two-time defending national champions' 32-game winning streak. Sciarra returned punts and kickoffs, leading the team in both categories while earning the nickname "Super Rook."

Each player brought enviable qualifications to the battle for playing time in 1973. Harmon possessed the pedigree, considering that his father, Tom, won the Heisman Trophy in 1940 as a half-back at Michigan. The younger Harmon also showed he was a star in his own right while becoming an All-American in two seasons at Pierce College and leading UCLA to an 8–3 record as a junior.

Even if he was a bit undersized at 5'11" and 180 pounds, Sciarra was a freakishly natural athlete who could run the 40-yard dash in 4.6 seconds. He didn't play contact football before high school, having competed on a seven-man flag team that helped him develop agility because he had to run away from defenders instead of through them. At Bishop Amat High in La Puente, Sciarra starred as a shortstop on the baseball team who was offered a con-tract by the Cleveland Indians and a quarterback on the football team who became one of the nation's most widely coveted recruits.

Each player could make a compelling case for why he should be running UCLA's wishbone offense heading into the 1973 season.

"He's two years older and you get in certain situations maybe you need a little bit more experience in dealing with that, a little more control," Sciarra said of Harmon, "and then you've got a younger guy who may have a little bit better skill sets in other areas that could break big plays and make certain throws and you just figure that out and it gets to be a competitive situation."

Harmon started the season opener against Nebraska, but the Bruins faltered badly during a 40–13 loss in which Sciarra would also play. The arrangement would become a trend the rest of the season, Harmon starting eight of 11 games and Sciarra appearing in relief when he wasn't starting. "We were pretty much sharing the position from about the third game on," Sciarra said. Sciarra showed his skill as a dual-threat quarterback, passing for 503 yards and rushing for 496 more as the Bruins finished 9–2 but did not go to a bowl game after losing to USC and finishing second, behind the Trojans, in the Pac-8 Conference.

The quarterbacks moved in together again after Harmon's college career was complete. Harmon bought a house, which was a bit of a financial stretch and necessitated roommates to help make payments at a time when he worked as a merchandising director.

"When it came to the utilities, it was like, 'Don't turn on the heater, don't do this, don't do that,'" Sciarra recalled of Harmon, who would become a renowned actor after starring in scores of film and television roles, including a longstanding part on *NCIS*. "He would leave notes everywhere and we would write back. It was quite comical. It was the typical kind of college scene that you would think it would be. We had BB gun fights in the house. It was crazy. It was a lot of fun."

Harmon's departure left Sciarra as the clear starting quarterback going into the 1974 season after new coach Dick Vermeil installed the veer offense, which featured a more versatile passing attack than the wishbone. The Bruins went 6–3–2 during a rebuilding season in which Sciarra broke his leg in the seventh game against California, forcing him to miss the balance of the season.

Sciarra's senior season was easily his best. He was a consensus All-American who finished seventh in the Heisman Trophy voting after passing for 1,313 yards and rushing for 787 more. UCLA went 9–2–1, capping its season with a 23–10 upset of top-ranked Ohio State in the Rose Bowl. Sciarra was selected in the fourth round of the 1976 NFL Draft by the Chicago Bears but opted to sign with the British Columbia Lions of the Canadian Football League after receiving a lucrative offer.

After two seasons in the CFL, where he won the league's Most Outstanding Rookie Award, Sciarra spent six seasons with the Philadelphia Eagles as a defensive back, reuniting with Vermeil and playing in Super Bowl XV. He eventually became president and CEO of National Retirement Services, but Bruins fans hadn't seen the last of John Sciarra. His son, John Sciarra, was a backup quarterback for UCLA in 2002, throwing a 14-yard touchdown pass at the end of a loss to USC.

Sciarra and Harmon never wavered in their friendship, even while living apart the one season they competed for the starting quarterback job. "We were always friends," Sciarra said. "It's just sometimes when the competition gets stiff, it's better to get space and get more focused during the season. We always rose above everything and our friendship was pretty unconditional."

64 The 1976 Rose Bowl

UCLA's 3–0 deficit felt more like three touchdowns when the team convened in its locker room at halftime of the 1976 Rose Bowl.

The Bruins had managed only 48 total yards in the first half against top-ranked, undefeated, and heavily favored Ohio State, forcing players to contemplate the possibility of a second defeat against the Buckeyes after getting trampled 41–20 when the teams had met only a few months before. "We had gotten the snot beat out of us by the same group of guys in the Coliseum earlier in the year," UCLA guard and center Randy Cross said, "and it wasn't hard to tell in all the events we did [leading up to the game] they figured it would be another one of those coming."

One takeaway from the first meeting that the Bruins thought would be helpful in the rematch was their ability to generate yardage with their option attack against Ohio State's vaunted defense. UCLA's 20 points were more than the Buckeyes' first three opponents had combined to score, and Ohio State would follow its early-season victory over the Bruins with back-to-back shutouts.

"Even though they kicked our butt, we moved the ball on them," recalled UCLA quarterback John Sciarra. "I think [Ohio State coach] Woody Hayes is sitting there going, 'Doggone it, these guys can really move the ball.' I mean, we took the lead right out of the chute that game. It wasn't like they just shut us down."

UCLA decided to use the same approach when the teams met on January 1, 1976, before a record crowd of 105,464 at the Rose Bowl, and it was as if Ohio State knew exactly what was coming. The Buckeyes put eight defenders in the box and shut down the option, holding the Bruins without a first down until late in the second quarter. "They just came in waves," Sciarra said, "and we were going nowhere fast." Fortunately for UCLA, its defense was nearly as stiff as that of its counterpart, shutting down Ohio State in the first half after the Buckeyes kicked a 42-yard field goal on their opening possession.

In the locker room, with his team trailing by three points, UCLA coach Dick Vermeil would unveil what Sciarra called "the greatest coaching adjustment" he had witnessed. "Vermeil brings the offense over," Sciarra recalled, "and says, 'We're scrapping the game plan. We're throwing the ball.'"

That's exactly what the Bruins did to start the second half, with the play-action pass complementing the running game as they drove for a tying field goal. After stopping the Buckeyes, UCLA went back to the air, Wally Henry taking a 16-yard touchdown pass from Sciarra to give the Bruins a 9–3 lead after they missed the extra point. "All of a sudden," Sciarra said, "we're moving the ball and boom—touchdown pass—and they're going, 'Oh, shoot, we better start backing off.'"

Ohio State switched defenses, allowing UCLA to effectively mix the run and the pass. On the Bruins' next possession, Sciarra connected with Henry again, this time on a 67-yard touchdown that gave UCLA a 16–3 lead.

The Buckeyes countered with some changes of their own after having passed the ball more than usual to that point. Going back to the running game, Ohio State cut its deficit to 16–10 early in the fourth quarter on Pete Johnson's three-yard touchdown run. Inexplicably, the Buckeyes went back to the air on their next possession and UCLA intercepted a pass to give the ball back to its offense.

With less than four minutes to play, UCLA running back Wendell Tyler took an option pitch and raced up the sideline before cutting back on the way to a 54-yard touchdown run that gave the Bruins a commanding 23–10 advantage. When another UCLA interception ended Ohio State's final threat, Hayes trudged across the field to offer congratulations before the game was over. "We were taking a knee at that point," Sciarra said, "and he had started walking across the field and we're all going, 'What's going on?'"

Hayes would concede he had been outcoached after his final appearance in the Rose Bowl, his players also saying as much. "We tried to pass the ball when we were averaging five yards per carry," Johnson told the *Cleveland Plain Dealer*, "and that made no sense.... In the first game we played them, we just killed UCLA by running the ball. Then we go out and try to pass. If we had just run the ball, we could have run all over them."

The Bruins held Johnson and Archie Griffin, the two-time Heisman Trophy winner, to under 100 yards rushing each, while getting 172 yards rushing of their own from Tyler. Sciarra was selected player of the game after completing 13 of 19 passes for 212 yards and two touchdowns with two interceptions. Sciarra would call it the most meaningful game of his college career, its outcome made possible by some savvy halftime tweaking. "That was a pretty good adjustment," Cross concurred. "And the best part of the adjustment was that John was pretty good at throwing, too."

65 Jerry Robinson

Jerry Robinson's coaches weren't surprised when he readily agreed to switch positions before the 1976 Rose Bowl, even if the change from wide receiver to linebacker was a most unusual one.

Wide receivers are usually reedy and speedy, while linebackers tend to be thicker and more muscular. But Robinson combined the perfect blend of both positions, possessing a slim waist, a strong upper body, and powerful legs. He had been a sprinter at Cardinal Newman High in Santa Rosa, California, and could run the 100 meters in 9.8 seconds. He also filled multiple needs for the football team as a running back, tight end, nose guard, and punter. Robinson even competed in the high jump for the track team when it needed the points, clearing 6'5" in the one and only time he jumped in a meet.

Robinson was recruited by a host of national football powers but had long since decided to attend UCLA if given the chance because of a dream he had in the eighth grade. It had nothing to do with football but involved the most prominent coach on campus. "I was playing at Pauley Pavilion," Robinson told the *Los Angeles Times*, "and coach John Wooden and I were real tight."

Robinson arrived in Westwood wanting to be the Bruins' starting tight end by his sophomore season, but the spot was manned by veterans Rick Walker and Don Pederson. Robinson moved to wide receiver once Norm Anderson suffered a leg injury and played sparingly as a freshman, making only two catches. Then Lynn Stiles, the Bruins defensive coordinator, asked Robinson if he'd like to play in the Rose Bowl. Sure, Robinson said. Even though he played only two downs during the team's 23–10 victory over Ohio State, it might have been the best decision he ever made.

Robinson found he enjoyed the read-and-react nature of playing linebacker, committing to defense permanently. "I'm having fun," Robinson told the *Los Angeles Herald-Examiner* early in the 1976 season. "Flying to the ball on every play." He made 12 tackles in his first start against Arizona State, leading the Bruins, and was so relentless in running sideline to sideline that he would regularly lose about 10 pounds during workouts with his team. "I'm 211 before practice," the 6'3" Robinson told the *Times*, "but only about 202 after it."

He showed his exceptional speed and agility during another showdown with Ohio State. With the Buckeyes driving for what would have been the go-ahead touchdown in the fourth quarter, they faced third-and-2 on UCLA's 7-yard line. That's when Buckeyes quarterback Rod Gerald, trying to spot an opening in the defense, instead found Robinson, who wrapped him up for a tackle. Ohio State was forced to kick a field goal, the final points in a 10–10 tie.

Robinson ended that season as the only sophomore All-American among 23 first-team selections after making 159 tackles, including a school-record 28 against Air Force. As a junior, he made 147 tackles and perhaps even more amazingly acknowledged afterward all the improvements that he needed to make. His senior season might have been his best, Robinson making 161 tackles, including 132 in the final eight regular-season games.

His three-year total of 468 tackles remained a school record until Eric Kendricks broke it with 481 from 2010 to '14. Robinson also scored three touchdowns on interception returns—69 and 72 yards as a sophomore and 95 yards as a junior. He finished 10th in voting for the 1978 Heisman Trophy and won the Pop Warner Award as the top player on the West Coast. Robinson concluded his UCLA career as the first three-time consensus All-American in school history and the first in the nation since Southern Methodist's Doak Walker from 1947 to '49.

Along the way, he helped restore UCLA's reputation on defense, which had been lagging since the Red Sanders era in the 1950s. The Philadelphia Eagles selected Robinson with the 21st pick of the first round of the 1979 NFL Draft and he went on to play in the 1981 Super Bowl as part of his 13-year career with the Eagles and Los Angeles Raiders. UCLA retired the No. 84 jersey he had worn as a Bruin.

Sing the Fight Songs

No UCLA touchdown or field goal feels complete until its soundtrack kicks in. As "The Mighty Bruins" wafts over the Rose Bowl, the UCLA Bruin Marching Band adds a finishing touch to the revelry that can induce goose bumps.

The fight song was created by Academy Award–winning composer Bill Conti in 1984 after being commissioned by the UCLA Alumni Association to commemorate its 50th anniversary. UCLA had previously shared a fight song with California, the Bruins' version called "Sons of Westwood." But alumni grew tired of hearing the same song played whenever UCLA faced Cal and decided to seek their own version. "It is not right for a top-caliber university like UCLA to be sharing a fight song," Conti told the *Daily Bruin*, "especially with the excellent athletic tradition that UCLA possesses."

Conti chose the lyrics from submissions by UCLA alumni Barbara Lamb and Don Holley as part of a contest featuring a

$1,000 prize before adding the music. The song made its debut on September 30, 1984, as part of a ceremony at Westwood Plaza in which the school's iconic 10-foot-long, 6-foot-high statue, "The Bruin," was also unveiled. Conti led the 250-member UCLA Bruin Marching Band in a spine-tingling introduction of "The Mighty Bruins" that day. He also conducted the band the following week when the Bruins played host to Stanford at the Rose Bowl.

UCLA's other primary fight song, "The Bruin Warriors," was updated in 2016 to include lyrics that would be appropriate for both male and female athletes. The melody was taken from Cal's "Big C," which dates to 1913.

In 1959, UCLA participated in a football doubleheader featuring schools in the University of California system, with the Bruins playing Cal and UC Santa Barbara facing UC Davis and the bands from all four schools performing together as part of the halftime shows. It was then that UCLA band director F. Kelly James, an alumnus of the Cal band, unveiled his own spin on his alma mater's song, which went over so well that the Bruins made it a permanent fixture despite the vehement objections of James Berdahl, then director of the Cal band. In 1969, the Copyright Office of the Library of Congress ruled that "Big C" had never been copyrighted and was in the public domain, meaning UCLA was within its rights to do whatever it wished with the song.

"The Mighty Bruins" is often accompanied today by an eight-clap cheer. "They're different arrangements," Gordon Henderson, who became director of the UCLA Bruin Marching Band in 1982, said when asked to compare the songs. "You would recognize them as being the same basic melody."

UCLA's fight songs are largely considered interchangeable, though "The Bruin Warriors" is played when the men's basketball team runs onto the court and "The Mighty Bruins" follows scoring plays by the football team.

The school has a handful of other traditional songs that are often played at sporting events. "By the Old Pacific" was composed in 1922 by Thomas Vickers Beall, then the newly appointed leader of the ROTC band. It served as the UCLA fight song until 1962 and is still rolled out from time to time by the marching band and performed by the cheer squad before every football game.

UCLA's alma mater, "Hail to the Hills of Westwood," was written by Bruins alumna Jeane Emerson in 1960 after students objected to a reference to their school as the "California of the South" that had been contained in a previous alma mater called "Hail Blue and Gold." UCLA and Cal had shared an earlier alma mater until 1925. The Band's current version of "Hail to the Hills of Westwood" was arranged by Dwayne Milburn while he was an undergraduate student in 1985.

Bruins basketball victories are followed by the alma mater and a rousing rendition of "Rover," which dates to the late 1960s. At that time, a band student wrote lyrics to accompany a tune being played at football games titled "I'm Looking Over a Four-Leaf Clover." The UCLA version was renamed "Rover" and initially played only after runaway Bruins basketball victories, which were routine during coach John Wooden's heyday. Now the song is played after every triumph.

One of UCLA's first songs included a touch of Hollywood. In 1936, composers George and Ira Gershwin moved to Beverly Hills to work on the Fred Astaire movie *Shall We Dance*, when they were approached about contributing a song to UCLA. The Gershwins revised the lyrics to "Strike Up the Band" and dubbed the new version "Strike Up the Band for UCLA," which became one of the school's primary songs. It is still played as part of the Band's pregame show at football games and occasionally at home basketball games.

The Mighty Bruins

We are the Mighty Bruins,
The best team in the West.
We're marching on to victory,
To conquer all the rest.
We are the Mighty Bruins,
Triumphant evermore.
You can hear from far and near,
The Mighty Bruin roar!
U! (3 claps)
C! (3 claps)
L! (3 claps)
A! (3 claps)
U-C-L-A! Fight! Fight! Fight!

The Bruin Warriors

Hail to all our Bruin Warriors,
Sons and daughters lead the way,
Who we are and what we stand for makes us proud today,
Fight! Fight! Fight!
Westwood is the home for Bruins,
L. A. is OUR town!
Ready for the test we're the best team in the West,
Future Champions we'll crown.
U-C-L-A! Fight! Fight! Fight!

Hail to the Hills of Westwood

Hail to the hills of Westwood,
To the mighty sea below;
Hail to our Alma Mater,
She will conquer every foe.
For we're loyal to the Southland,
Her honor we'll uphold;

We'll gladly give our hearts to thee,
To the Blue and to the Gold.

Rover

We're looking over our dead dog, Rover,
That we overran tonight (all right!)
One leg is broken, the other is bent,
And in his head, there's a great big dent.
No need explaining the parts remaining
Are scattered all over the court (next page).
We're looking over our dead dog, Rover,
That we overran tonight!

Strike Up the Band for UCLA

Let the drums roll out!
Let the trumpets call, Let the whole world shout UCLA.
With our battle cry Bruin! Conquer all! We will do or die! UCLA!
There's a game to be won, to be won!
Put the foe on the run, on the run!
And it's got to be done, To be done here today!
With our flag unfurled, we can lick the world!
You see, we're UCLA!

67 Gerrit Cole

UCLA's baseball team faced a competitor far more intimidating than any Pac-10 Conference rival in the summer of 2008. The Bruins had to take on the New York Yankees.

The Yankees had taken star recruit Gerrit Cole with the 28th pick of the amateur draft, setting up an epic battle for the services of the player who was considered the top high school pitcher in the nation. It didn't seem like a fair fight given that the Yankees had more than a potential multi-million-dollar signing bonus going for them.

Cole had been a huge Yankees fan since playing T-ball as a six-year-old for the Tustin Western Little League Rockies. He wrote a sixth-grade report on Yankees legend Lou Gehrig and considered shortstop Derek Jeter his favorite player. Cole had even attended Games 6 and 7 of the 2001 World Series between the Yankees and Arizona Diamondbacks, with a newspaper printing a photo of an 11-year-old Cole holding a sign that read "YANKEES FAN TODAY, TOMORROW, FOREVER."

Luckily for UCLA, Cole was also a huge fan of Bruins coach John Savage. Cole believed in Savage's ability to lay the groundwork for his major league career, having already produced a number of successful big leaguers. He also liked the idea of matching wits with college classmates while attending school just far enough away from his Orange County home.

By the time the Yankees decided to open negotiations with Scott Boras, Cole's advisor, Cole had already picked Blue and Gold over the famed pinstripes, becoming the first high school player drafted in the first round to attend UCLA. "It would have been a different decision," Cole said, "if I didn't have as much confidence in Coach Savage."

That confidence was rewarded early in his freshman season when Cole was made a Friday-night starter, the collegiate equivalent of being the ace of the rotation. The right-hander didn't disappoint, compiling a 3.49 earned-run average while establishing a school freshman single-season record with 104 strikeouts. His 4–8 record was largely a function of meager offensive support, the Bruins combining for just 14 runs in his seven losses as a starter. UCLA finished the season with a 27–29 record, failing to make the NCAA tournament.

Cole's sophomore season was much more enjoyable. He went 11–4 with a 3.37 ERA, leading the Bruins to their first College World Series appearance since 1997. He allowed one hit in five scoreless innings during UCLA's 15–1 victory over Kent State in the opener of their regional at Jackie Robinson Stadium. Cole was the losing pitcher in the opener of the Bruins' super regional against Cal State Fullerton, and UCLA was one out from elimination in the second game. But Tyler Rahmatulla's two-run homer extended the game into extra innings and the Bruins prevailed 11–7 in 10 innings. UCLA won the deciding game 8–1 to advance to the College World Series.

Cole struck out 13 batters in eight innings during a 6–3 victory over Texas Christian as the Bruins won three of their first four games during the final College World Series played at old Rosenblatt Stadium, setting up a best-of-three championship series with South Carolina. Cole lost the opener of that series and the Gamecocks won the next game 2–1 in 11 innings to win the title. Nevertheless, Cole described the experience as one of the most memorable of his baseball career.

"It's just like the most attention that any of us had been exposed to ever," Cole said. "It was the biggest stage that anyone had ever played on. Really, it was the biggest stage I had played on until I got to the big leagues."

Cole had an up-and-down junior season. He opened the season with his first career complete-game shutout, during a 1–0 victory over San Francisco, and carried a perfect game into the seventh inning of back-to-back games. But he finished 6–8 with a 3.31 ERA and was the losing pitcher in the opener of UCLA's regional against San Francisco. The Bruins rallied with consecutive victories before suffering a season-ending loss to UC Irvine.

Gerrit Cole delivers a pitch against TCU in the first inning of the College World Series in Omaha, Nebraska, on Monday, June 21, 2010. (AP Photo/Nati Harnik)

Cole finished his UCLA career ranked second in school history in strikeouts (376), third in games started (49), and fifth in innings (322⅓). He was a two-time All-Pac-10 selection (2009, 2010), greatly enhancing his draft stock. The Pittsburgh Pirates selected him No. 1 overall in the 2011 Draft, making him the only player in UCLA history to have twice been selected in the first round. He credited his career as a Bruin for making him into a major league ace. "Even though we didn't get rewarded as often as we wanted to pitching inside with metal bats," Cole said early in the 2017 season, "we still did it and it's been a core value that helped me develop and get me to the point where I am now."

68 Visit Jackie Robinson Stadium

One of the most intimate college baseball stadiums in the country comes with a larger-than-life name. Jackie Robinson Stadium holds its occupants in awe by serving as a constant reminder of the four-sport standout at UCLA who went on to break the color barrier in Major League Baseball when he made his debut for the Brooklyn Dodgers in 1947.

"It's amazing," said Gerrit Cole, a former Bruins pitcher who was selected No. 1 overall in the 2011 MLB Draft by the Pittsburgh Pirates. "I mean, it's Jackie Robinson Stadium."

The stadium is also a tribute of sorts to Dodger Stadium because of the way it plays—preventing some hard-hit balls from becoming home runs during cool nights while allowing scores of fly balls to clear the outfield fence during hot afternoons. The symmetrical field features 8-foot-high fences that stand 330 feet from home plate down the foul lines, 370 feet in the power alleys, and

395 feet in straightaway center field. A padded backstop built into the base of the stands is 55 feet from home plate, providing ample foul territory behind home plate.

Sitting about a mile from UCLA's campus on the grounds of the Los Angeles Veterans Health Administration and the site of old Sawtelle Field, Jackie Robinson Stadium opened for the 1981 season with a construction cost of $900,000. The tree-lined stadium that has been expanded to seat 1,820 was made possible with a private gift from Hoyt Pardee, a 1941 UCLA graduate and classmate of Robinson's who requested that the facility be named in honor of the Hall of Famer.

The stadium was dedicated on February 7, 1981, with an exhibition game between the Bruins and the Los Angeles Dodgers. UCLA played its first college game there a week later, losing 9–6 to Pepperdine. A bronze statue of Robinson located near the concession stand on the concourse level was dedicated on April 27, 1985, before the Bruins played Arizona State.

Rachel Robinson, Jackie's widow, has been a regular visitor over the years, her presence another powerful reminder of what her husband symbolized. UCLA's coaches have also ensured that their players try to represent the famous alumnus with distinction.

"We remind them constantly of the pioneer that Jackie was and what he stood for and what he went through, so they feel very honored," UCLA baseball coach John Savage said. "There's no entitlement. They know it's a very big honor and privilege to play at the stadium named after him."

Upgrades since 2006 have provided many of the amenities expected of a modern stadium, including comfortable seats, state-of-the-art backstop netting, and a digital video board that was updated in 2013. Other improvements followed, including a new playing surface, batter's eye, and netting behind home plate. The playing surface was named Steele Field in honor of donors Ethel and Horace Steele. A 10,500-square-foot hitting complex was added behind right field in 2009 and named after donors Jack and Rhodine Gifford.

The stadium has not been without controversy. The American Civil Liberties Union filed a lawsuit against the Veterans Health Administration on behalf of homeless disabled veterans in 2011, alleging that leasing parts of the campus to organizations that did not directly benefit veterans was a misuse of the land. UCLA's lease of Jackie Robinson Stadium was cited as an example of the alleged misuse.

UCLA agreed in 2016 to pay $1.15 million annually for medical, legal, and recreational services to the VA's West Los Angeles campus. The school also agreed to pay $300,000 per year for its renewed lease of the stadium as part of a 10-year agreement. Savage said the Bruins have forged a strong relationship with many veterans who come to games to support the team; Robinson himself had served in an Army cavalry unit during World War II. "We love the relationship with the veterans," Savage said, "and we also feel honored to play on their property."

The stadium has played host to NCAA regionals in 1986, 2010, 2011, 2012, 2013, and 2015, as well as super regionals in 2010 and 2012, regularly drawing overflow crowds of more than 2,000 fans and creating enduring memories for the Bruins. "To take that field with those four letters on the front of your chest trying to represent all the things that Jackie did," Cole said, "it was an unbelievable honor and very special."

69 2013 College World Series Champions

What do you call a team that batted .250, didn't feature a .300 hitter in its regular lineup, and averaged one home run every 3½ games? The 2013 College World Series champions.

UCLA won it all with pitching and defense that season, relying on two dominant starters and a strong back end of the bullpen to capture the first national championship in the history of a storied program that had produced scores of first-round draft picks, not to mention racial pioneers Jackie Robinson and Dave Roberts. The one thing the Bruins hadn't done was prevail on college baseball's biggest stage, having lost during trips to the College World Series in 1969, 1997, 2010, and 2012.

The Bruins finished only third in the Pac-12 Conference in 2013, behind Oregon State and Oregon, but coach John Savage knew his team was built for a deep postseason run because of a pitching staff that featured dual aces in Adam Plutko and Nick Vander Tuig and a bullpen constructed like that of a quality major league team. There was closer David Berg, sidearming right-handed setup man Zack Weiss, and star freshman James Kaprielian, who could also handle late-inning pressure.

"We had a lot of power in that bullpen and it was really a six-inning game a lot of times," Savage recalled. "If we could get to that sixth or seventh inning with a lead, if you look at that year and what we did with leads after the seventh, it was pretty lockdown stuff."

Top-seeded UCLA opened regional play at Jackie Robinson Stadium with a 5–3 victory over San Diego State. Things looked dire in the second game against Cal Poly when the Bruins faced a four-run deficit before Kevin Williams' three-run, game-tying triple in the sixth inning propelled them to a 6–4 victory. The regional final against San Diego wasn't much of a contest, with Grant Watson, Weiss, and Berg combining to throw a one-hitter during a 6–0 triumph.

UCLA only had to venture down a few Southern California freeways for the super regional against Cal State Fullerton, one of the nation's top teams. The Bruins scrapped their way to a win in the opener of the best-of-three series, with sophomore right fielder Eric Filia's flare to right field in the 10th inning driving in the go-ahead run in an eventual 5–3 victory. The game was indicative of the way UCLA won all season, getting solid pitching and timely hitting.

It was Vander Tuig's turn to star in the second game. He pitched 6⅓ scoreless innings to lead UCLA to a 3–0 triumph that propelled the Bruins into the College World Series for the third time in four years. In some respects, Savage felt his team had already won by beating the Titans to get there.

"I say to this day, whoever would have won that super regional was going to go on and win the World Series and I think Fullerton would have, I really do," Savage said. "They were 51–8 [entering the super regional], they were the No. 1 team in the country and we went in there and beat them and I think that was kind of a sign of the times that we had a special team."

UCLA's joyride continued upon its arrival at TD Ameritrade Park in Omaha, a 2–1 victory over Louisiana State in the opener turning when the Tigers hit into a double play during a sacrifice situation. The Bruins edged North Carolina State 2–1 in their second game thanks to another strong start from Vander Tuig. Berg completed his team's 4–1 tightrope victory over North Carolina after allowing one run while facing two bases-loaded situations in the ninth inning.

That advanced UCLA into the best-of-three championship series against Mississippi State. At that point, the Bruins were 8–0 in the postseason and felt they were on the verge of something special, even if no one would openly acknowledge it. "It's like a pitcher with a no-hitter; you don't go near him," Savage said. "It's just one of those things where it flows and our routine flowed and our practices and our preparation and it just seemed like we were winning pitches and winning innings and at the end of the day, we were the best team."

No one could question that at the end of the two games against the Bulldogs. Filia was the offensive hero in the first game, hitting an opposite-field double to set up UCLA's first run and adding a two-run single in the fourth inning. Berg secured an inning-ending double play in the eighth inning and stranded the tying runs in the ninth to record his NCAA-record-setting 24th save of the season while completing the Bruins' 3–1 victory.

The clincher was a laugher. UCLA took a 5–0 lead in the fourth inning and was never threatened on the way to an 8–0 triumph in which Vander Tuig pitched eight scoreless innings. The Bruins let Berg finish the lopsided game as a tribute to his season-long dominance. "I remember him telling the third baseman, 'Hey, you've got bunt and I've got the first-base line,' and it was just a telling sign that they were still playing the game," Savage said. "I still look at that and I'm like, 'Okay, we played the right way and at the end of the day we got rewarded.'"

When Berg induced a grounder to first baseman Pat Gallagher for the final out, it triggered a celebration nearly a century in the making for a program that had played its first game in 1920. UCLA's postseason dominance had been practically unrivaled, the Bruins going 10–0. They also posted the lowest team earned-run average (0.80) in the College World Series' aluminum bat era and became the first team to complete the Series without allowing more than one run in each game.

The celebrants included former longtime UCLA coach Gary Adams and Bruins athletic director Dan Guerrero, a second baseman on the team in the 1970s. "It was just a sense of accomplishment for a lot of people," Savage said, "for coach Adams and Dan Guerrero, just a lot of people who put a lot of time into this program, they finally could carry the flag."

70 Woody Strode

Woody Strode's first starring role came far away from the glow of the silver screen, on a field of manicured grass inside the Los Angeles Memorial Coliseum. His chiseled physique and square jaw were every bit as imposing as they would be in his more than 100 film appearances, striking fear into those who tried to stop him as the standout end for UCLA.

The son of a brick mason who grew up in the shadow of the Coliseum and attended nearby Jefferson High, Strode was a young man of many talents. While most ends specialized in pass receiving, blocking, or defense, Strode excelled in all three areas as a two-way player. "He haunts his end like a departed spirit," read one account in the *Los Angeles Examiner*, "taking out four men on one play if need be."

Strode teamed with All-American tailback Kenny Washington, who was adept at both passing and running the football in the days when the position required a healthy mix of both. Strode and Washington became such a powerful duo that a local sportswriter dubbed them the "Goal Dust Twins," in what was at the time considered an acceptable twist on the two black children featured on the box of Fairbank's Gold Dust, a widely used soap powder. They were hailed as the greatest passing-catching tandem in Pacific

Coast football history while operating out of the single wing offense from 1937 to '39.

Strode and Washington were joined in 1939 by Jackie Robinson, forming three of the four backfield players. Also, counting Ray Bartlett, the Bruins had four black players at a time when only a few dozen others played at other schools across the country.

Standing 6'3" and weighing 205 pounds, Strode led UCLA in receiving in 1938 (with seven catches for 73 yards) and 1939 (with 15 catches for 218 yards). He was selected honorable mention All-Coast by United Press in 1938 before making the Associated Press All-Coast first team in 1939. The Bruins went undefeated during the latter season, going 6–0–4 and battling archrival USC to a scoreless tie at the Coliseum. UCLA rose as high as No. 7 in the national rankings.

Strode also excelled in track, pushing the shot put 51'6½", a distance that won the 1938 conference championship and stood as a school record until 1947. He threw the discus 161 feet 10 inches to set another school record. A sociable sort, despite his brooding appearance, Strode was a member of Alpha Phi Alpha, the first black intercollegiate Greek fraternity.

His groundbreaking ways couldn't immediately continue in the NFL after his college career because there were no black players in the league at that time despite no formal regulations forbidding them. Black players had competed in the NFL as early as 1920, but from 1934 to 1945 the league comprised only white players after NFL owners acceded to their complaints about job competition. So Strode spent the first seven years after he left UCLA playing semipro football for the Hollywood Bears, wrestling professionally, and serving in the Air Corps in World War II.

The door to the NFL finally re-opened after the fledgling All-American Football Conference embraced black players, forcing the NFL to do the same. That allowed Strode and Washington to break the NFL's color barrier in 1946 when they signed as a package deal with the Los Angeles Rams for their debut season in the city. Prodded by sports columnist William Harding and local officials who insisted the team sign Washington as a condition for letting them play in the Coliseum, Washington signed with the Rams after they also agreed to take Strode. A 32-year-old rookie, Strode played sparingly with the Rams, catching four passes, and was released at the end of his one and only NFL season.

He would enjoy more long-lasting success as an actor during a career that spanned nearly a half century. He often played muscle-men and tough-guy characters as a result of his imposing presence. Strode participated in one of the most famous movie fight scenes when he played Ethiopian gladiator Draba and faced off against Kirk Douglas in *Spartacus*, earning Strode a Golden Globe nomination in 1960 for best supporting actor. His last film appearance came more than three decades later in *The Quick and the Dead*, alongside Sharon Stone and Gene Hackman.

When Strode died of lung cancer in 1994 at age 80, *Sports Illustrated* dubbed him a "Forgotten Pioneer." "Integrating the NFL was the low point of my life," Strode told the magazine before his death. "There was nothing nice about it. History doesn't know who we are. Kenny was one of the greatest backs in the history of the game, and kids today have no idea who he is. If I have to integrate heaven, I don't want to go." Strode's impact alongside his former UCLA teammate was more widely recognized after his death. They had led the way for so many other black players in the NFL, an everlasting testament to their steely resolve.

71 Don Barksdale

The blowback from becoming the NBA's first black All-Star was hardly an introduction to racial discrimination for Don Barksdale.

He was cut three times from his Berkeley High basketball team despite having shown the potential to be one of its best players. The director of the playground that Barksdale frequented, Dutch Rudquist, asked the Berkeley coach why the budding star wasn't good enough to make his team. "The coach told Dutch," Barksdale later recalled in an interview with the *San Jose Mercury News*, "'I've already got one black player.'"

Barksdale would go on to star in track and basketball at San Marin Junior College before arriving at UCLA for the final five games of the 1942–43 season. His impact was immediate. Utilizing his superior passing skills and speed on the fast-break—not to mention his famed turnaround jump shot—the 6'6", 200-pound center helped the Bruins beat crosstown rival USC for the first time in 11 years.

A headline in the *Los Angeles Times* on March 6, 1943, said it all: "TOO MUCH BARKSDALE." "For 42 straight games," Al Wolf wrote in the *Times*, "Troy had invariably vanquished Bruin quintets. But this was the first time the Trojans ran into... Barksdale... and that made the difference. He thumped in 18 big points for high point honors and was an awful ball hog beneath the rim."

Barksdale's career with the Bruins was brief but prolific, interrupted by a stint in the military during World War II. He returned to UCLA in 1946, running the 100-yard dash in under 10 seconds as a member of the track team while also becoming the Bruins' top high jumper and long jumper. But he made his biggest impact in basketball, becoming UCLA's first black All-American in the sport and only the third overall. He led the Pacific Coast Conference's Southern Division in scoring by averaging 16.5 points per game during the 1946–47 season, while helping the Bruins record their second division championship and first conference playoff appearance. His 198 points in division play broke a record that had been shared by Johnny Ball (1936) and Jackie Robinson (1940), the latter being one of Barksdale's mentors.

Robinson had visited Barksdale in 1938 while Barksdale attended Berkeley High and the Bruins were in town to play California. Nine years later, after Robinson had broken the color barrier in Major League Baseball, he convinced Barksdale that he could handle whatever slights came his way in his attempts to help integrate the NBA. There would be many. When Barksdale became the first black Olympic basketball player in 1948, he could not stay in the same hotel as his white teammates or eat in the same restaurants. Someone threatened to shoot him if he played.

But a turning point came during an exhibition game in Lexington, Kentucky, deep in the Jim Crow South. A white teammate took a drink from a water bottle during a timeout and passed it to Barksdale, who took his own swig before passing the bottle to another white teammate named Shorty Carpenter, a burly 6'7", 250-pound center. The crowd of 16,000 held its breath… needlessly. "Shorty didn't even hesitate," Barksdale told the *Mercury News*. "He held it out and drank. Nothing happened, but it was just about the scariest moment of my life."

Barksdale was co-captain of the undefeated gold-medal-winning team in London but couldn't go directly to the NBA upon his return because black players weren't allowed in the league until 1950, when the Boston Celtics drafted Chuck Cooper, a forward from Duquesne. Not long after, the New York Knicks signed Nat Clifton and the Baltimore Bullets did the same by bringing in Barksdale as a 28-year-old rookie.

Barksdale was considered the best of his early black contemporaries, becoming the league's first black All-Star in 1953 while playing in a game that featured 13 eventual Hall of Famers. He is widely considered the NBA's version of Robinson for his pioneering role. "Watching Don play basketball was like watching a ballet," Red Auerbach, who coached Barksdale for two seasons after Barksdale was traded to the Boston Celtics, told the *Mercury News*.

Barksdale became a Hall of Famer himself despite playing only four seasons, retiring after the 1954–55 season because of severe ankle problems. His UCLA ties proved fortuitous in one of his most enduring post-retirement endeavors. Dismayed by an article detailing the financial hurdles facing underprivileged children who wanted to play after-school sports, Barksdale approached Cornell Maier, then the chairman of Kaiser Industries. Maier had attended UCLA while Barksdale starred there and eagerly supported Barksdale's efforts to provide financial support. Barksdale died in March 1993 in Oakland. UCLA retired his jersey (No. 11) in 2013.

72 Alumni Game for the Ages

The rosters were so flush with talent that Michael Jordan had to come off the bench.

On one side, North Carolina featured a starting lineup representing four decades of Tar Heels greatness with James Worthy, Kenny Smith, Bob McAdoo, Tom Kearns, and Charlie Scott. On the other side, UCLA rolled out starters Reggie Miller, Lucius Allen, Walt Hazzard, Kiki Vandeweghe, and Curtis Rowe, who had won six national titles between them.

Nobody seemed to mind that Kearns, a starter on North Carolina's 1957 national championship team, had silver-gray hair, or that Hazzard, the star player-turned-roly-poly coach of the Bruins, appeared winded after running about a dozen steps from the bench onto the court during player introductions.

The event was dubbed the Collegiate Legends Classic, and the only figures more legendary than the players were the coaches who roamed the sideline inside Pauley Pavilion on June 28, 1987. There was UCLA's John Wooden, winner of a record 10 national championships, versus North Carolina's Dean Smith, who would go on to surpass his counterpart with an unprecedented 879 victories at the time of his retirement in 1997. The coaches had previously faced off in the 1968 national title game, with UCLA prevailing in a 78–55 runaway.

The alumni game was held to honor Wooden and to establish the Nell and John Wooden Scholarship Fund for postgraduate studies by UCLA students. It also benefited the University Fund at North Carolina that assisted minority students. The game was orchestrated by former Wake Forest player and coach Billy Packer, who played for a team that beat Wooden's Bruins in the 1962 Final Four's third-place game and wanted to pay tribute to the legendary coach.

The game was televised nationally by ABC, with Miller's sister, Cheryl, handling sideline reporting duties. North Carolina might not have felt completely in enemy territory given that Worthy, only two weeks removed from leading the Los Angeles Lakers to an NBA championship, received one of the loudest ovations during player introductions before the crowd of 4,828.

The Bruins were a bit short-handed considering that their two greatest stars—Lew Alcindor (now Kareem Abdul-Jabbar) and Bill Walton—did not play. Alcindor was traveling abroad at the time of the game and Walton was only able to attend and not take part.

Several older players who participated might have wished they had scheduled a trip to Ecuador. Kearns fired up an airball from beyond the three-point arc, though broadcaster Keith Jackson went easy on him. "Tommy Kearns, a little short on that shot," Jackson said. Then again, North Carolina's Lennie Rosenbluth showed that his sweeping hook shot remained a revelation at 54, making three baskets for the Tar Heels.

The game largely belonged to the youngsters. Jordan finally got to play on the court he once hoped to call home, telling *Playboy* in 1992 that UCLA had been his dream school. "By the time they wanted to recruit me," Jordan told the magazine, "they had heard that I was going to stay close to home, which was not necessarily true."

Jordan made Bruins fans wonder what might have been, throwing down a tongue-wagging dunk in the first half. He added a hanging, one-handed shot contested by future Chicago Bulls teammate Jack Haley that Jordan banked off the glass while being fouled to give North Carolina a four-point lead with 42 seconds left after Jordan made the free throw. Jordan's 18 points helped the Tar Heels complete a comeback from 18 points down for a 116–111 victory. Haley finished with 18 points, six more than his career high as a Bruin. "I think he's trying to show me what he can do," Jordan said afterward.

It would be the first of many memorable matchups between Jordan and Miller, who was just beginning to harness his greatness after having been recently drafted by the Indiana Pacers. "MJ was MJ and I was young and brash," Miller recalled 30 years later. "I was going 100 miles per hour and I couldn't control my super powers at the time. It was one of those X-Men things where you can't control it and you need to go to the school to control your super powers, but it was great."

Mostly, the game was about what had been rather than what was or what would be. After Rosenbluth repeatedly blistered UCLA's

Denny Miller, who had played for Wooden in the 1950s, Miller didn't try to hide his advancing years. "Who is this Rosenbluth?" Miller asked the *Los Angeles Times'* Mike Downey, laughing. "He was my man. I could have stopped him, but somebody attached these old legs to my body when I wasn't looking."

73 Bob Waterfield

The romance wasn't all that glamorous, considering it involved the country's most acclaimed quarterback and a budding movie starlet. The lack of pizzazz probably had something to do with the fact that Bob Waterfield and Jane Russell were essentially just a pair of homebodies from Van Nuys.

Their idea of a vacation was a five-day outing to Bishop, an outpost on the California-Nevada border where they camped out on the ground in sleeping bags for five snow-dusted nights while fishing for bass. They once lived in the same small stucco house on an unpaved road that Waterfield had called home as a child—at a time when the former UCLA star turned NFL Most Valuable Player made what was then the princely sum of $20,000 a year after leading the Cleveland Rams to the 1945 league championship as a rookie.

Russell, a leading sex symbol of the silver screen, had fawned over Waterfield (who was a year older) since she was in the eighth grade. He finally returned the favor once Russell became a senior in high school, and the two began to date. Waterfield worked odd jobs for several summers at Warner Brothers just to make enough money to buy Russell hot dogs and soft drinks at Van Nuys bistros, though he was eventually discovered as an actor himself and appeared in Johnny Weissmuller's *Jungle Manhunt*.

Date nights included outings to the local movie theater, fights at the Olympic auditorium, and a small bar in Hollywood where Russell was the only celebrity customer, immediately recognized for her roles in films such as *Gentlemen Prefer Blondes*. A writer from *Look* magazine noted that the adult Russell adored her husband as if they were still in the dizzy infancy of their courtship, writing that "she looks at him is if she were still in the eighth grade."

The only thing their marriage lacked was a Hollywood ending. After nearly a quarter century of matrimony, they separated in 1967, with Russell alleging in her divorce suit that in their final year together Waterfield "was out until 2:00 and 3:00 in the morning almost continuously" and returned home only to sleep. Russell received custody of two of the couple's three children, all of whom were adopted because a botched abortion had left Russell infertile.

Waterfield's first marriage—and a three-year stint coaching the Los Angeles Rams from 1960–62 in which the team went 9–24–1— was about the only part of his life that wasn't a resounding success. He came to UCLA on a gymnastics scholarship, getting chided by the school's coach when he went out for football. Picking a sport became its own pursuit. Waterfield was a world-class swimmer, scratch golfer, and ace handball player who also could handle a rifle, often stopping on his way from Van Nuys to Westwood to hunt rabbits or birds. Waterfield would have also played basketball during his final year in college had he not separated his shoulder during the East-West Shrine game on January 1, 1945.

The 6'1", 191-pound dynamo was equally versatile on the football field, playing offense and defense as well as handling punting and placekicking duties. He became known for his bootleg plays, placing the ball on his hip and running upfield, often for touchdowns. "The secret of that," Waterfield told the *Los Angeles Daily*

News, "was never telling my blockers. They didn't even know. I would just say to the back involved, 'Don't take it.'" He distinguished himself in the rivalry against USC in 1942 by throwing a 42-yard pass to All-American end Burr Baldwin for the go-ahead touchdown in UCLA's 14–7 victory—its first triumph in the history of the series.

Waterfield played in the Bruins' first Rose Bowl at the conclusion of that season—a 9–0 loss to Georgia—before serving in the Army in World War II, being honorably discharged as a lieutenant for a knee injury he had suffered while playing football. Ironically, that allowed him to return to Westwood for one more season with the Bruins in 1944.

Waterfield wasn't a national sensation while at UCLA, despite setting school single-game records for most passing yards (308), completions (15), and total offense (308); season records for passing yards (1,095) and touchdown passes (24); and the career record for passing yards (2,824)—all of which were later broken. The Rams drafted him in the fifth round in 1945 and he quickly became known from coast to coast.

He was the NFL's MVP in 1945 and 1950, and also led the Rams to a second NFL championship in 1951 after the team had moved to Los Angeles. Waterfield was known as the strong, silent type, though he preferred his voice to be the only one heard in the huddle. When some teammates chattered on the field several games into his rookie season, he shouted, "Shut up. I'll call the plays."

Waterfield retired at age 32 after only eight NFL seasons, later explaining that he "just felt like I wasn't improving any." He was inducted into the Pro Football Hall of Fame in 1965, remarried in 1976, and died in 1983 at age 62 of respiratory failure following a lengthy illness. Russell died in 2011, also from a respiratory-related illness.

74 Myles Jack

UCLA was running out of running backs when it turned to Myles Jack against Arizona in November 2013. Jordon James and Steven Manfro were sidelined by ankle injuries. Damien Thigpen left the game with a leg injury that would require a walking boot.

That left Jack as an enticing option at running back alongside regulars Paul Perkins and Malcolm Jones. At the time, Jack was a freshman linebacker with experience playing tailback as a two-way standout in high school. The Bruins coaches asked Jack to become Mr. Versatility once more against the Wildcats.

"They were like, 'Do you want to try something?'" Jack recalled of the suggestion he play running back. "I thought they were playing at first—I didn't think they were serious until we ran the plays and everything—but we ended up doing it."

And it ended up saving the Bruins. Jack ran for 120 yards on only six carries, including a 66-yard touchdown in the fourth quarter that gave UCLA a 31–19 lead in an eventual 31–26 victory. His first carry came in the second quarter, the Bruins unveiling an inverted wishbone formation that helped Jack gain 29 yards on third-and-1.

It was just the start of something big. Jack added 25 yards rushing during a 90-yard touchdown drive late in the first half. Then came his signature moment on the fourth-quarter touchdown run, the powerfully built, 6'1", 225-pound phenom sweeping right before cutting up the field and through the Arizona defense.

"It kind of felt like high school all over again once I started running the ball, so it wasn't like a big deal to me," Jack said. "It was just cool seeing yourself on ESPN Top 10 [plays of the day.]"

UCLA coaches revealed afterward that they had considered using Jack at running back since training camp but only did it as a result of the injuries. Jack also had eight tackles against the Wildcats and recovered a fumble in the end zone while playing linebacker. Offensive coordinator Noel Mazzone told reporters that linebackers coach Jeff Ulbrich had said during the game that Mazzone was wearing his guy out. Retorted Mazzone: "Too bad."

Actually, Jack recalled not being overly fatigued. "It wasn't that tiring because of the way they split up my reps," he explained. "I would get a couple of carries here and there and they would split it up between series."

Jack reprised his role as an offensive catalyst the following week. He scored four touchdowns against Washington on runs

Myles Jack breaks free during a 2013 game against Arizona State at the Rose Bowl. (Charles Baus/Cal Sport Media via AP Images)

of eight, two, one, and one yards while collecting 59 yards in 13 carries. The performance was all the more special for Jack because he had played at Bellevue (WA) High and was heavily recruited by the Huskies before picking UCLA in part because of the relationship he had forged with Bruins coach Jim Mora, who had coached Jack's younger brother Jahlen in youth football.

The buzz created by Jack went national, with *USA Today* creating the portmanteau "runningbacker" to describe his play. Jack's allegiance to defense never waned, despite his newfound stardom on the other side of the ball. "To make plays on defense and be a dominant defense, that just has an aura about it," Jack said. "When you see teams in NFL and college and they have a really good defense, it's like an intimidation factor that it has, so I always liked to be a part of that."

Jack continued to make plays on defense, intercepting a pass on Utah's final drive to preserve a victory over the Utes and returning an interception 24 yards for a touchdown against Virginia Tech in the Sun Bowl. He also blocked a punt against Oregon while playing special teams. Jack was selected the Pac-12 Conference's Freshman of the Year on defense *and* offense after rushing for seven touchdowns, the most by a UCLA freshman since DeShaun Foster had 10 as a full-time tailback in 1998.

Jack mostly stuck to defense as a sophomore after UCLA replenished its fleet of running backs, appearing sporadically on offense in short-yardage situations and finishing the season with 28 carries for 113 yards and three touchdowns. He made 87 tackles and returned an interception 41 yards against Kansas State in the Alamo Bowl.

Jack's playmaking ability was again on display early in his junior year when he intercepted a pass against Brigham Young to help the Bruins hold on for a 24–23 triumph. At the time, no one knew it would be his final game at the Rose Bowl. "That was the last play anybody ever saw me play in college," said Jack, who tore the meniscus in his knee in practice the following week, ending his college career. Jack contemplated returning for his senior season but decided to enter the NFL draft. Concerns about his knee caused him to slip to the second round, where the Jacksonville Jaguars selected him with the 36th pick overall.

Jack packed plenty of electric plays into his two-plus seasons as a Bruin, upholding the tradition of top-shelf linebackers that had been started by elder teammates Anthony Barr and Eric Kendricks. "It's hard for me to throw myself in there," Jack said, "but I definitely think those two guys really started the whole pride that we take in being a linebacker at UCLA. I just tried to uphold their standard and that's what we're trying to continue at UCLA."

75 Donn Moomaw

One of the most meaningful conversions in college football history didn't involve a football flying through the uprights, even though it came after UCLA center and linebacker Donn Moomaw scored a touchdown against USC in the final game of the 1951 season.

His girlfriend had asked him to accompany her to a religious rally a few weeks before the rivalry game, Moomaw attending somewhat skeptically. But his outlook changed when he heard Bill Bright, the campus director of the "Crusade for Christ" movement, explain the power of prayer. Taking the cue, Moomaw prayed that the Bruins would beat the favored Trojans. He prayed even harder during the game.

In the third quarter, with UCLA holding a 14–0 lead, Moomaw intercepted a pass and ran it back for a touchdown, securing what would become a 21–7 victory. It was a moment that changed the trajectory of his life. "I don't know why I was over there where the ball was," Moomaw said afterward. "I intercepted it and when I stepped into the end zone, my heart was crying.… It's strange how a simple thing like my scoring a touchdown in that game, for the first time all season, changed my life. But that's what happened. If I'd had a good year, I might never have become interested in religion. But I had a bad one."

Moomaw was referring to the leg and shoulder injuries that had hampered him for most of his junior season. He had already established himself as a standout as a sophomore, earning first team All-American honors. Standing 6'4" and weighing 220 pounds, he was known as the "Mighty Moo" and the "Wild Bull of the Campus." Whenever he made a tackle, the UCLA cheerleaders would lead the crowd in a "MoooooooooMAW!" chant, remembered lifelong Bruins fan Edward Steinhaus, the volume increasing with each spectacular play Moomaw made.

He was never more imposing than he was on October 25, 1952, before what was then a record crowd of 52,131 at Wisconsin's Camp Randall Stadium. It was there that Moomaw helped shut down Badgers running back Alan Ameche, holding him to 31 yards in 14 carries. The Bruins manhandled Wisconsin, limiting a team that had been averaging 240 rushing yards per game to only 48. UCLA won the game 20–7 over one of the eventual Rose Bowl participants. Afterward, UCLA coach Red Sanders praised Moomaw, saying "that's the greatest game I ever saw a linebacker play."

By then, Moomaw was well into another endeavor that he found even more fulfilling than football. After his spiritual awakening following his touchdown against USC, Moomaw began speaking to Youth for Christ rallies and other congregations across California despite a busy schedule that included classes, waiting on tables, and performing other odd jobs. "My plea for athletic redemption had been answered," Moomaw explained at the time, "so I determined to do something in return. Religion isn't a one-way game; it works both ways. I'd only thought of prayer before as a medium for asking for what I wanted, kinda in a hurry. I'd never considered that I was in a position to give something too."

Moomaw said religion gave him the direction he was missing in life, despite attaining athletic stardom. "I know now that joy in Christianity is supreme over all," he told the *Pasadena Star-News*. His football stardom had certainly been impressive enough. He was a two-time first-team All-American and UCLA's second unanimous All-American, after Burr Baldwin. His No. 80 was retired by the school and he was inducted into the College Football Hall of Fame in 1973.

The Bruins went 8–1 during Moomaw's senior season, losing only to USC, 14–12. After the game, Marv Goux, a sophomore linebacker for USC, complimented Moomaw, a longtime friend who had attended the same church. "I said to him, 'Great game, Donn,'" Goux told the *Los Angeles Times*. "'You have a great team and we just happened to come out on top at the end.' And I'll never forget the classy thing he said to me. He looked me in the eye and said, 'Marv, I'll always be a winner because I'll always have my faith.'"

That faith prompted Moomaw to continue his studies after he graduated from UCLA with a bachelor's degree in physical education. He went on to receive his bachelor of divinity degree at Princeton Theological Seminary and his doctor of divinity degree at Sterling College in Kansas. He was drafted by the Los Angeles Rams in 1953 but refused to play football on Sundays, instead spending seven games with the Toronto Argonauts of the Canadian Football League (at a salary of $600 a game) in 1953 and a few more games with the Ottawa Rough Riders in 1955.

Moomaw's true calling was in the pulpit. He was part of the group that organized the Fellowship of Christian Athletes and served as pastor to president Ronald Reagan, individually giving the invocation and benediction for Reagan's inauguration in 1981 and serving as one of four clergymen at his 1985 inauguration.

Moomaw served as Minister of Bel-Air Presbyterian Church for 29 years before resigning in 1993 because of sexual misconduct with five women, acknowledging he had "stepped over the line of acceptable behavior with some members of the congregation." He later returned to active ministry in Rancho Santa Fe with the blessings of Presbyterian officials after serving a suspension imposed by the church.

76 Dick Linthicum

The lengthy list of UCLA basketball All-Americans, which includes Walt Hazzard, Lew Alcindor, Bill Walton, and many, many others, started with a player who could have been described as a Bruin blur. Richard "Dick" Linthicum possessed terrific speed and could handle the basketball with either hand, traits that would help make him the school's first All-American in any sport in 1931.

Los Angeles Times columnist Paul Lowry noted that the lanky forward, who stood 6'1½" and weighed 170 pounds, was the best player on a West Coast team in a decade, but there didn't seem to be much debate. "Coaches in the [Pacific] Coast Conference are almost universally agreed on this point," wrote Lowry, who described Linthicum as a team player who could "diagnose plays of opposing teams, guard effectively, hound the ball, and keep possession of it in the heaviest going."

For all his talent, Linthicum made bigger news off the court as a sophomore when he eloped to Ventura to marry Florence Louise Moore with the blessings of both families. During Linthicum's senior season, *L.A. Times* writer Braven Dyer quipped that he had been married for two years, "which has served to improve his aim." Not that Linthicum had struggled much as a junior. During a victory over Stanford on January 9, 1931, Dyer wrote that "the Bruins were peppering the bucket from all angles with brilliant Dick Linthicum leading the attack." UCLA beat the Indians (then Stanford's nickname) 32–23 after Linthicum helped hold them scoreless for the game's first 10 minutes.

The Bruins' opponents might have wondered if Linthicum ever missed, particularly in the final moments of a close game. He scored from underneath the basket with less than 30 seconds left to give UCLA a 29–28 victory over Montana on December 29, 1930, at the Olympic Auditorium, where the Bruins played their home games in those days. He made a basket and a free throw to help UCLA edge USC 26–24 late in the 1931–32 season, helping the Bruins overcome a three-point deficit in the final 100 seconds.

Linthicum was the Bruins' captain during the 1931–1932 season and led the PCC's Southern Division in scoring over a three-year period. He was twice selected an All–Southern Division forward, once made All-PCC, and was eventually chosen as a member of the All-Time PCC third team. He was an All-American in 1931 and 1932, gracing the same list as Purdue's John Wooden, who would go on to guide the Bruins to 10 national championships as perhaps the most famous coach in college history.

Linthicum served as a UCLA assistant coach and scout for five years after his college career ended, though his playing days weren't over. At the request of the Japanese government, Linthicum toured the Far East in 1935 as a player-coach for an undefeated American All-Star team, whose nucleus formed the roster that would eventually win the gold medal in the 1936 Olympics (Linthicum was not a member of that team).

His career after basketball might have been even more thrilling. After spending eight years as a business manager for Columbia

Pictures, Linthicum embarked on a lengthy career with the U.S. Navy and the Central Intelligence Agency. Cmdr. Linthicum served as an intelligence officer with the Navy in the South Pacific during World War II before holding posts in Asia, Europe, and the Mediterranean. His duties with the CIA involved executive-level assignments in Washington, D.C.; Europe; and the Middle East overseeing various operations. He was awarded the CIA Certificate of Merit for superior performance of duty upon his retirement in 1968. Linthicum died from cancer in 1979.

A letter written by John T. McCann, chief of the CIA's retirement service branch, to the UCLA athletics department in 1986 detailed Linthicum's value to the U.S. government; it also sounded like a coach praising his star player. "A very hard worker," McCann wrote, "Mr. Linthicum is never satisfied with a second-rate performance, but always strives for excellence. His ingrained feeling for team-play, his respect for authority, and his strong sense of discipline, combined with natural modesty, great restraint, exceptional fair-mindedness, and a highly cooperative attitude, contribute to making him a most respected and valued staff officer."

77 Burr Baldwin

Burr Baldwin was a man of many firsts at UCLA. He was part of the first Bruins team to beat USC, in 1942, after UCLA had gone 0–5–3 against its archrival in the series' early years. Playing end on offense and defense, he was the school's first consensus All-American, in 1946, after the Bruins had completed their first unbeaten and untied regular season. Thus, he was part of UCLA's first two Rose Bowl teams, in 1943 and 1947.

He also may have been the first Bruin to poke fun at himself in a first-person account of his play. Writing for the *Los Angeles Mirror*, Baldwin detailed his role in the 1947 Rose Bowl five years after the game.

"I wish I could say that I caught a pass and ran 95 yards or so in that 1947 Rose Bowl game between UCLA and Illinois," Baldwin wrote. "I can't. I couldn't even catch Buddy Young. But the game was still the most thrilling I ever played. There's something about being in a Bowl game, representing your school and your section against the best from the East, that can't be matched anywhere else... even when you lose, as we did, by a score of 45–14."

Baldwin noted that the Illini had reached UCLA's 16-yard line in the first quarter when he had his first chance to stop Young, Illinois' star halfback. But Young took the ball and bowled over him for 10 yards to set up the Illini's first touchdown. "For the rest of the afternoon," Baldwin wrote, "I don't think I laid my hands on him. He was a real ball of fire."

Illinois went on to run away with the game with three fourth-quarter scores. Baldwin caught three passes for 57 yards in a losing effort. "So I finished my college career without the cheers of the multitude ringing in my ears. I did not get a Morley Drury ovation," Baldwin wrote, referring to the legendary USC tailback who left his final game at the Los Angeles Memorial Coliseum to rousing cheers in 1927. "Did it get formal recognition? It sure did—in the hospital records. I was carried off the field on a stretcher, victim of a concussion."

For most of his college career, Baldwin was the one inflicting the hurt. He took a pass from teammate Bob Waterfield and scored on a 42-yard touchdown that helped the Bruins secure their first-ever win over USC, a 14–7 triumph on December 12, 1942. UCLA players celebrated afterward at the Glen, a local watering hole.

Baldwin's football career was interrupted by World War II. He served in the U.S. Army with the 85th Infantry Division in the Battle of the Bulge in December 1944, receiving a Bronze Star and the Combat Infantryman's Badge. He attained the rank of captain and was discharged in April 1946, returning to UCLA the following September.

Baldwin's most impressive college game came against Stanford on October 12, 1946. He caught six passes for 115 yards, with one of his receptions leading to a touchdown after he lateraled to teammate Roy Kurrasch. Baldwin was selected Lineman of the Week by the Associated Press following the Bruins' 26–6 victory, an honor he earned again three weeks later after catching two touchdown passes against St. Mary's and scoring another touchdown on a blocked kick.

Baldwin finished the season having made 15 catches for 317 yards and four touchdowns as UCLA went 10–0 before its Rose Bowl loss to Illinois. Bruins coach Bert La Brucherie called the 6'1", 196-pound Baldwin the best end he had ever seen. Baldwin finished seventh in the 1946 Heisman Trophy voting won by Glenn Davis of Army and later had his jersey (No. 38) retired. He played in the 1947 College All-Star Game in Chicago, where the collegians beat the NFL's Chicago Bears. Baldwin's jersey from that game remains on display inside UCLA's Athletic Hall of Fame.

Baldwin was chosen in the first round of the 1947 NFL Draft by the Green Bay Packers but decided to remain in Southern California to play for the Los Angeles Dons of the All-America Football Conference. He spent three seasons with the Dons before serving a stint as an ROTC Military Science Instructor at UCLA during the Korean War and embarking on a 50-year career in the insurance business, opening his own agency. Baldwin died in 2007 of complications from cancer.

78 Jonathan Ogden

From the moment Jonathan Ogden first set foot on campus, UCLA could no longer go by its longtime moniker, the "gutty little Bruins." The offensive tackle checked in at 6'2" and 270 pounds— as a high school freshman. By the time he reached UCLA, Ogden cut a Bunyanesque figure at 6'8" and 340.

"I came in eating a lot of candy and stuff that you shouldn't be eating in high school," said Ogden, the biggest player Terry Donahue recruited in his two decades as the Bruins' head coach, "but you come to college and your budget gets a little lighter, you eat a little better in the dorm."

Ogden's size wasn't the only factor that put him in position to play as a true freshman during the 1992 season. He quickly mastered the playbook after making a deal with coaches that he could skip spring football and compete in track and field throwing the shot put and discus if he made first or second team on the depth chart. He solidified his standing when he knocked defensive lineman Mike Chalinsky off the ball in practice and battled standout teammate Arnold Ale to a stalemate.

"As a true freshman," Ogden said, "when you do pretty good against the top guys on the defense, you've got to feel like, 'You know what, maybe I've got a shot at this.'"

Ogden played sporadically but exceptionally in the Bruins' first few games, prompting coaches to anoint him a starter midway through the season by moving Craig Novitsky from tackle to guard. But Ogden found that all that weight he was carrying around came with a downside. Arizona State's Shante Carver beat him badly, prompting some reflection. "I was 340 pounds, give or take,"

Ogden said, "and I realized I wasn't quick enough to compete at the level that I should be."

He slimmed down to 295 pounds by his sophomore season before playing the balance of his college career at around 310. His quick first step was partially a function of all the basketball he had played since childhood, when he dreamed of becoming a point guard, and his field events for the UCLA track team enhanced his strength.

Playing left tackle meant going against an opponent's best pass rusher each week during a golden age for defensive ends in college football. Ogden faced—and often bested—USC's Willie McGinest, Arizona's Tedy Bruschi, and Washington State's DeWayne Patterson, among many others. He also developed a preference for pulling, which allowed him to showcase his athleticism while winning mismatches against undersized defenders. "It's really cool to come around a corner and see a little defensive back or a linebacker and know I'm about to wear them out," Ogden said. "Those were the fun ones."

Ogden had a blast during UCLA's season opener against Miami in 1995, repeatedly pulling from the left to shuffle in front of running back Karim Abdul-Jabbar on sweeps to the right side. "I talk to Ray Lewis about that game to this day," Ogden said in 2017, referencing the star Hurricanes linebacker who would later become his teammate with the Baltimore Ravens. "I blocked him."

Abdul-Jabbar finished the Bruins' 31–8 victory over Miami with 180 yards and two touchdowns, but it was Ogden who was selected the Pac-10 Conference's Offensive Player of the Week. It was the first time in at least a decade, going back to the start of available records for the award, that an offensive lineman had been honored.

There would be more recognition to come during a senior season in which Ogden became UCLA's first winner of the Outland Trophy, awarded to the nation's top interior lineman. He viewed the award as a team honor, belonging to the players and coaches who helped him develop into such a fearsome presence as well as sports information director Marc Dellins, who helped promote his prowess at a time when football awards voters tended to favor players from the East Coast.

Ogden also excelled in his other sport, winning the 1996 NCAA Division I indoor national championship in the shot put with a personal best of 19.42 meters. But there was no doubt about where his future would lie.

The Ravens made Ogden the first draft pick in their franchise's history, selecting him fourth overall in 1996. He would become an 11-time Pro Bowler and 10-time All-Pro during his 12-year NFL career, helping Baltimore win Super Bowl XXXV in 2000. That triumph came three years after UCLA had retired his No. 79 jersey, signifying that size did matter, along with all the other traits that made Ogden one of the best linemen in school history. "It was good for UCLA," said Ogden, who was elected to both the National Football Foundation and Pro Football halls of fame, "to finally shed that 'gutty little Bruin' image of sorts for never having good offensive linemen."

79 Terry Donahue

Long before Terry Donahue participated in UCLA's first Rose Bowl triumph and broke the Pac-10 Conference record for coaching victories, he was the Improbable Bruin.

Donahue was an undersized, 175-pound linebacker when he left Notre Dame High in the Los Angeles suburb of Sherman Oaks, forced to spend an unhappy season as a walk-on at San Jose State. He returned home and attended L.A. Valley College for a year while taking up boxing in an effort to stay in shape, winning an amateur bout against an opponent who outweighed him by 40 pounds. That prompted his handlers to plan another fight against a young heavyweight named Jerry Quarry.

But those plans were scuttled when Donahue brought home the trophy he had won from his first bout. His father, a doctor, insisted that his son quit fighting. It was back to football for Donahue, who ate and trained his way to 197 pounds before enrolling at UCLA and going out for football. He made the team but only as a walk-on, redshirting a year and serving as a blocking dummy before rising up the depth chart to starting defensive tackle during the 1965 and '66 seasons under coach Tommy Prothro.

There were plenty of times when Donahue still felt anonymous, especially when Prothro would call him Donny Donovan. But Prothro had no trouble recalling his name when Donahue got into a tussle with the Stanford quarterback, much to Prothro's delight. "I'll take losing the opponent's quarterback and Terry Donahue anytime!" UCLA quarterback Gary Beban remembered Prothro cracking.

Donahue's teams won big, going 17–3–1 and upsetting undefeated and top-ranked Michigan State in the 1966 Rose Bowl for UCLA's first bowl victory in school history.

Donahue eventually followed UCLA assistant Pepper Rodgers to Kansas, where Rodgers had become head coach, as a graduate assistant who worked with the freshman team. It was initially an unpaid position, Donahue scraping by thanks to free meals at the players' training table and the meager salary he earned managing an apartment building.

By his second year, Donahue was on the payroll for $7,500 a year as the defensive line coach. After four years at Kansas, having met his wife, Andrea, he returned to UCLA in 1971 along with Rodgers to help coach the offensive line. Donahue remained in that role under Rodgers and his successor, Dick Vermeil, until the latter coach abruptly departed in 1976 to coach the NFL's Philadelphia Eagles.

That prompted UCLA athletic director J.D. Morgan to hire Donahue, at age 31, in what seemed like an act of desperation to many, given Donahue's lack of experience. Morgan explained that the Bruins needed to move quickly with the recruiting period fast approaching, but even Morgan seemed to harbor modest expectations.

"Terry, if you make it till you're 40 here, you'll probably be a good coach by then," Morgan told Donahue the day he promoted him.

In his first game, Donahue faced third-ranked Arizona State and the Sun Devils' gruff coach, Frank Kush, in Tempe in what seemed like the ultimate mismatch. But Donahue was emboldened by the advice of Rodgers, his longtime mentor.

"Donahoo," Rodgers said, repeating the pronunciation he had long used as a way of teasing his protégé, "you and Kush aren't playing. Your players are playing."

The Bruins players were superior that day, beating the Sun Devils 28–10. UCLA started that season 9–0–1, steamrolling its first 10 opponents by a combined score of 371–113 before losses to USC in the final regular-season game and Alabama in the Liberty Bowl.

Donahue's early success gave way to some struggles when his run-oriented teams ran up against more dynamic opponents. After the Bruins went 5–6 in 1979, Donahue hired Homer Smith as his offensive coordinator, heralding a glorious era in which UCLA thrived under quarterbacks Troy Aikman, Steve Bono, Tommy Maddox, Jay Schroeder, and Tom Ramsey.

Donahue remained an ageless wonder, always tan and appearing at ease on the way to winning a UCLA-record 151 games and a Pac-10 record 98 conference games in his 20 seasons. There were five conference titles and the same number of top 10 finishes. The Bruins made 13 bowl appearances under Donahue, winning eight consecutive bowls and four straight New Year's Day bowls. UCLA also won five straight games over USC, including the triumph in 1995 that allowed Donahue to surpass Washington's Don James for the most conference victories in Pac-10 history.

Along the way, Donahue rejected an offer to coach the Atlanta Falcons in 1987 and seriously contemplated becoming coach of the Los Angeles Rams in 1994 before learning they would move to St. Louis for the following season.

His players suspected he might finally leave when he followed them by jumping over the wall adjacent to the practice field in a season-ending ritual in 1995. Donahue wasn't sure himself until the day he announced he was leaving to take a job as an analyst with CBS Sports. UCLA prepared two news releases, one saying he was staying and the other saying he was going.

Donahue left, but not before having become the gold standard for Bruins football coaches. "Ever since I walked onto the UCLA campus to play football, my dream was to be head football coach at UCLA," Donahue said not long after his hiring. "I'd hate to leave this place even for heaven."

80 The Unlikely Rose Bowl

Terry Donahue was never happier to see a banner bearing the name of a Pac-10 Conference rival. It meant that UCLA was headed to the 1983 Rose Bowl, culminating an improbable set of circumstances that all went in the Bruins' favor.

UCLA appeared bound for a midtier bowl after losing to Washington in Seattle in early November. That defeat left the Bruins tied for fourth in the Pac-10 with a 3–1–1 conference record. All sorts of things would need to go their way in the coming weeks for them to make the Rose Bowl after making the eponymous stadium their permanent home for the first time that season.

For starters, UCLA would need to win its last two games, both at home, against Stanford and USC. The rest was out of the Bruins' control. Arizona State, which started 5–0 in the Pac-10, had to lose its last two conference games. Washington, which was 5–1, had to lose to rival Washington State, which was already well on its way to a losing record.

Even Donahue conceded it was unlikely. "Well," Donahue said at the time, "you can always have hope. But I just don't think it can happen. I hope I'm wrong."

The dominoes started to fall the following week. UCLA pulled out a 38–35 victory over Stanford and Arizona State lost to Washington. The Bruins needed to beat rival USC to keep their implausible dream alive. That seemed in doubt when Trojans quarterback Scott Tinsley tossed a one-yard touchdown to Mark Boyer with three seconds left in the game, cutting their deficit to 20–19.

UCLA nose guard Karl Morgan momentarily thought that score had sunk the Bruins. "I didn't realize what the score was," Morgan told the *Los Angeles Times*. "I thought we were trailing and had to hold them. So, when they scored, I thought we'd lost the game. Then, I saw the look in everybody's eyes and I knew we had one more chance."

Morgan made the most of it when the Trojans went for a two-point conversion in an attempt to win the game, sacking Tinsley to preserve his team's triumph. Washington State would also upset Washington, whose roster included eventual UCLA coach Jim Mora. That left the Bruins needing Arizona to beat Arizona State the following week to give them the Rose Bowl berth.

There was also plenty on the line for the Sun Devils, who were seeking their first Pac-10 championship and what would have been their first trip to the Rose Bowl. The odds seemed to favor

Arizona State, which had won 15 of the preceding 17 games in its cross-state rivalry. Michigan coach Bo Schembechler, whose team had already clinched a Rose Bowl berth, watched the Arizona State–Arizona game from the press box in Tucson, assuming he was scouting his bowl opponent.

Donahue decided not to follow the game on television or radio, holing up at his condominium in Palm Springs. "We figured that at about 9:30 [at night] we'd hear," Donahue would later recall. "The doorbell rang then and it was my brother, Dan, holding an Arizona banner. He told us that Arizona was up by 18 with nine minutes to go."

Donahue learned that Arizona had held on for a 28–18 triumph during a subsequent call from former UCLA associate athletic director Angelo Mazzone. Donahue would be going to the Rose Bowl for the first time in his seven years as the Bruins coach. The headline in the *Times* read: "IT'S NO MIRAGE... UCLA FINDS ROSES IN THE DESERT." "I don't feel we backed into it," Donahue said, "because I felt we had the best team in the conference."

UCLA finished the regular season 9–1–1, a tick better than the 9–2 records compiled by Washington and Arizona State. Washington would go on to the Aloha Bowl and Arizona State its hometown Fiesta Bowl. Had Arizona State beaten Arizona, it would have been UCLA going to the Aloha Bowl.

"My wife might be disappointed at missing a trip to Hawaii," Donahue said. "But I told her I'd take her on my own... We'll be up all night boogying."

Schembechler also didn't seem to mind the unlikely turn of events. When the irascible coach learned he would be playing UCLA instead of Arizona State, he told reporters, "That's fine, too."

The Bruins and Wolverines were certainly familiar with each other, having already met twice in the previous year. Michigan had beaten UCLA 33–14 in the 1981 Bluebonnet Bowl before squandering a 21-point lead during a 31–27 loss to the Bruins in September 1982 in Ann Arbor.

There would not be as much drama in the Rose Bowl. UCLA built leads of 10–0 and 24–7 on the way to a 24–14 victory that served as the perfect capper to so much good fortune.

"Sometimes," Donahue said, "it's just your year to have a lot of good things happen."

81 Meet Joe and Josephine Bruin

You never know where Joe Bruin might work his furry magic. An early version of the UCLA mascot costume is stationed inside the school's Athletic Hall of Fame as a static tribute to its frenzied antics through the years. One summer day, the current Joe Bruin stood nearby, waiting for his moment, before springing to life as students walked past.

"You could hear the screams throughout the whole building," said Emily S. Knox, senior art director and curator of the Hall of Fame.

Joe Bruin can usually be found roaming the Rose Bowl, Pauley Pavilion, and other athletic venues. He bared all—save for the fur—during an epic comeback by UCLA's basketball team against Oregon in February 2017, standing next to the basket stanchion and turning his back toward Ducks forward Jordan Bell as Bell prepared to shoot the second of two free throws.

Before Bell could release the shot, Joe Bruin bent over and pulled his shorts down while gyrating and spanking his rear end. Bell somehow made the free throw but UCLA completed its comeback from 19 points down and prevailed 82–79, thanks in part to an equally unlikely assist from its mascot.

UCLA has a proud history of its mascot going wild, perhaps because the early Bruins were actual live bears rented from Hollywood studios in the 1930s. Concerns about safety and handling prompted the Los Angeles Memorial Coliseum to ban the live animals from the stadium in the early 1940s.

UCLA tried again in 1950 with Little Joe Bruin, a female black Himalayan bear cub outfitted with a yellow sweater with "Bruins" spelled out in blue that would bound onto the field, much to the delight of fans. Having grown to 200 pounds within a year, however, the not-so-little mascot was sold to a circus, necessitating the purchase of a new bear from Griffith Park Zoo. A live

Joe and Josephine Bruin prepare to perform with the UCLA cheerleaders.
(Ben Liebenberg via AP Images)

bear always seemed to go over well with fans, if not its handlers. "It was with the cheer squad," recalled linebacker and center John Peterson, captain of the 1954 team. "Everybody got a big bang out of it."

Josephine Bruin made her debut in 1961 after arriving from India as a four-month-old, 18-pound Malayan sun bear who resided in the backyard of UCLA's rally committee chairman. But she suffered a similar fate as Little Joe, sprouting more quickly than expected and being given to the San Diego Zoo in 1962.

Costumed student mascots began appearing in the mid-1950s and took over the sole responsibility of representing UCLA at athletic events a decade later. In 1967, the first costumed Josephine Bruin appeared alongside Joe, making UCLA one of only a few universities to feature both male and female mascots. Various revisions of the costume designs were made over the years, including a stern-looking Joe, a 7-foot-tall version designed by Walt Disney Productions, and a brawny, broad-shouldered adaptation.

UCLA's first mascot wasn't much of a Bruin—or a Bruin at all. A stray dog named Rags that roamed the fledgling Southern Branch of the University of California campus on Vermont Avenue was adopted as the first unofficial mascot in 1919, but students soon wanted something more representative of the Cubs moniker that had been chosen by the student body as an offshoot of sister school California Berkeley's Golden Bear mascot.

Initially, a teddy bear toted by students to games sufficed, before Prunes made his debut in 1922 as the first live bear cub on campus. The unveiling was eventful for all the wrong reasons: Prunes bit a basketball player. UCLA became the Grizzlies in 1924, the new nickname more symbolic of a school that was now awarding four-year degrees and eager to come into its own. But UCLA's entry into the Pacific Coast Conference two years later sent it in search of a new moniker because Grizzlies was taken by the University of Montana, already entrenched in the PCC. UCLA formally became the Bruins in October 1926 after Berkeley student leaders vowed to bequeath that nickname to UCLA while retaining their moniker as the Bears. It's a name that has endured for nearly a century.

82 Randy Cross

Randy Cross was a first team All-American at UCLA, a versatile offensive lineman who could switch between center and guard without missing a block. It might surprise those who watched him manhandle whoever stood in his way that Cross didn't regularly lift weights.

"I absolutely hated lifting weights," Cross said. "I mean, I never lifted weights in high school; I lifted weights whenever a coach was in the weight room and we were supposed to be lifting weights, but when nobody was supervising, I didn't touch them. I just hated it. It was for a silly reason: Every time I lifted, I got sore, so I figured if I didn't lift, I'd never get sore."

Cross had intended to compete in the shot put at UCLA as well as blow defenders off the line of scrimmage after starring in both endeavors at nearby Crespi High. Then a field coach showed him the weight room underneath the stands at Drake Stadium, where he was expected to build strength, and that was the end of his collegiate track and field career. "I looked at [the coach] and I was like, 'There is no way,'" Cross said.

He almost always managed to overpower his counterparts even without hitting the weights. It helped that Cross was 6'4" and weighed as much as 260 pounds, he recalled, "depending on which barbecue or frat party I'd gone to the night before." An even bigger factor was his firm grounding in fundamentals that started in high school under coaches Steve Butler and Morris Freedman, who had both played on UCLA's 1966 Rose Bowl team.

Cross recalled watching that team play USC on television in the family living room as a child. His early love for UCLA was bolstered by a father who took him to games at the Los Angeles Memorial Coliseum and a mother who worked on the school's campus as a manager at a couple of residence halls. He narrowed his college choices to UCLA and Nebraska before deciding to become a Bruin, in part because the Cornhuskers weren't crazy about letting him play two sports.

Cross spent his freshman season in 1972 as a guard on the junior varsity team. In spring practice, he was moved to center because of his agility and was taught to long snap, allowing him to handle punts, field goals, and extra points. He started five games as a sophomore before moving to left guard during a breakthrough junior season in which he started every game, becoming second-team All-Pac-8 Conference and winning UCLA's George W. Dickerson Award for outstanding offensive lineman.

Heading into his senior season in 1975, Cross was asked to man multiple positions. His coaches decided that their team had nine starter-caliber offensive linemen and wanted to rotate them to take advantage of the depth, though Cross remained a constant. He would play guard with the first unit for two or three series before moving to center with the second unit and then back to guard when the first-teamers returned to the field. He preferred guard because it didn't require him to coordinate the offense or worry about getting the ball to the quarterback before he hit someone. "I loved it when I didn't have to snap," Cross said, "because I could just tee off."

UCLA reached the Rose Bowl that season, beating top-ranked Ohio State, just as Cross' career was heading into full bloom. The All-American was selected in the second round of the 1976 Draft by the San Francisco 49ers and then ushered into the weight room to show how much he could bench press in the days before there was a pre-draft combine. "I did 325 pounds twice and one chin-up, one pull-up," Cross said, referring to his less-than-impressive results in the weight room. "Monte Clark, who was the coach that year, looked at me and goes, 'Are you trying to get me fired?' I'm like, 'No, sir, I just don't touch that stuff.' He goes, 'Shit.'"

Cross would go on to lift plenty of weights during a 13-year professional career in which he was a four-time All-Pro, three-time Pro Bowl selection, and part of three teams that won Super Bowls, including his final game in Super Bowl XXIII in 1989. He capitalized on the versatility he had developed at UCLA, playing both center and guard, while showing that being a top-notch lineman goes well beyond being able to rule the weight room.

"You've got to have a little bit of a crazy, nasty edge to you," explained Cross, who was selected to the National Football Foundation College Football Hall of Fame in 2010. "You have to be blessed with a sort of hyperactive protective gene where everybody that carries the ball or handles the ball for your team, you've got to treat them like somebody's picking on your little brother. Then there's the other traits—you've got to have quick hands and quick feet and you've got to keep your head about you when things can get kind of crazy. What I'm describing, I guess, is that you have to be a really stable maniac."

After his playing career ended, Cross became a football analyst for CBS Sports and NBC Sports before co-hosting shows on Sirius NFL Radio. He returned to the Rose Bowl in 2013 when his son Brendan, a quarterback who had spent the previous four years at Wake Forest, completed his college eligibility as a graduate transfer at UCLA. It was a happy homecoming for the father whose love for his alma mater only grew over the years. "In general," Randy said, "UCLA was probably the best thing that's ever happened to me."

83 Bill Kilmer

The headline above a column by famed sportswriter Jim Murray read "Call Him Bill Killer." The words contained a touch of irony considering that for much of William Orland Kilmer's abbreviated UCLA career, it was as if someone else was out to get *him*.

As a sophomore in 1958, the tailback who came to be known as "Wild Bill" broke a wrist in his third game and couldn't play again until the season finale against USC. He made the most of the opportunity, helping the Bruins forge a 15–15 tie.

Kilmer lost most of his junior season after being hit on the ankle with a wayward foul ball while umpiring a UCLA intramural baseball game, of all things. Having broken the ankle, Kilmer had to play the final three games of the 1959 football season in soft shoes that prevented him from running the ball. He showed he was still plenty skilled at passing, throwing for the winning touchdown in the Bruins' 10–3 upset victory over second-ranked and previously undefeated USC.

By the time he completed his career the following season, Kilmer was considered one of the greatest players in UCLA history; the only unknown was how prolific he might have been had he been able to play a full slate of games.

Kilmer's injuries left him with some catching up to do. He wasn't listed as a starter before fall practice his senior year, that designation going to Bobby Smith until Kilmer overtook him on the depth chart.

"I was plenty worried about Smith," Kilmer told the *Los Angeles Times* later that season. "I knew I had to knuckle down. Last year I weighed 208. So this year I cut down on eating and ran a lot more. I got down to 187. I could feel that I was much quicker."

Kilmer's role as the tailback in the single-wing offense was to be UCLA's primary kicker, passer, and rusher. He showed that he was equally adept in each of those roles.

He accounted for four touchdowns in a 27–27 tie with Purdue, including scoring passes that went for 76 and 70 yards to flanker-back Gene Gaines, and outdueled eventual All-Pro quarterback Roman Gabriel during a 7–0 victory over North Carolina State. Kilmer also rushed for 180 yards against Utah, at the time a school record.

The yardage added up to some impressive totals. Kilmer led the nation in total offense in 1960 with a combined 1,889 yards rushing and passing (1,086 passing and 803 rushing). His average of 42.3 yards per punt was also fifth best in the nation. He played in the East-West Shrine Game and Hula Bowl and was most valuable player of the 1961 Chicago All-Star Classic, completing 11 of 20 passes for 173 yards and a touchdown.

Kilmer was selected No. 11 overall in the first round of the 1961 Draft by the San Francisco 49ers and played four seasons each with the 49ers and New Orleans Saints before spending his final eight seasons with the Washington Redskins.

He wasn't done with unfortunate injuries. He plowed his 1957 Chevrolet into the San Francisco Bay after falling asleep while driving up the Bayshore Freeway and missed the end of the 1962 season as well as the entire 1963 season with a fractured leg. He rebounded to become a Pro Bowl selection in 1972 and helped the Redskins reach the Super Bowl in 1973.

84 The Steve Lavin Years

His boss fired, his future uncertain, Steve Lavin found something he could rely on when he became UCLA's interim basketball coach in November 1996: the wisdom of John Wooden. The legendary former Bruins coach, by whom a parade of unfortunate successors would be judged, told Lavin that this was his moment, even if it didn't come as he had hoped.

Lavin was a 32-year-old assistant coach promoted after the sudden dismissal of the man who had brought him to Westwood six years earlier. UCLA ousted coach Jim Harrick over a falsified expense report and a botched cover-up, elevating Lavin into his position for what was expected to be just a short stay. Bruins athletic director Peter Dalis told Lavin as much, explaining that the school's national search for a permanent coach might last a week or a month.

Lavin lasted seven seasons, a wild ride that encompassed five appearances in the Sweet 16 and one trip to the Elite Eight as well as the losing season that cost him his job. There were enough rocky moments interspersed with deep NCAA tournament runs to leave fans disillusioned long before Lavin was fired in March 2003. His teams wildly vacillated between heady success (victories over top-ranked Arizona and Stanford) and head-scratching defeats (a home loss to Cal State Northridge and a 48-point setback against the Cardinal that represented the most lopsided margin in school history).

It appeared as if Lavin might not have that interim tag removed from his title after the Bruins started the 1996–97 season with a 3–3 record. That's when Lavin took the advice of Jim Milhorn, an associate athletic director and former player under Wooden who coaxed Lavin into using the matchup zone that helped the Bruins notch a pivotal victory over Saint Louis. Only two years removed from making $16,000 per year as the restricted-earnings coach, Lavin was made the permanent head coach in February after the Bruins avenged that historic drubbing against Stanford with a 19-point victory over the Cardinal, boosting their record to 13–7.

Lavin also won over the UCLA administration by displaying steely discipline that his predecessor lacked, benching stars Jelani McCoy and Kris Johnson twice for minor infractions and benching forward J.R. Henderson three times. Lavin became the fifth-youngest active coach in the country and the second youngest to follow Wooden at UCLA, trailing only Larry Farmer, who was 30 when he got the job.

With his slicked-back hair and sweat-soaked shirts, Lavin rewarded his bosses with a Pac-10 Conference title and a 12-game winning streak that included point guard Cameron Dollar's finger-roll layup with 1.9 seconds left in overtime that gave UCLA a 74–73 victory over Iowa State in a Midwest Regional semifinal. The Bruins might have advanced to the Final Four had McCoy not sustained a bruised breastbone that limited him to 13 minutes during an 80–72 loss to Minnesota in the regional final.

UCLA went 24–9 the following year, advancing to the Sweet 16, before Lavin guided an exceedingly young team to a 22–9 record in his third season. Those Bruins lost to Detroit Mercy in the first round of the NCAA tournament but featured almost no postseason experience and were missing center Dan Gadzuric, still recovering from knee surgery, largely issuing Lavin a free pass. Three consecutive trips to the Sweet 16 ensued, helping Lavin become the second-fastest UCLA coach to reach 100 victories (in 142 games), trailing only Harrick's 136 games. (For comparison's sake, it took Wooden 144 games to reach that milestone.)

But discontent grew among fans and athletic department officials amid upset losses to the likes of Cal State Northridge and Pepperdine, as well as fourth- and sixth-place finishes in the Pac-10. Dalis acknowledged he courted Rick Pitino as a potential replacement in the middle of the 2000–01 season after Pitino had resigned from the Boston Celtics, an embarrassing development for Lavin. His fate was sealed when the Bruins went 10–19 in 2002–03, triggering criticism from many of the same columnists who had been mesmerized by his improbable rise from volunteer assistant to coach of the most storied program in college basketball.

"Steve Lavin deserves to go," the *Los Angeles Times'* Bill Plaschke wrote. "In his seven years at UCLA, the players stopped learning, the recruits stopped coming, the fans stopped cheering, and the tradition of consistency stopped, period."

Lavin remained classy to the end, which came in a fashion befitting his UCLA career. One day after knocking off top-ranked Arizona in the Pac-10 tournament, the Bruins were outscored 13–1 over the final 3:12 of a loss to Oregon. Lavin's destiny was so obvious that new athletic director Dan Guerrero didn't even have to tell him he was fired. The men merely discussed the future of a program that would not include Lavin over lunch at Junior's Deli in Westwood. Lavin had long figured this was how things were probably going to end for him at UCLA.

"If you take over at 32 years old, [you'd be] naive in thinking this is going to be your final stop and they're going to name the court after you or anything," said Lavin, who would go on to coach at St. John's between stints as a basketball analyst for ESPN, ABC, and Fox. "When you're at UCLA, you know that you get one or two terms and you do the best you can… be grateful that you got to participate in some small way relative to the significant achievements of Coach Wooden, and then you move on with grace and give thanks and look for the next opportunity or gift where you can add some value or do something meaningful."

85 Kevin Love

There was a reason UCLA coach Ben Howland began pursuing Kevin Love when Love was in the eighth grade. In addition to possessing traditional big man skills, the 6'10" McDonald's All-American with size 18 feet could throw a two-handed chest pass from behind one baseline through the basket on the other end of the court. Before Love had even played in his first college game, Howland called him the "best passing and outletting big guy I've seen since [Bill] Walton."

Howland engaged in a fierce recruiting battle over Love that essentially came down to UCLA and North Carolina. Like a perfectly positioned pop-up restaurant, the Bruins had three things going for them: location, location, location. Love's father, Stan, had played at Inglewood Morningside High for eventual UCLA coach Jim Harrick before going on to become a power forward for the Los Angeles Lakers; his mother, Karen, grew up in Costa Mesa in nearby Orange County; and his uncle Mike Love and his cousins, the Wilsons, formed the Beach Boys (Kevin's favorite song by the group was "Good Vibrations").

"They're West Coast people," said Howland, who emerged the big winner when Love signed a letter of intent with UCLA in November 2006.

Love was widely seen as the missing piece the Bruins needed coming off two consecutive Final Fours in which they had been manhandled inside by Florida. Love brought much more than scoring and rebounding. His passing seemed innate for someone whose middle name—Wesley—was a tribute to Wes Unseld, a former Baltimore Bullets teammate of Stan Love's who was a gifted outlet passer.

Bruins fans weren't disappointed when Love scored 22 points and grabbed 13 rebounds against Portland State in his college debut, the most rebounds ever by a UCLA freshman in his first game. Love topped that with a school-freshman-record 16 rebounds during a victory over Maryland while playing with a broken left finger. It seemed like there was nothing Love couldn't do by the time he collected 21 points and 11 rebounds the next day against Michigan State, becoming Most Valuable Player of the O'Reilly Auto Parts CBE Classic.

But there would soon be a touch of discord. Love took only six shots and sat on the bench in the final minutes of a 63–61 loss to Texas in early December, Howland favoring the defensive presence of senior Lorenzo Mata-Real. Howland and Love agreed that Love needed to improve his conditioning. "Game shape is a lot different than practice shape," Love acknowledged afterward. "Hopefully by the Pac-10 [schedule] I'll really be where I want to be."

Love's irritation appeared to grow later that month during victories over Davidson and Idaho State, *Los Angeles Times* writer Diane Pucin noting that "there were at least four times when Love was visibly frustrated, throwing his arms in the air or dawdling on his way back to play defense."

Love got back on track during a sweep of Stanford and California in which he combined for 34 points and 21 rebounds, outplaying Stanford's 7-foot twins Brook and Robin Lopez and Cal's 6'11" DeVon Hardin and 6'10" Ryan Anderson. But lingering holes in Love's defense were apparent during a 72–63 loss to rival USC in which the Trojans' Davon Jefferson drove past and dunked over his Bruins counterpart on the way to 25 points.

An entirely different sort of challenge awaited Love when the Bruins traveled to play Oregon in Eugene, about a two-hour drive from his high school in Lake Oswego. Booing and cursing were the least of the insults inflicted by the crowd at McArthur Court. Signs alluded to past issues with drug abuse and mental illness suffered by Stan Love's cousin Brian Wilson. Other signs called Kevin "fat" and still others questioned his and Stan's sexuality. Howland said Love even received death threats on his cell phone.

Love responded by setting a UCLA freshman record with 18 rebounds to go with 26 points during the Bruins' 80–75 victory. "What more can you ask for?" UCLA guard Darren Collison said after the game. "He's not an average freshman. He plays like a senior."

Love's strong play continued in the NCAA tournament, where he logged 19 points, 11 rebounds, and seven blocked shots during a tight victory over Texas A&M in the second round. His fallaway jump shot from near the foul line with three minutes left tied the score after UCLA had trailed by 10 points earlier in the second half. He set a career high with 29 points during a victory over Western Kentucky in the West Region semifinal and gave Collison a piggyback ride after the Bruins defeated Xavier 76–57 to reach a third consecutive Final Four.

It came with a sadly familiar ending. UCLA fell short, this time a 78–63 loss to Memphis in a national semifinal the fateful blow. "I had to keep my emotions in check," Love said after finishing with 12 points on 4-for-11 shooting and nine rebounds while fighting double teams the entire game, "because we had such a special year."

Love was selected as the Pac-10 Conference Player of the Year, joining Cal's Shareef Abdur-Rahim as the only freshmen to win the award. He was also made the conference's Freshman of the Year and a first-team All-American by the Associated Press after leading the Bruins in scoring (17.5 points per game) and rebounding (10.6). He would become a five-time All-Star with the Minnesota Timberwolves and Cleveland Cavaliers, winning an NBA title with the Cavaliers in 2016, after being the No. 5 pick in the 2008 Draft. He once called his time at UCLA the best year of his life. "It truly has been special," he said.

86 Three Consecutive Final Fours

The sequence is usually shown during any montage of memorable NCAA basketball tournament comebacks.

UCLA guards Cedric Bozeman and Jordan Farmar trap Gonzaga's J.P. Batista in the backcourt, arms flailing wildly. The ball gets poked away and Farmar picks it up, firing a pass to teammate Luc Richard Mbah a Moute on a back cut for the layup that puts UCLA ahead by a point with only eight seconds left.

UCLA's comeback from a 17-point deficit in a West regional semifinal in March 2006 was completed moments later, forcing Gonzaga star Adam Morrison, openly weeping, to pull his jersey over his head and roll over on the court in an attempt to hide his anguish.

"It was unbelievable," UCLA coach Ben Howland said more than a decade after his team's 73–71 triumph at Oracle Arena in Oakland. "It was so loud in that building. It was really an incredible feeling to be a part of that."

It was the flashpoint for the first of three consecutive Final Four appearances that UCLA made under Howland, a high-water mark for the program in the first two-plus decades since its most recent national title in 1995.

Scrappiness was a trait of all three Final Four teams. Center Ryan Hollins, a 60 percent free-throw shooter on the season, made six of six free throws to help the Bruins complete their comeback against Gonzaga. Rather than celebrate his go-ahead basket, Mbah a Moute sprinted back on defense and forced a loose ball that led to a jump ball with the possession arrow pointing in his team's direction.

Lorenzo Mata-Real uses his fingers to make the letter "A" for Atlanta, where the 2007 NCAA Final Four would be held, after UCLA's 68–55 victory over Kansas in the West Regional final sent them to their second straight Final Four. (AP Photo/Marcio Jose Sanchez)

"I just think they were tough," Howland said of his players during a run of consistency that UCLA had not enjoyed since the heyday of John Wooden. "They were hard-nosed, tough, we won with defense first and the guys were incredibly unselfish. It was all about the team and all about winning and they supported each other, they were coachable. It's something that I will always treasure just because it was a special time of greatness."

The Bruins followed their epic comeback against Gonzaga with a grinding 50–45 victory over Memphis that propelled them to their first Final Four since 1995. UCLA won rather easily against Louisiana State in a national semifinal, its 59–45 victory made possible in large part by the Bruins double-teaming ball screens, a tactic they had not previously used all season that surprised the Tigers and led to a flurry of turnovers.

UCLA was back in the national championship game. Unfortunately for the Bruins, so were the Florida Gators, who featured eventual NBA All-Stars Al Horford and Joakim Noah as well as Corey Brewer. UCLA struggled to score and fell 73–57. "We just ran into the Florida buzzsaw," Howland said, uttering words he would be able to repeat a year later.

UCLA lost Farmar, Hollins, and Bozeman for the 2006–07 season, but welcomed the return of Josh Shipp from hip surgery as well as the arrival of freshman guard Russell Westbrook, still far removed from the form that would make him the NBA's Most Valuable Player. The Bruins won the Pac-10 Conference championship for a second consecutive season, going 15–3 in conference play, before suffering their first back-to-back losses of the season heading into the NCAA tournament. Howland didn't mind an early exit from the Pac-10 tournament. "It really gave us some time to regroup," he said.

UCLA's first three games in the NCAA tournament were largely uneventful, leading to a showdown with top-seeded Kansas in the West Regional final. Bruins guard Arron Afflalo poured in a game-high 24 points and a memorable assist on a pass to Shipp that resulted in a three-pointer just before halftime, leading his team to a runaway 68–55 triumph.

That led to a rematch with Florida in a national semifinal, the Gators' roster still graced by Noah, Horford, and Brewer. "Who has everybody come back from an NCAA championship team?" Howland wondered rhetorically. UCLA was no better equipped to handle Florida than it had been a year earlier, the Gators' 76–66 victory a prelude to a second consecutive national championship.

UCLA was left to contemplate a roster that would need to replace the scoring and savvy of Afflalo, who departed for the NBA after his junior season. It helped that the Bruins had won a furious recruiting battle for Kevin Love and could pair the fresh-man forward with Westbrook, who moved into a more prominent role his sophomore season. It was a combination that proved nearly unbeatable, UCLA winning a third consecutive Pac-10 title with a 16–2 conference record while facing a loaded field that included future NBA players James Harden, Brook and Robin Lopez, Chase Budinger, O.J. Mayo, and Jerryd Bayless.

The top-seeded Bruins survived a second-round NCAA tour-nament scare against Texas A&M, with Shipp rising in the lane to block a shot by Donald Sloan in the final seconds, before rela-tively easy victories over Western Kentucky and Xavier sent them to a third consecutive Final Four. Florida was not awaiting this time, but there were three other No. 1 seeds, the first time since the current seeding system started in 1979 that all four top seeds advanced to the Final Four.

UCLA faced a Memphis team that featured Derrick Rose and Chris Douglas-Roberts, who would combine for 53 points to lead the Tigers to a 78–63 triumph. For the Bruins, the setback was every bit as deflating as those losses to Florida, maybe even more so given that it was their third consecutive defeat on college basketball's biggest stage. "This one hurt more than the others," Collison said after scoring a season-low two points before fouling out.

The Bruins had repeatedly reached the pinnacle only to stumble, three consecutive 30-win teams and trips to the Final Four leaving Howland with an empty feeling. "It was disappointing," Howland said after his team became the first to depart three straight Final Fours without a title since Duke from 1988 to '90. "I really wanted to win one in the worst way."

Howland would soon field a consoling phone call from Michigan State coach Tom Izzo, who told Howland that it was more amazing to reach three consecutive Final Fours than to win one national championship. "I listened to him," Howland said, "but I would have liked to have won one."

87 Meet at *The Bruin*

For all the back-and-forth intrigue of the UCLA-USC rivalry, with the archenemies finding increasingly creative ways to upstage each other, there was one area in which the Trojans undeniably trumped the Bruins for more than half a century: USC could delight in Tommy Trojan, the statue erected in 1930 that served as the ultimate symbol of campus pride.

UCLA had nothing of the sort.

That changed on September 30, 1984, when the 50th Anniversary Committee organized by the UCLA Alumni Association unveiled *The Bruin* in Westwood Plaza (later renamed Bruin Plaza) as a snarling testament to school spirit. Measuring 10 feet long, 6 feet tall, and 3 feet across, *The Bruin* weighed more than two tons and was said at the time of its construction to be the largest bear sculpture in the United States.

The open-mouthed bronze statue cost $47,000—$37,000 to cast and an additional $10,000 for artist Billy Fitzgerald's fee—and struck an imposing presence, planting its four feet on an elevated pedestal. *The Bruin* was meant to display a fluid forward movement representing the strength and progress of UCLA.

"You'll notice that it's formidable," Alexander Hamilton, a graduate of the Class of 1924 and a founding member of the Alumni Association, told the *Los Angeles Times*. "It's the antithesis of fragility."

The vicious statue hardly resembled school mascot Joe Bruin, which cast a far friendlier appearance at the time. The Bruin, located across from the Ackerman student union, became a prominent campus landmark and gathering place. It led to a common refrain heard countless times among both students and alumni in the years to come: "Meet me at the Bruin."

The statue became a symbol of hope and possibilities. A giant wreath of roses was placed around the Bruin's head prior to the 1986 Rose Bowl, a 45–28 UCLA victory over Iowa. Students have long been known to rub the statue's back paw for good luck before final exams.

Of course, the Bruin has also unwittingly become part of the epic series of pranks between UCLA and USC that has included the Trojans' stealing of the Victory Bell in 1941 and "USC" being burned into campus lawns in Westwood. A massive new statue required a nearly around-the-clock security detail during rivalry week, prompting students to camp out while guarding their precious talisman.

At one point, the Bruin was covered with a protective blue-and-gold tarp reading, "THE BRUIN BEAR IS HIBERNATING," with Rally Committee members standing at the ready to defend its well-being. But in 2009, some ruffians from USC broke through the tarp and drenched the statue with red and yellow paint, resulting in thousands of dollars in damage. That led to the construction of a wooden structure that housed *The Bruin* before the rivalry game, with security cameras monitoring the surrounding area.

UCLA students were no innocents themselves, having vandalized Tommy Trojan with various schemes, including dousing it in blue and gold paint and repeatedly taking its sword. But the construction of *The Bruin* put UCLA on equal footing with its rival, leading to the game before the game and a new source of one-upping each another.

88 Ducky Drake

For every ankle he taped and elbow he iced, Elvin C. "Ducky" Drake soothed a psyche.

Whether it was homesickness, lovesickness, fear of losing playing time, or anxiety over an assortment of other issues associated with playing major college sports while attending one of the top public universities in the country, Drake was there for thousands of UCLA athletes over a career that spanned parts of seven decades. Perhaps it was no coincidence that he had been born in Friend, Nebraska, of all places.

"A lot of people think maybe all you do in the training room is tape ankles and so forth," the longtime track coach and trainer told the *San Bernardino Sun-Telegram* in 1976. "But in the training room, you can do an awful lot for the mental condition of athletes. Sometimes I know more about the kids than their coaches do. They'll talk to me about things they won't talk to their coaches about. I probably get them at the times they're lowest mentally. They have to have someone to talk to."

Drake always seemed to know what to say. When star basketball player Larry Farmer, a native of Denver, was suffering from severe homesickness during his first year on campus, Drake sat and talked to him about Colorado, which was also his home state. Farmer went on to be a part of teams that went 89–1 while winning three national championships.

"Ducky was just like the rock of the program," said Jamaal Wilkes, who went by Keith Wilkes when he was a forward for the Bruins in the early 1970s. "That's the best way I could describe him. He was very understated, like coach [John] Wooden. He didn't want to draw a lot of interest to himself but he was kind of like the rock of the program."

Drake would also get players out of being caught between a rock and a hard place. One time, guard Lucius Allen came back to his hotel room past curfew and found Drake asleep in his bed. Drake never told Wooden, but Allen spent the night on the floor. "If Ducky caught you doing something wrong, he never told the coach," Farmer told the *Sun-Telegram*. "But he would scare you so much that you'd never do it again."

Drake also was beloved for his diligence in the basics of his job requirements. He helped Heisman Trophy–winning quarterback Gary Beban quickly return to a game against USC in 1967 despite bruised ribs that ached whenever he twisted his body or took a hit, and became known for his tirelessness in treating every ailment.

"I've had a pulled hamstring a couple of times, and the first person I go to see is Ducky," Cormac Carney, a receiver for the team that won the 1983 Rose Bowl, told the *Los Angeles Times*. "The other guys would want to put you on the machines, but Ducky will just do a rubdown and work on it for hours and hours. He's not lazy. He'll just keep working on it. You just lie there and fall asleep. He's something."

Drake was a man of many talents and responsibilities. He was also involved with the athletes' training table, keeping team buses running on time, and travel plans, in addition to the curfew checks that occasionally required him to hop into a strange bed.

Drake told *Ventura County Star* columnist Woody Woodburn that his nickname came from his last name also being the word for a male duck. His friends had called him Ducky since childhood. Drake first arrived at UCLA as a student in 1923, when the school was known as the Southern Branch and its campus was located at Vermont Avenue and Santa Monica Boulevard. The sports teams' mascot back then was the Grizzlies.

Drake had a job delivering newspapers and would practice around his work schedule. His schedule became even more crammed during meets, when he would run the 880, mile, two mile, and relay, becoming team captain as a junior in 1926. Drake returned to UCLA as coach Harry Trotter's assistant in 1929. He went on to become cross-country coach (1935–42) and freshman track coach (1935–45) before succeeding Trotter as the head track coach in 1947. He was already five years into his career as head athletic trainer by then and gave up coaching in 1964 to focus full time on training, saying he wanted to help more athletes. His 19-year record as track coach was 107–48, and included the school's first NCAA title in the sport in 1956.

Drake always said his biggest thrill was having two of his decathletes, Rafer Johnson and C.K. Yang, finish one-two in the 1960 Olympics in Rome, an unprecedented accomplishment for a coach and a university. Drake's allegiances weren't torn. "They were both my boys," Drake said at the time. Yang's mistake was committing a foul on his best effort in the shot put. In the last event, Johnson only needed to stay close to Yang in the 1,500 to protect his lead in points and win the gold medal. That's exactly what happened, with Johnson finishing 1.2 seconds behind his UCLA teammate.

UCLA named its 12,000-seat track stadium in Drake's honor in 1973, a year after his retirement. "Naturally, it's a big thrill," said Drake, who would remain a fixture on campus until his death from a heart attack in 1988 at age 85. "But it makes me a little embarrassed. I wonder if I really deserve it. I think of all the things that went undone, but, perhaps, there wasn't enough time. But then you have to be mighty proud that someone thinks you deserve it."

89 Eat at John Wooden's Breakfast Spot

The same scene would repeat itself every time John Wooden stepped into his favorite breakfast spot. Paul Ma, owner of VIP's Cafe, a cozy diner along Ventura Boulevard in Tarzana that was only a short drive from Wooden's condominium, would act like he had not saved the coach's preferred booth.

Which, of course, he always had.

"Coach, he didn't like for us to treat him special," Ma said. "Coach is very humble. He just wanted to be treated like a regular customer, so I had to play some tricky stuff. I didn't want to let him know, but whenever he got here he could sit down right away."

Wooden would arrive around 8:00 each morning, settling into Table No. 2, a booth one spot over from the corner of the restaurant and across from a counter lined with stools that faced the kitchen. The wood laminate table was marked on its outermost edge with a "2," just as each table was adorned with its own number. There was symmetry between where Wooden sat and what he ate. Ma said Wooden preferred to order the No. 2, which was two eggs, two strips of bacon, and a sliced English muffin. The coach liked his eggs over easy, and his bacon brittle, and would pair them with hot tea. In a ritual that delighted Ma, Wooden would place his spoon over his teacup and squeeze out a spoonful of honey before placing the spoon into the cup and stirring it. "It was really wonderful," Ma said. "It cheered me up."

The coach's dining companions included his daughter Nan and other family members, as well as various former players and coaching colleagues. He was also usually accompanied by Tony Spino, the UCLA trainer who helped care for Wooden in his final years. Cafe regulars always felt like they were dining with Wooden because of his graciousness. Ma said he never saw the coach turn down a request for an autograph or to pose for a picture even on days when he wasn't feeling well. Pictures of Wooden standing alongside friends and luminaries still adorn the walls of the cafe to this day. One is of a smiling Wooden, holding a blue California license plate reading "UCLA WON."

Wooden first ate at VIP's a few years before Ma became owner in 1998. Ma, who is of Chinese descent but immigrated to the United States from Spain, didn't know Wooden from a wooden spoon, unaware of his wild success at UCLA or his famed Pyramid of Success until the previous owner made the introduction. It was not until after Wooden gave Ma one of his books that the cafe owner began to appreciate who was in his midst. "At the beginning, I thought he was all about basketball," Ma said, "but after I read his book, I found out he is a coach for life, not only a coach for sports. I really love his philosophy."

VIP's is open for breakfast and lunch, seven days a week, with one exception. Ma closed the cafe so that all of his employees could attend Wooden's memorial service in 2010. Ma also honored his most famous patron with a plaque above his preferred spot that reads "Coach John Wooden's favorite booth." Patrons still clamor to sit there, with Ma noting that many have traveled from Indiana, Wooden's home state. "Even after Coach passed away," Ma said, "they still come here, call me before they come and say, 'Hey, can you reserve the booth, Coach's booth?'" Those who lose out can at least order his favorite meal, which has been renamed "Coach Wooden's special" while still being is listed as the No. 2: two eggs, two strips of bacon, and an English muffin. Just the way Coach liked it.

90 John Barnes

By the time he started what came to be known as "The Game," UCLA quarterback John Barnes owned a more extensive resume than many of his veteran coaches.

There was the season he had spent at Saddleback College in hopes of going on to greater things, resulting in nothing more than a weeklong stopover at Long Beach State. From there it was on to Western Oregon, an NAIA Division II school where coaches informed Barnes that his future was at tight end. That prompted a move to UC Santa Barbara, where he thrived as the starting quarterback, throwing for 2,100 yards and 23 touchdowns, only for the school to announce it was killing its football program.

The next day, beer in hand while seated on the sofa, Barnes watched on television as UCLA quarterback Tommy Maddox announced he was turning pro. It was the only inducement Barnes needed. He put on a suit and met with Bruins coaches in the spring of 1992, dropping back to show his footwork while in dress shoes.

The next few months weren't storybook stuff, even after Barnes was allowed to join the team. "I was quite clear when he asked me for a chance to walk on," Bruins coach Terry Donahue told the *Los Angeles Daily News*. "I told him, 'It's very, very doubtful you will ever get a chance to actually play.'"

Barnes spent a week living out of his car except at night, when he slept on a friend's couch, and rode his bike down Wilshire Boulevard to be with his new teammates. He was so low on the depth chart during spring ball that his responsibilities included holding the dummy during tackling and blocking drills. An injury to starter Rob Walker did nothing to change Barnes' status, Donahue reminding him that he would remain the fifth-stringer because the scholarship players needed their repetitions.

But the dream inside Barnes never died. As he rode his bike home every night, stopping it with his feet because the brakes didn't work, Barnes envisioned what it would be like to play and how he would handle it.

He got his chance against Washington State after several quarterbacks ahead of him were injured, and it didn't go well. Barnes turned the ball over twice and was replaced in the fourth series of an eventual defeat. "He walked back to sit next to me on the bus," Charlie Smith, then a student manager, told the *Los Angeles Times*, "and you could tell he had been crying, his career was over."

Not even close. Barnes came off the bench the next week against Arizona State to complete nine of 13 passes, albeit while facing a prevent defense in another UCLA loss. He also sparked an upset victory over Oregon by throwing a 28-yard touchdown pass to receiver J.J. Stokes. Along the way, Barnes confided in receivers coach Rick Neuheisel that he had a learning disability that was preventing him from mastering the intricacies of the team's offense. They worked out a system that helped Barnes memorize the plays, with Neuheisel twisting his body into the form of a "Y" or a "Z" to remind the quarterback of his primary receivers.

Eventually, Barnes was told to simply nod to Stokes to signify he intended to hit him on a deep pass. That would prove pivotal during UCLA's season-ending rivalry game against USC, one Barnes had attended the year before as a fan after his girlfriend slipped him her student ID through a fence, allowing him to gain admission. This time, Barnes was on the Rose Bowl field as the starting quarterback. And his team was losing big, USC taking a 31–17 lead into the fourth quarter.

That's when Barnes cemented his legacy. He connected with Stokes for a 29-yard touchdown early in the fourth quarter before hitting his favorite target again on a 59-yard pass play that set up the tying score. The onetime fifth-stringer was becoming a leading man. "The confidence he exuded in the huddle that day," left tackle Jonathan Ogden recalled, "I couldn't have told you that he hadn't been there before."

Facing third-and-4 at their own 10-yard line, Barnes and Stokes acknowledged their intentions to one another, Stokes giving Barnes a hand signal to let him know he was running a streak route and Barnes nodding in return. Neuheisel recognized the quarterback's signal but was stunned by its timing. "I didn't think he would do it on third down on our 10-yard line!" Neuheisel told the *Times*. "I about died."

UCLA survived because of the play, a 90-yard touchdown that included a medium pass and a long, zigzagging run that gave the Bruins the go-ahead score. USC scored a touchdown with 41 seconds to play before Bruins linebacker Nkosi Littleton knocked away a pass on the two-point conversion attempt, preserving a most improbable 38–37 triumph for Barnes and his team that made a 6–5 season unusually special.

"All this taught me that you never give up, that good things will happen if you hang in there long enough," Barnes told the *Times* a decade after having thrown for 385 yards on that afternoon, including 204 during the fourth-quarter comeback.

His college career complete, he was soon awarded a scholarship for the balance of his senior year. Barnes played football professionally in Italy for a year before working in the computer industry in the Bay Area. He would experience one more moment of glory. In 1994, Barnes pulled on an Alabama jersey, fielded a kickoff, and stuck the ball into the belly of actor Tom Hanks. "Forrest, run!" Barnes shouted in the movie *Forrest Gump*, the second Hollywood ending of his career.

91 First to 100 NCAA Team Titles

After the UCLA women's water polo team held on for a 5–4 victory over Stanford on May 13, 2007, at the Joint Forces Training Base in Los Alamitos, California, Bruins players gleefully pushed coach Adam Krikorian into the pool. This wasn't just any national championship celebration. It was the 100th NCAA team title in UCLA's history, making the Bruins the first school in the country to hit triple digits in championships.

The achievement was all the more remarkable considering that when UCLA had won its first NCAA title, in men's tennis in 1950, it had some serious catching up to do. Yale had won the first NCAA team championship 53 years earlier, in the spring of 1897. The Bruins also faced a steep uphill climb considering that Stanford and USC were more firmly established powerhouse programs on the West Coast.

But no one would have more championship fun than UCLA starting with the latter half of the 20th century. It began with a slew of upsets, including Bruins co-captain Glenn Bassett defeating 1951 Wimbledon champion Dick Savitt of Cornell on the way to that first UCLA team title the previous year. "I remember we were just so happy that it was darn beyond description," said Bassett, who would become a trendsetter as the Bruins men's tennis team went on to win the school's first five NCAA titles.

There were several reasons widely touted for UCLA's across-the-board dominance. The school benefited from near-perfect weather, a picturesque campus, a strong academic reputation, and a vast pool of local high school talent. There was also what felt like a palpable carryover effect from one winning UCLA team to another.

UCLA'S NCAA Team Championships*

Men's sports (75)

Baseball (1): 2013
Basketball (11): 1964, 1965, 1967, 1968, 1969, 1970, 1971, 1972, 1973, 1975, 1995
Golf (2): 1988, 2008
Gymnastics (2): 1984, 1987
Outdoor Track & Field (8): 1956, 1966, 1971, 1972, 1973, 1978, 1987, 1988
Soccer (4): 1985, 1990, 1997, 2002
Swimming (1): 1982
Tennis (16): 1950, 1952, 1953, 1954, 1956, 1960, 1961, 1965, 1970, 1971, 1975, 1976 (co), 1979, 1982, 1984, 2005
Volleyball (19): 1970, 1971, 1972, 1974, 1975, 1976, 1979, 1981, 1982, 1983, 1984, 1987, 1989, 1993, 1995, 1996, 1998, 2000, 2006
Water Polo (11): 1969, 1971, 1972, 1995, 1996, 1999, 2000, 2004, 2014, 2015, 2017

Women's sports (41)

Golf (3): 1991, 2004, 2011
Gymnastics (7): 1997, 2000, 2001, 2003, 2004, 2010, 2018
Indoor Track & Field (2): 2000, 2001
Outdoor Track & Field (3): 1982, 1983, 2004
Soccer (1): 2013
Softball (11): 1982, 1984, 1985, 1988, 1989, 1990, 1992, 1999, 2003, 2004, 2010
Tennis (2): 2008, 2014
Volleyball (5): 1984, 1990, 1991, 2011, 2018
Water Polo (7): 2001, 2003, 2005, 2006, 2007, 2008, 2009

*As of Publication

"There's always a buzz in this department," Bruins athletic director Dan Guerrero told *USA Today*. "And the expectations here are very, very high. We expect to win national championships."

The Bruins rarely disappointed. UCLA enjoyed so much success that John Wooden won 10 championships as coach of the men's basketball team and wasn't even close to the winningest coach on his own campus. That distinction went to Al Scates, the coach of a men's volleyball team that won 19 NCAA titles between 1970 and 2006.

Wooden's championship run was unprecedented in his sport, his 10 titles covering a 12-year span, including seven straight from 1967 to 1973. Legends such as Lew Alcindor (later Kareem Abdul-Jabbar), Bill Walton, and Gail Goodrich graced the basketball team's roster during its glorious run.

But UCLA's sprint to 100 titles was largely fueled by more anonymous athletes in lower-profile sports. Since Wooden retired in 1975, the men's basketball team has won only one additional title, in 1995. There is also no official NCAA Division I champion in football. That has left most of the winning to other teams. UCLA pulled off a double-double in 2000–01 and 2004–05 when its men's and women's water polo teams won NCAA titles in the same calendar year.

The Bruins women's teams were instrumental in the school reaching triple digits in championships. They contributed 30 of the first 100 NCAA titles over a 25-year span after becoming official members of the NCAA starting with the 1981–82 season. In the five years immediately preceding UCLA's milestone, the school's women's teams outpaced the men, 10 titles to three.

The women's water polo team won UCLA's 99th NCAA title in 2006, leading school officials to make plans for a giant blue-and-gold banner commemorating No. 100. They wouldn't get to unfurl it until the following year, when the women's water polo team won a third consecutive championship.

UCLA celebrated its 100th title with a special trophy approved by the NCAA, similar to the one the organization gives to team champions, only significantly larger. It rests inside the school's Athletic Hall of Fame.

"It's pretty special and it's great to be No. 100," Courtney Mathewson told the *Los Angeles Times* after scoring a game-high three goals during the Bruins' victory over Stanford in 2007, "but there's going to be 100 more."

92 Anthony Barr

For two years, Anthony Barr was UCLA's "F-back," a hybrid tight end–wide receiver–running back whose role was to create mismatches. It's just as confusing as it sounds. "It's funny because I still don't know what it is either," Barr quipped more than three years after his final college game.

Playing the position made Barr wonder whether his college was the right fit. He seemed destined to go to Notre Dame, having been born in South Bend, Indiana. There was also the matter of his father and uncle both having played running back for the Fighting Irish and his mother having attended St. Mary's College right across U.S. Highway 31 from Notre Dame.

Barr picked UCLA because he liked coach Rick Neuheisel and offensive coordinator Norm Chow and clicked with the recruits who were in his class. But he questioned his choice almost from the start of his college career. He didn't have a position coach his first season, attending meetings with Chow in the quarterbacks room. The offensive coordinator would quickly touch on Barr's responsibilities before switching his attention back to the quarterbacks. "I didn't really have a clear understanding as to what my role was on the team or where I fit in and I was kind of lost," Barr said.

Barr played sporadically, making a handful of carries and catches, but didn't come close to producing the expected impact. When Neuheisel was fired in November 2011 after a 50–0 loss to USC, Barr contemplated an exit strategy. "That's when I started thinking like, maybe this isn't for me, maybe football isn't where I belong, maybe I need to switch schools," Barr said.

The arrival of Jim Mora as Neuheisel's replacement changed the fortunes of the program and the trajectory of Barr's career. The coach and player agreed that Barr would switch to linebacker, allowing the 6'5", 230-pound junior to feast on his athletic advantage over linemen and fullbacks. Barr saw a lot of similarities between running back and linebacker—find the hole, attack the hole, and then make the tackle instead of running through it.

Barr's transition was eased by fellow linebacker Eric Kendricks, who taught him the nuances of the position, and he was pushed by linebackers coach Jeff Ulbrich and strength coach Sal Alosi, each of whom demanded maximum effort and held him accountable for any slipups.

Barr started low on the depth chart but rose quickly. "I didn't like being third string and being kind of the cleanup guy getting the B.S. minutes in practice," Barr said, "but I took a liking to it pretty quickly. I felt like I was making an impact almost right away and I felt like after the first couple of weeks at the position, I was saying, 'This might have been the best move I made in my career.'"

By the third day of fall camp, Barr had won the job as starting outside linebacker. Not even a broken finger could stop him from a monster season in which he led the team in sacks (13.5) and tackles for loss (21.5) while ranking second in tackles (83). His finest moment might have come in the rivalry game against USC when he drilled Trojans quarterback Matt Barkley on a blitz in the final minutes of UCLA's 38–28 victory at the Rose Bowl. Barkley fell on his right shoulder, suffering a sprain, and would not appear in another game during his senior season.

"It was one of our new blitzes we had put in," Barr recalled. "It was an interesting front and I think the offensive line was confused by it and they just turned me loose and I didn't get didn't touched and I got a clean shot."

Anthony Barr sacks USC quarterback Matt Barkley during the second half of a 2012 game in Pasadena, which UCLA won 38–28. (AP Photo/Mark J. Terrill)

UCLA finished the season 9–5, reaching the Pac-12 Conference title game before losing to Stanford. Barr's NFL stock was soaring in the wake of a season in which he had become a first-team All-Pac-12 selection, but he decided to return for his senior year because he was enjoying college so much and felt like he wasn't ready for professional football.

Another standout season followed, with Barr making a career-high 11 tackles against Nebraska to help the Bruins complete an emotional comeback from a 21–3 deficit less than a week after teammate Nick Pasquale died from injuries sustained while being hit by a car. Barr finished the season with 10 sacks, 20 tackles for loss, and six forced fumbles, winning the Lott IMPACT Trophy as college's top defensive player in character and performance during a season in which UCLA went 10–3.

"I was like, 'Wow, I'm winning a college football award,'" Barr said of his reaction, "which, two years earlier, I didn't think that was possible."

Barr was selected ninth overall in the 2014 Draft by the Minnesota Vikings, becoming a Pro Bowl selection in 2015, '16, and '17. He was joined by a familiar face in 2015, when the Vikings also drafted Kendricks, his former teammate.

"I think it's kind of funny because when I first became a linebacker in college, he was kind of showing me what to do and where to go," Barr said. "Then when he got to the NFL, it was my turn to help him out and give him a few pointers here and there. So it kind of came full circle and it's been real fun and enjoyable."

93 Johnathan Franklin

The tailback who would go on to become UCLA's all-time leading rusher once fought just to get a single carry. In practice.

Johnathan Franklin arrived in Westwood designated as an athlete, meaning he did not have a specialty and could play a wide range of positions. He was first slotted as a safety before realizing he wanted to go back to running back because it was a position he had starred at while playing for nearby Dorsey High. Franklin approached the Bruins' running backs coach, Wayne Moses, who agreed to give him an opportunity. There just weren't many chances in practice.

Franklin was fifth on the depth chart, trailing Milton Knox, Derrick Coleman, Christian Ramirez, and Chane Moline. For the first few weeks, Franklin and Knox, a fellow freshman, would get only one rep each at tailback in practice. "We used to get pissed off," said Franklin, who questioned whether he had made the right decision by attending UCLA. "We used to say a few choice words, but we just kept each other afloat. We kept pushing each other and we just said, 'Let's keep working hard, let's keep competing, and whatever rep we get, let's just take advantage of it.'" Their dedication was rewarded as their reps increased from one to two to three.

Fast but compact at 5'11" and 195 pounds, Franklin became a part-time starter as a redshirt freshman in 2009, scoring a 12-yard touchdown on his first carry against San Diego State. Big rushes would become an early trend as Franklin compiled 100-yard games against Kansas State and California while leading the team with 556 yards rushing, the sixth-best total by a Bruins freshman. Franklin followed it with an even stronger sophomore season, though he temporarily lost the starter's job to Coleman. Franklin still managed to lead the team with 1,127 yards rushing, becoming the school's first 1,000-yard rusher since Chris Markey in 2006.

Franklin continued to run wild during his junior season, averaging a career-high 5.9 yards per carry on the way to a team-high 976 yards. That set the stage for his record-breaking senior season in 2012 after the arrival of coach Jim Mora. Franklin said that's when Gaston Green's school record of 3,731 yards rushing from 1984 to '87 finally seemed breakable. "The vision came within reach my senior season," Franklin said, "when I believed in myself and had great mentors and my faith became my foundation and I was truly focused."

Franklin entered his final college season needing 1,062 yards to make the record his own. He looked like he might get there by midseason after opening with back-to-back 200-yard rushing games against Rice (214) and Nebraska (217). Franklin entered UCLA's game against Arizona on November 3, 2012, at the Rose Bowl needing only 21 yards to pass Green. He did it on the Bruins' first possession, zipping past two defenders after taking the handoff before blowing by another would-be tackler about 10 yards downfield en route to a 37-yard touchdown run. Franklin took a knee as he always did after scoring, consumed with prayer and unaware of the significance of the moment.

"Shaq Evans and another teammate came up and were like, 'You broke the record!' before it even hit me," Franklin recalled. "They just hugged me and I walked to the sideline and got so much love from my teammates and when I got the bench, Coach Mora was like, 'No, this is your moment. Get out there!'"

Mora called timeout so that the home crowd could shower Franklin with an ovation. A video tribute from Green was then shown on the video board. "They played the video and I was like, 'Oh my gosh.' It was just so humbling," Franklin said. "A freshman who started [fifth] on the depth chart and from starting and losing my job and so much adversity from struggling and fumbling the ball and so many doubters to getting to that moment it was like, wow, dreams do exist, you know?"

Franklin wasn't finished, going on to run for 171 yards during a victory over archrival USC as well as 194 yards in the Pac-12 Conference championship game against Stanford. He finished the season with 1,734 yards and nine 100-yard games, both new school records, while becoming a finalist for the Doak Walker Award that went to the nation's top running back.

Franklin's final tally of 4,369 yards rushing for his career placed him fifth on the all-time Pac-12 list. He was selected in the fourth round of the 2013 NFL Draft by the Green Bay Packers and was off to a promising start when he suffered a career-ending neck injury while returning a kickoff late in his rookie season. His charismatic personality having earned him the nickname "The Mayor," Franklin worked for the Packers before Notre Dame hired him as an administrator for student welfare and development. He returned home in September 2016 to work for the Los Angeles Rams in community and external relations.

His UCLA career was a story of dedication and perseverance, from turning one practice rep into an all-time school record. "It was disappointing at times," Franklin said of his humble beginnings, "but if you stay focused, who knows what can happen?"

94 Walk the Concourse Inside Pauley Pavilion

The renovation of Pauley Pavilion involved more than cushier seats, a high-definition video scoreboard, and a redesigned court. It also included new historic exhibits inside the enclosed concourse that are deserving of a leisurely stroll before or after a game.

Unveiled upon the reopening of Pauley Pavilion for the 2013–14 season, the centerpiece of the exhibits are three large glass-enclosed display cases on one side of the arena known as "Wooden Way" that tell the story of John Wooden as a teacher, coach, and legend.

The first case, dubbed "The Teacher," details Wooden's early life before arriving at UCLA and his initial success coaching the Bruins in the men's gym, a rudimentary arena nicknamed the "B.O. Barn" for its close quarters that produced sweaty aromas whenever it was packed. There are black-and-white photographs of Wooden from his childhood and quotes that encapsulate his values and virtues. "You can never acquire happiness," Wooden says in one quote on display, "without giving yourself to someone else without the expectation of getting something back." The backstory of Wooden's courtship of Nellie Riley that resulted in their marriage in 1932 is also described. "I met Nellie Riley freshman year at a carnival… she was the prettiest girl I'd ever seen… I don't know why she liked me, she was probably the most popular girl in school, but she did and I'm grateful for it." The most visually appealing aspect of the display is a giant wooden Pyramid of Success and a rudimentary black-and-white television set.

The second case, labeled "The Coach," examines Wooden's heyday at UCLA alongside star players such as Lew Alcindor and Bill Walton. A television shows highlight videos of each of his 10 championships next to photos of every team. There is the original chalkboard Wooden used in Pauley Pavilion, complete with two plays drawn up by the coach, as well as his letterman's jacket and half of the center circle that was used inside Pauley Pavilion prior to its $136-million renovation.

Wooden lists some of his most memorable games in a handwritten letter included in the display and tells the story of giving Walton a choice between keeping the beard he had grown during a 10-day break and remaining a member of the team. "I looked at him and said politely, 'Bill, I have a great respect for individuals who stand up for those things in which they believe. I really do. And the team is going to miss you,'" Wooden recalls. "Bill went to the locker room and shaved the beard off before practice began." The story of Pauley Pavilion is also told, including photos of the original construction as well as the renovations. The building was designated a California Historical Landmark, one of the reasons it was not razed but instead renovated and expanded to include the new surrounding concourse.

The third case, called "The Legend," is dedicated to Wooden's life after his 1975 retirement, when he became a widely coveted speaker who was known as a life coach. "Clearly, the championships created a platform for him," Andy Hill, one of Wooden's players who went on to a successful career in the entertainment industry before becoming an author and motivational speaker, said in a quote included in the display, "but it's quite unique that a prominent public figure retires from a professional career and starts a second career in which he was more successful than he was in the first; that was the case with Coach." The seat Wooden occupied during UCLA games in his final years is on display, as is a large section of what was dedicated as Nell and John Wooden Court in 2003. A television shows tributes to Wooden's greatness as a person next to a banner listing all 11 of the school's national championships in basketball, including its most recent in 1995.

The concourse also serves as an extension of the school's Athletic Hall of Fame through other exhibits. Twenty-four "Incredible moment" displays detail memorable events such as UCLA's freshman basketball team, led by Alcindor, defeating its varsity counterparts in 1965. Giant photos of greats from the basketball, volleyball, and gymnastics teams that competed inside Pauley Pavilion adorn one entryway across from a welcome wall listing all of the school's national championship teams. There are displays for each of UCLA's All-Americans in each of the six sports that have called Pauley Pavilion home through the years.

Large block letters affixed to one wall declaring "Champions made here" do not exaggerate. Only a few steps outside of the Northeast Entrance stands a bronzed statue of Wooden with his arms folded, game program in hand. One of his guiding philosophies is included in an accompanying plaque: "Success is peace of mind, which is a direct result of self-satisfaction in knowing you made the effort to become the best of which you are capable."

95 Eric Kendricks

Brothers being hard on each other isn't always a bad thing. It helped make Eric Kendricks the leading tackler in UCLA history.

He was barely out of the crib when his sibling Mychal, who was 17 months older, tussled with him in front of the Christmas tree. The family has it on video. Their fights weren't always playful, Mychal leaving scars below his little brother's left eye and on the back of his head. Eric got his revenge, twice casting a rock that knocked out Mychal's front teeth. They were exchanges that gave Eric toughness before he played his first down of football.

Eric's relentlessness came from another older brother who attended many of Eric's practices and games. As soon as the ball was snapped, Chad Kendricks could be heard across the field. "I would just hear his voice over everyone else's screaming, 'Run to the ball!'" Eric recalled. Failing to make the play had consequences beyond letting the other team get positive yardage.

"He would give me crap for it," Eric said of Chad. "I hated it and I felt like he was singling me out at the time, but I'm more thankful for that than just about anything because even when I'm tired and I'm gassing for breath, I feel like as soon as the ball is snapped, my mentality is to get the ballcarrier."

Eric's lifelong love of UCLA came from his father. Marvin Kendricks was the Bruins' leading rusher during the 1970 and '71 seasons who went on to play in the Canadian Football League. His struggles with crack cocaine addiction that he eventually overcame caused him to be an inconsistent presence in his sons' lives, but he always imparted his love of UCLA whenever he was around. "I grew up knowing that my dad went to UCLA," Eric said, "and it was always my vision to go there and do better than he did."

Eric arrived at UCLA far from a finished product as a linebacker. He was an undersized prospect who received three stars on Rivals.com's five-star scale. He redshirted his first season on campus but quickly blossomed in 2011, starting the final three games of the season and finishing second on the team with 77 tackles.

Kendricks nearly doubled that total as a sophomore, leading the Pac-12 Conference with 150 tackles. He also sparked UCLA's 38–28 victory over USC that ended the Bruins' five-game losing streak in the rivalry, blocking a punt when he wasn't even supposed to be on the field. "We had a guy injured and I was the backup and I was kind of running in as I was buckling my chin strap," Kendricks recalled. "I went in right when the ball was snapped and I ran back there and blocked the punt, so it was pretty crazy."

Kendricks also made his first career interception on a pass from USC quarterback Matt Barkley, a function of having studied the defense's tendencies the week before the game. "It was a third-down route and I knew exactly what they were running," Kendricks said. "I had seen the formation and I kind of just jumped right to the spot and Matt Barkley threw it right to me."

Kendricks reached triple digits in tackles again as a junior in 2013 while becoming a co-captain of a team that also featured standout linebacker Anthony Barr. Kendricks' senior season was history-making from start to finish. Coming off a pair of surgeries, he made 16 tackles, returned an interception for a touchdown, and forced another fumble that resulted in a touchdown in the opener against Virginia, making him the national defensive player of the week. He reached double digits in tackles a school-record 11 times and needed nine tackles in UCLA's regular-season finale against Stanford to break Jerry Robinson's school career record of 468. Kendricks got there in the fourth quarter but couldn't fully enjoy the accomplishment because the Bruins lost the game, depriving themselves of a chance to play in the Pac-12 title game. "It was kind of bittersweet for me," said Kendricks, who finished his career with 476 tackles after UCLA's victory over Kansas State in the Alamo Bowl. "I knew I had worked so hard for that, but at the same time we didn't get our team objective."

There was more of a feel-good moment a few weeks later when Bruins strength and conditioning coach Sal Alosi asked Kendricks some seemingly random football trivia after a workout. Alosi then pointed to the answer: NFL Hall of Famer Dick Butkus, who had walked onto the practice field. Kendricks immediately realized he was UCLA's first winner of the Butkus Award, given each year to the top linebacker in college football. "I was completely shocked and I can't even explain it," Kendricks said. "It gets me emotional thinking about it because I worked so hard for that moment." Kendricks also won the Lott IMPACT Trophy, named in honor of Hall of Fame defensive back Ronnie Lott and awarded for personal character as well as athletic excellence as the defensive player of the year.

Kendricks was selected in the second round of the 2015 NFL Draft by the Minnesota Vikings, where he rejoined Barr. He also reunited in a sense with Mychal Kendricks, the brother who had become a linebacker with the Philadelphia Eagles. It was brotherly love that had nudged Eric toward stardom. "I've never been the hardest hitter," Eric said, "but I've always kind of been in the right place at the right time to make the tackle."

96 The Game That Would Never End

Sigi Schmid devised a plan to calm his team's nerves in the biggest game of its season. The UCLA men's soccer coach told his players that he wanted everyone to get a touch in the opening minute of the 1985 NCAA championship. So the ball went from the forwards to the midfielders to the left fullback to the left center back to the right center back, the Bruins making no initial attempt to mount an assault on the American University goal.

There would be plenty of time for that. The game would go on for eight overtimes, giving both teams more touches than they could physically handle during the longest game in NCAA soccer history. In the eighth overtime, American star Michael Brady limped to the sideline with muscle cramps. That left the Eagles two men short because Serge Torreilles had been ejected for butting heads with UCLA captain Dale Ervine in the third overtime.

By now, with the game more than 160 minutes old and nearing the length of two full regulation contests in an era before penalty kicks, the Bruins also felt at something less than full strength. It didn't help that the teams were running on the rigid artificial turf inside Seattle's Kingdome that was laid over concrete, exacerbating sore joints.

On the bench, UCLA coaches figured some fresh legs might be in order. In the seventh overtime, they inserted Andy Burke, a seldom-used sophomore who had not appeared in any of the Bruins' previous four playoff games after breaking a bone in his left foot earlier in the season. Burke had spoken the night before with his father, John, who relayed a story he had read in the *Wall Street Journal* about the last man on the bench winning a game.

It might as well have been about his son. Burke took a long lead pass from senior Paul Krumpe and booted a left-footed shot from about 15 yards out past American goalkeeper Steven Pheil for the only goal in UCLA's 1–0 victory. Burke's first goal of the season would give the Bruins their first and most improbable men's soccer championship. His teammates weren't too weary to mob him in celebration.

"Just the sheer joy that they had for him getting the game-winning goal," recalled Jorge Salcedo, then UCLA's 12-year-old ballboy, "you could just see how happy they were for him but also obviously so excited to have won the first national championship for men's soccer at UCLA."

The game lasted 166 minutes and five seconds, nearly seven minutes longer than the 159:16 that Indiana had needed to beat Duke in eight overtimes in the 1982 championship. "I've never been this tired," Krumpe said after the game. "My legs are so drained. I'm so tired I can't even think."

In the locker room, the triumphant Bruins mustered the energy to sing ad-libbed songs about every player on the roster, in addition to Schmid, whose early-game strategy had nearly backfired. American's Brady, realizing what UCLA was doing with its pass-happy exchanges in the opening minute, came up with a steal and a breakaway but couldn't convert. "We gave them a great chance," said Salcedo, who was watching from the stands alongside a reporter from the *Daily Bruin*, "and they didn't score."

Schmid acknowledged afterward that he had considered red-shirting Burke that season but was overjoyed he had not. The team's new star concurred. "I told the coach that I wanted a shot to play in the playoff," Burke told the *New York Times*. "I got it at just the right time."

The game's legacy transcended all the longests and firsts for UCLA. It inspired Salcedo to want to play for the Bruins, especially after the team awarded him a championship ring at its postseason banquet. "It was an impression that I'll never forget; it was one that made me love UCLA even more and made me want to be at UCLA five years later as a freshman." Salcedo gave the Bruins their second national championship in 1990 when he scored the game-winning penalty kick against Rutgers and was an assistant coach when the team won it all again in 2002.

Salcedo became UCLA's head coach in 2004, his lifelong allegiance to the Bruins owing an assist to Burke. "UCLA soccer always stood for very talented, gifted young men and young soccer players," Salcedo said, "but there's always opportunities in soccer to go and to add to what your team does and that's exactly what he did. He found a way to contribute and ultimately he contributed in one of the greatest fashions you can, scoring a game-winning goal."

97 Visit John Wooden's Den

There's no need to imagine where John Wooden spent much of his time after retiring in 1975. You can see it for yourself inside the UCLA Athletic Hall of Fame. Wooden's den from his Encino condominium was meticulously re-created after his death in 2010, every item transported to Westwood for its final resting spot behind glass windows that provide a touching glimpse into the legendary coach's final years.

This was the place where Wooden would pen his monthly love letters to his wife, Nell, after her death in 1985. It's where he would sit at his desk and autograph mountains of pictures and lounge in a leather recliner while watching his favorite Western movies and baseball games. That same television is here, showing some of those same movies and games in addition to UCLA basketball highlights and a tribute from legendary Los Angeles Dodgers broadcaster Vin Scully. "It's as if he was here watching," said Emily S. Knox, senior art director and curator of the UCLA Athletic Hall of Fame, not exaggerating in the least considering there's a picture of Wooden seated in the recliner posted on one wall.

UCLA senior associate athletic director Ken Weiner visualized the exhibit and fellow senior associate athletic director Bobby Field, a close friend of the Woodens, received permission from the family to relocate the contents of the den on campus. Knox used photos and a floor plan to replicate the living space, placing every item in the exact spot it had previously occupied. "We put all the stuff back in within two days," Knox said. "We were pretty motivated and excited. It wasn't that hard because we had pictures and we had gone to his house and we had put everything back in the boxes the way it should be, so we just took it back out, placed it on a shelf or on a table. You'd look at the photo and make sure you were doing it the exact same way."

Scores of books line a bookshelf that also holds autographed basketballs from Wooden's 500th and 1,000th coaching victories. Hanging above the television are photographs of the coach's 10 national championship teams arranged in a pyramid by Nell Wooden, presumably a tribute to her husband's famed Pyramid of Success. One wall is adorned with congratulatory letters from Presidents Nixon and Ford. There are also mugs and plates adorned with the scribbles of his grandchildren. "My favorite part is just how much prominence he gives to his grandkids' plates and he has all these keys to the city in this wishing well, like, 'Eh, no big deal,'" Knox said. Wooden's Pyramid of Success is included in a display across from the den, as well as his extensive collection of books from President Lincoln, one of his role models.

Wooden's lair is considered the most popular exhibit inside the Hall of Fame, leading to extended hours in which it is now open on the first Saturday of every month in addition to its regular hours

Monday through Friday. Tyler Trapani, Wooden's grandson who made the last basket inside Pauley Pavilion in 2011 before it was closed for extensive renovations, was a regular at the exhibit during his time on campus. "Daily, I hear people come and have this reaction like, 'Wow, this is exactly like it was,'" Knox said. "It's our most popular exhibit for sure."

98 Lonzo Ball

Lonzo Ball was an international sensation before he even played his first game for UCLA.

The wiry point guard drew a crowd everywhere he went during the team's exhibition tour of Australia in the summer of 2016. Fans chanted his name on every stop from Sydney to Melbourne to Brisbane. "Lonzo! Lonzo! Lonzo!" was the constant refrain, more than three months before Ball played in a game that actually counted as a freshman.

He showed that the hype was justified during the Bruins' season opener. Ball made his first three-pointer only 10 seconds into the game and logged his first assist slightly more than a minute later. UCLA made a school-record 18 three-pointers during a 39-point rout of Pacific, largely because of the impact of its ball-moving newcomer. "It's fun," Bruins forward TJ Leaf had said before the game of his team's style of play. "I mean, if you run, you're going to get the ball."

Ball brought more than passing wizardry with him to Westwood. His 6'6" frame gave the Bruins the lengthy perimeter defender they had lacked in recent seasons and allowed Bryce Alford to move back to shooting guard, his natural position. Ball's presence also shifted the Bruins' offense into hyperdrive. "You can't really measure his pace," Kory Alford, UCLA's video and analytics coordinator, said. "I would love to with a camera because he's probably the fastest player I've witnessed on the basketball court."

Ball's status as one of the nation's best players was cemented in early December against then–No. 1 Kentucky at famed Rupp Arena. Ball struggled throughout much of the first half, committing five turnovers and missing his first four shots. Then he drained a deep three-pointer in the seconds before halftime, providing a glimpse at what would become one of his signature shots. Ball was stellar in the second half, making four of seven shots and handing out four of his seven assists to help engineer the No. 11 Bruins' 97–92 victory. The most indelible moment came when Ball held an upright finger in front of his mouth to shush Wildcats fans after making a three-pointer in the final minutes. "It just came natural, you know?" Ball said. "I didn't think about it, I just did it."

UCLA rose to No. 2 in the national rankings and finished its nonconference season a perfect 13–0, the first time it had gone unbeaten before conference play since the 1994–95 team, which went on to win the national championship. Fans and celebrities such as Jessica Alba, Pete Sampras, and Sugar Ray Leonard flocked to Pauley Pavilion, with the team selling out almost every game the rest of the season.

The most memorable home game came when the Bruins avenged a last-second loss to Oregon. Ball sidestepped defender Dylan Ennis for a three-pointer with 32 seconds left, completing a comeback from 19 points down during a wild 82–79 victory. It was a further rebuttal to the criticisms of a funky shooting motion in which Ball pulled the ball up to the left side of his head before releasing it, reminding some of the style used by former NBA player Kevin Martin.

UCLA would go on to earn a No. 3 seeding in the NCAA tournament and a first-round game against Kent State that it won

Lonzo Ball goes up for a dunk over Pacific's D.J. Ursery during a 2016 game in Los Angeles. (AP Photo/Jae C. Hong)

with relative ease. But the Bruins struggled early in their second-round game against Cincinnati, falling behind 33–30 at halftime. Ball's back-to-back three-pointers propelled his team to a 79–67 victory and into a regional semifinal rematch against Kentucky. UCLA was competitive in the game's opening minutes and trailed by only three points at halftime. But Ball had pulled a hamstring in the game's early going and struggled to keep up with Kentucky counterpart De'Aaron Fox, who set an NCAA tournament freshman record by scoring 39 points. The Wildcats pulled away by midway through the second half, going on to an 86–75 triumph. Ball spared the media any suspense about his future in the locker room afterward, announcing that his college career was over and he was headed to the NBA.

It was quite the career despite the unhappy ending. Ball's 274 assists were easily the most for a freshman in Pac-12 Conference history, surpassing Gary Payton's 229 from the 1986–87 season. Ball was selected Pac-12 Freshman of the Year as well as national Freshman of the Year by *USA Today*, the *Sporting News*, and the United States Basketball Writers Association. He was also one of five finalists for the John R. Wooden Award and a first-team All-American as selected by the Associated Press.

Ball didn't harbor any regrets despite finishing well short of his stated goal of a national championship. "Any time you go from 15–17 [the previous season] to a Sweet 16, that's a big jump," Ball said before the Los Angeles Lakers selected him with the No. 2 pick in the 2017 NBA Draft. "Obviously, I'm a winner, I love to win, but looking back on it, I just smile because I'm grateful I got to go there. I'm thankful for everything that happened. Unfortunately, we didn't go all the way but we gave it our best and that's all you can live with."

99 The Comeback

As UCLA's deficit mounted in its season opener against Texas A&M at the Rose Bowl, it seemed that no one connected with the Bruins football team was safe from fan angst. Coach Jim Mora was already fired on social media, with Chip Kelly being widely touted as his replacement. Athletic director Dan Guerrero felt the heat more directly, getting booed while being shown accepting an award on the stadium's video board during a timeout.

By the time the third quarter ended on September 3, 2017, gleeful Texas A&M fans locked arms and swayed to the Aggie War Hymn, making the fast-emptying Rose Bowl feel more like Kyle Field back in College Station, Texas. The Aggies certainly made themselves at home for most of the first three quarters, building a 38–10 halftime lead that they extended to 44–10 late in the third quarter. After UCLA's opening drive produced a field goal, Texas A&M would dominate in all facets.

A fast, aggressive Aggies defense pressured Bruins quarterback Josh Rosen, forced turnovers on back-to-back plays late in the first quarter, and almost completely shut down UCLA's running game. Meanwhile, Texas A&M's spread offense forced UCLA to abandon its 4-3 base defense in favor of nickel and dime formations that proved susceptible to the run. And run the Aggies did. Tailbacks Trayveon Williams and Keith Ford helped their team stomp its way to 286 rushing yards in the first half alone.

Rosen's first game in nearly 11 months after returning from a season-ending shoulder injury was shaping up as a dud. He couldn't sustain any rhythm, partly the result of breakdowns among blockers and partly the result of receivers struggling to get open. Rosen also displayed spotty touch with his passes, overthrowing a few receivers.

The quarterback rose slowly after getting mashed to the turf late in the second quarter, his efforts on a fourth-down scramble resulting in a sack and more disappointment for a team that had already endured plenty. Rosen limped toward the sideline, his team trailing by four touchdowns.

The second half started with a familiar feel. On UCLA's first drive of the third quarter, Rosen was sacked and fumbled. Two Texas A&M field goals extended the Aggies' lead to 44–10 and it seemed as if the balance of the game would amount to an attempt by the Bruins to pretty things up a bit.

They certainly did.

The biggest comeback in school history started with a connection from Rosen to tight end Caleb Wilson that put UCLA near midfield. The Bruins eventually scored on tailback Soso Jamabo's six-yard touchdown run but still trailed 44–17. The possibility of what was to come started percolating only after UCLA receiver Darren Andrews scored on a hitch pattern to make it 44–24. "Stranger things have happened," Fox broadcaster Gus Johnson said as the game went to commercial.

The oddities started in earnest once Rosen floated a pass on UCLA's next possession toward Andrews, with Texas A&M nickel back Deshawn Capers-Smith in perfect position to make the interception. The ball slipped through Capers-Smith's hands and into those of a stunned Andrews, who scooted into the end zone for a 42-yard touchdown that pulled his team to within 44–31 with 8:12 left in the game.

It was at this point, Mora would later acknowledge, that he thought a comeback was possible. The Bruins defense had started to stiffen by shedding its extra defensive back and reverting to its base defense, making it more stout against the run. It also probably didn't hurt that Texas A&M starting quarterback Nick Starkel was forced out of the game in the third quarter with an ankle injury. The Aggies still could have extended their lead had UCLA safety Adarius Pickett not broke through to get his left thumb on a 43-yard field goal attempt that fell short with 4:41 left.

"We were an inch away from losing that game probably 10 times," Rosen would say later.

Rosen benefited from more luck when he tried to throw away a pass with a defender in his face and the ball fell into the hands of UCLA receiver Theo Howard in the front of the end zone for a 16-yard touchdown. Now it was 44–38 and the Rose Bowl was rocking with 3:10 left. The Bruins got another defensive stop, with defensive end Jacob Tuioti-Mariner sacking backup quarterback Kellen Mond on third down.

UCLA drove quickly downfield before facing a fourth down after receiver Jordan Lasley dropped a pass. Rosen found Jamabo on a swing pass for a first down at the Texas A&M 10-yard line with less than a minute to play. The Bruins raced to the line of scrimmage as if they intended to spike the ball. Rosen pantomimed throwing the ball to the ground before pulling it back in and firing a pass into the corner of the end zone for Lasley, who made a twisting catch while getting one foot in bounds.

Pandemonium broke out. UCLA had tied the score before kicker J.J. Molson's extra-point nudged his team ahead with 43 seconds left. The Bruins needed only one more stop and got it when they held Mond a yard short of the spot he needed to reach on fourth down. The second-biggest comeback in the history of major college football was complete.

The same fans who had been so critical only minutes earlier were fully embracing their team. "The outcome was a lot of fun," Mora said afterward. "This team grew up throughout that game."

100 The Hiring of Chip Kelly

Chip Kelly surveyed the more than 300 boosters, season ticket-holders, and media who crammed into a club room and sat before him inside Pauley Pavilion.

"Not a lot going on in L.A. today, as I can see from this crowd," Kelly cracked from his spot behind a table positioned on an elevated platform. The joke hit its mark, prompting laughter even from reporters.

UCLA's football program was in dire need of some levity by the time Kelly was introduced as its new coach on November 27, 2017. Predecessor Jim Mora had gone 10–17 over his final two-plus seasons, leading a group of fans to pay for a banner that was flown over the Rose Bowl calling for his dismissal prior to his final home game as coach.

The Bruins were in danger of missing a bowl game in back-to-back seasons for the first time since 1989 and 1990 before beating California under the guidance of interim coach Jedd Fisch to notch the sixth win they needed to secure an invitation to the Cactus Bowl.

There were hopes for much greater things to come under Kelly, whose arrival former Bruins quarterback Troy Aikman hailed as the greatest hire in UCLA history. Kelly had gone 46–7 in four seasons at Oregon from 2009 to 2012, leading the Ducks to two Rose Bowls and an appearance in the 2011 national championship game before losing to Auburn on a last-second field goal.

The Bruins had not appeared in a Rose Bowl game since January 1, 1999, and had won only one national championship in their first century of football, in 1954.

Kelly had achieved more modest success during four seasons in the NFL, twice winning 10 games with the Philadelphia Eagles before being ousted with his team holding a 6–9 record in 2015. He then bottomed out with a 2–14 season with the San Francisco 49ers in 2016 that led to his firing. He spent the 2017 season as an ESPN analyst who had gained a new perspective after speaking with Duke coach David Cutcliffe. "He just said when you come back that you find the right fit," Kelly said. "That was extremely important to me."

Kelly found that his vision aligned with that of UCLA chancellor Gene Block and athletic director Dan Guerrero during a whirlwind courtship that lasted less than a week following the dismissal of Mora. Kelly was the only candidate that Bruins officials interviewed before awarding him a five-year, $23.3-million contract that was the richest in school history.

Kelly was known for running offenses that spread the field and operated at a breakneck pace, tiring defenses while generating scads of points. He suggested that he would tailor his initial schemes to the players already in place.

"We're going to open up next year and we're not going to say, 'In two or three years when we get our guys in here,'" Kelly said. "I met with my guys today and I'm excited about those guys that are currently part of this program."

Aikman had been part of a UCLA search committee that also included sports executive and megadonor Casey Wasserman in addition to Guerrero and senior associate athletic director Josh Rebholz. Aikman had previously gotten to know Kelly while doing his prep work as a football analyst for games involving Kelly's NFL teams and said his reputation as solely a football savant was misguided.

"A lot of people might think that Chip thinks of himself as a guru because of his style and I think really nothing could be further from the truth," Aikman said. "I think he's a guy who's always seeking information, he wants to know how other people do it, he wants to then conclude for himself whether or not it works for him but I think he's sensational."

Kelly kept the crowd laughing beyond his opening remarks during his introduction, repeatedly rolling off one-liners and making references to legendary UCLA basketball coach John Wooden. He compared the role of his coaching staff to that of professors at the renowned public university.

"Our exam happens to be every Saturday and they know the syllabus before the season starts, they know how many tests they're going to have," Kelly said. "The only difference between the guys we have and the common student here is 90,000 people aren't going to watch them take that test."

As the Bruins prepared to enter their most anticipated era in school history, it was clear no one would be watched more closely than Kelly.

Acknowledgments

The prospect of writing a book always seemed overwhelming. What? You want more than 70,000 words? From me? As a veteran newspaper reporter used to knocking out relatively short stories each day and then moving on to something else, I didn't think I would know where to start such a massive undertaking. Fortunately, the concept of *100 Things UCLA Fans Should Know & Do Before They Die* made it seem infinitely more feasible if I thought of it as writing 100 stories for my job at the *Los Angeles Times*. By that measure, I could complete one chapter a day.

It also helped that I had a formidable team to guide me every step of the way. Marc Dellins, the former longtime sports information director at UCLA, helped me brainstorm possible chapter topics (there were well over 100) and connected me with numerous players and coaches. Current UCLA staffers Alex Timiraos and Liza David provided access to the school's sports archive room inside the J.D. Morgan Center, my home away from home while completing this project. Timiraos helped fact-check several chapters and provided suggestions for improvements. Jesse Jordan, my editor at Triumph Books, supplied sharp editing and kept me on track for more than a year.

A couple of friends also nudged me toward the finish line. Myvan Bui helped with the laborious transcribing and provided encouragement during times when the dual strain of the project and work life took hold. Renowned author and lifelong UCLA fan Jim Bendat saved me from embarrassment by catching scores of errors that would have made it past even the most seasoned copy editor. Bendat also suggested added context that immensely improved several chapters.

I would like to extend a special thanks to my children, Emma and Max, who showed tremendous patience with me while I was trying and often failing to simultaneously be a father, journalist, and author. And, of course, the many Bruins coaches and athletes who spoke with me vastly enhanced the authenticity of the book. I would like to thank everyone who made *100 Things UCLA Fans Should Know & Do Before They Die* a reality.

Sources

Books

The College World Series: A Baseball History, 1947–2003 (W.C. Madden and Patrick J. Stewart)

Total Basketball: The Ultimate Basketball Encyclopedia (Leonard Koppett)

UCLA: The First Century (Marina Dundjerski)

Magazines

Collier's (Arthur Mann)

Inside Sports (Bob Rubin)

Look (Cameron Shipp)

Sport (Phil Berger, Claude Lewis)

Sports Illustrated (Lew Alcindor, Peter Carry, Anthony Cotton, Seth Davis, Frank Deford, Melvin Durslag, Joe Jares, Dan Jenkins, Curry Kirkpatrick, Bruce Newman, Richard O'Brien, Jack Olsen, William F. Reed, Rick Telander, John Underwood, Alexander Wolff)

The Hoop (Paul Farhi)

The Sporting News (Dave Kindred)

Touchdown Illustrated (Nick Peters)

Newspapers

Argus Leader (Melissa Elrod-Miller)

Chicago Tribune (Andrew Bagnato, Skip Myslenski)

Chicago Tribune Press Service (Roy Damer)

Daily Bruin (Brent Boyd, Doug Kelly, Cynthia Lee, Karen Mack, Laura Mishima, Kristina Wilcox)

Indianapolis Star (Dana Hunsinger Benbow)

Long Beach Press-Telegram (Gary Rausch, Loel Schrader)

Los Angeles Daily News (Erik Boal, Vincent Bonsignore, Steve Dilbeck, Tom Hoffarth, Bob Hunter, Billy Witz)

Los Angeles Herald-Examiner (Ed Kociela, Don Page, Tom Singer)

Los Angeles Times (Chris Baker, Ben Bolch, Thomas Bonk, Dwight Chapin, John Cherwa, Jerry Crowe, Jamie Curran, John Dart, Tracy Dodds, Mike Downey, Braven Dyer, Gordon Edes, Helene Elliott, Nathan Fenno, Mal Florence, Andrea Ford, Shav Glick, Earl Gustkey, Jim Hodges, Richard Hoffer, Gale Holland, Scott Howard-Cooper, Tim Kawakami, Alan Malamud, Jim Murray, Robyn Norwood, Scott Ostler, Mike Penner, Bill Plaschke, Jeff Prugh, Diane Pucin, Mark Purdy, Terry Shepard, Steve Springer, Larry Stewart, Pete Thomas, David Wharton, Lonnie White, Wendy Witherspoon, Peter Yoon)

Morning Call (Don Bostrom)

Milwaukee Journal (Terry Bledsoe)

New York Times (Tyler Kepner, John Polis, William C. Rhoden)

Orange County Register (Damian Calhoun, K.J.M. Singleton, Marcia C. Smith, Mark Whicker)

Pasadena Star-News (Rube Samuelsen)

Riverside Press-Enterprise (Lew Price)

San Bernardino Sun-Telegram (Betty Cuniberti)

San Diego Union-Tribune (Bryce Miller)

San Francisco Chronicle (Bill Leiser)

San Gabriel Valley Tribune (Steve Ramirez)

San Jose Mercury News (Charles Bricker)

Sun-Sentinel (Shandel Richardson)

The Globe and Mail

USA Today (David Leon Moore)

USA Today Baseball Weekly (Tim Wendel)

Valley News (Terry Wood)

Ventura County Star (Woody Woodburn)

The Washington Post (Donald Huff, Sally Jenkins)

News Services
The Associated Press (Hal Bock, Jim Cour, William J. Kole)
United Press International (Art Spander, Rich Tosches)

Other Sources
Central Intelligence Agency letter (John T. McCann)
Ducky Drake tribute program (Jerry Weiner)
Jackie Robinson memorial program
J.D. Morgan tribute program (Gary Rausch)
Personal résumé (Richard Linthicum)
UCLA 1964 National Collegiate Basketball Champions tribute
    program ("Ski" Wagner)
UCLA Athletics Archives (Bill Bennett)
UCLA Athletics Media Guides
UCLA News Bureau (Vic Kelley)
Los Angeles Hall of Legends Museum
Los Angeles Rams Thumbnail Sketches (Maxwell Stiles)

Videos
The 1970 National Collegiate Basketball Championships (Ray Scott)

Websites
Alumni.ucla.edu
AthlonSports.com
Calband.berkeley.edu
Collegehoopedia.com
Footballfoundation.org
Jockbio.com
MLB.com (Adam Berry)
Philadelphia.CBSlocal.com (Joseph Santoliquito)
Rosebowlstadium.com
UclaBruins.com

Personal Interviews

Joe B. Hall (November 30, 2016)

Pete Trgovich (November 30, 2016)

Richard Washington (November 30, 2016)

Tyus Edney (February 7, 2017)

Dick Enberg (February 9, 2017)

Larry "Frisbee" Davis (February 15, 2017)

Paul Ma (February 17, 2017)

Johnathan Franklin (March 4, 2017)

Lonzo Ball (April 7, 2017)

Emily S. Knox (April 17, 2017)

Al Scates (May 1, 2017)

Gordon Henderson (May 8, 2017)

Sinjin Smith (May 9, 2017)

Gerrit Cole (May 9, 2017)

Dave Roberts (May 9, 2017)

Eric Kendricks (May 16, 2017)

Brett Hundley (May 19, 2017)

Kenny Easley (May 22, 2017)

Cade McNown (May 24, 2017)

John Savage (May 31, 2017)

David Greenwood (June 5, 2017)

John Peterson (June 5, 2017)

John Sciarra (June 6, 2017)

Keith Erickson (June 6, 2017)

Karch Kiraly (June 7, 2017)

Ben Howland (June 8, 2017)

Anthony Barr (June 8, 2017)

Gail Goodrich (June 9, 2017)

Meb Keflezighi (June 13, 2017)

Ann Meyers (June 13, 2017)

Sidney Wicks (June 15, 2017)

Myles Jack (June 16, 2017)

Chris Chambliss (June 24, 2017)
Don MacLean (June 26, 2017)
Reggie Miller (June 30, 2017)
Steve Lavin (July 1, 2017)
Jorge Salcedo (July 5, 2017)
Lisa Fernandez (July 6, 2017)
Randy Cross (July 10, 2017)
Jonathan Ogden (July 18, 2017)
Gary Beban (July 20, 2017)
Jamaal Wilkes (July 20, 2017)
Dan Guerrero (January 10, 2018)
Jackie Joyner-Kersee (January 29, 2018)